To my dearest old fr[iend]
heslie, and the won[derful]
Mary —

You have made us feel so
warmly welcome that I feel
able to leave a little bit
of me to reside forever with
you — I hope, in your
wonderful old bookcase.

With great affection

Alan Jay

London
21·07·01

Pulse of the nation

A PORTRAIT OF AUSTRALIA

Pulse of the nation

A PORTRAIT OF AUSTRALIA

MARK DAY

HarperCollinsPublishers

HarperCollins_Publishers_

First published in Australia in 1999
by HarperCollins_Publishers_ Pty Limited
ACN 009 913 517
A member of the HarperCollins_Publishers_ (Australia) Pty Limited Group
http://www.harpercollins.com.au

Copyright © Mark Day 1999

mday@ozemail.com.au

HarperCollins_Publishers_
25 Ryde Road, Pymble, Sydney, NSW 2073, Australia
31 View Road, Glenfield, Auckland 10, New Zealand
77-85 Fulham Palace Road, London W6 8JB, United Kingdom
Hazelton Lanes, 55 Avenue Road, Suite 2900, Toronto, Ontario M5R 3L2
and 1995 Markham Road, Scarborough, Ontario M1B 5M8, Canada
10 East 53rd Street, New York NY 10032, USA

A CIP record for this title is available from the National Library of Australia

Reprinted with permission of John Williamson & Emusic Pty Ltd:
    "RIP RIP WOODCHIP" John Williamson © 1989 Emusic Pty. Ltd.
    "ONE MORE FOR THE ROAD" John Williamson © 1987 Emusic Pty. Ltd.
    "EVERYBODY'S SEARCHING FOR A REASON" John Williamson © 1998 Emusic Pty. Ltd.
    "YES I FEEL ABORIGINE" John Williamson © 1998 Emusic Pty. Ltd.

Cover painting: Ken Done
All photography by Mark Day and Wendy Day, except those which appear on pages
7, 20, 85, 86, 167, 272, 273 (News Limited); 177, 185, 194 (Ken Done); 244 (right),
245 (bottom) (F.S. Falkiner & Sons); 124 (Roger Fishman); 129 (Lex Silvester);
200, 202 (Woodside Petroleum); 117 (NT Tourist Commission); 277 (Ansett Australia); 13, 17 (top) (Unknown)
Internal Design: Melanie Feddersen
Printed in China by Toppan Printing Co. Ltd. on 113gsm Matt Art

9 8 7 6 5 4 3 2 1   99 00 01 02

Foreword

In the nineteenth century it was customary for journeying commentators to enter and try to define countries other than their own. It worked for the Frenchman de Tocqueville with his famous work on the fledgling United States, *Democracy in America*. The novelist Anthony Trollope also wrote a large work on North America, and two volumes on exotic Australia and New Zealand as he perceived them at the beginning of the 1870s. The formula is still alive in this era, but now, when most places on earth can be reached by people in the 'developed world' in little more than a day from any point of departure, when we are all our own travel writers and photographers, there is a tendency to look within, for the traveller to try to explore inner — rather than outer — space.

In Australia, as Mark Day here shows, inner space is massive, both in geographic and spiritual terms. The roads into the Australian landscape, and into the Australian soul (what we have tentatively called identity) are near-to-endless, and require skilled maps and a subtle eye. This invigorating, stylish account shows that Mark has both of these gifts, and has the humility, energy, and imagination adequate to the huge Australian rainbow serpent of an equation he wrestles with in these pages.

Mark grew up in the quintessentially named Merino in the western district of Victoria, worked, and made and lost fortunes, in journalism and radio, and since I first met him, by a mike at 3AW nearly two decades past, has always been teased by Australia, by its politics, the inroads it makes on the imagination of the immigrant, its mysteries and atmospherics, its character, its glories and sins, its future direction. He became an early, genial and brave republican and took part in the public debate on constitutional issues, but he never lost sight of the sensibilities of the countryside, Australia's older loyalties and fervours, many of them examined in this work. I remember (and he remembers, since he mentions it in these pages) a time we spent — by permission of Aboriginal owners — on the Goomadeer River in Arnhem Land, painting the estuary, the mangroves, the noble escarpments, and going out each day to fish in a river graced by the kind of animals commemorated in Northern Australian rock art — barramundi, crocodile, shark, jabiru.

Even there, as the sun fell and the sandflies came up to plague us, Mark went on worrying out, in conversations sometimes primed with rum and wine, the larger questions. How was this remote square kilometre of apparent wilderness connected to the splendid, polluted realities of the urban Australia where most of us live? How was the Aboriginal imagination reflected in the rest of us? Why had this place always lain at the bottom of our Australian souls, part of our psychic equipment as Australians, so that we arrived at it with instant recognition even though we were now visiting it for only the first time? And then, to what extent should Australia make us brave, to what extent wary? To what extent has its enormous landscape liberated us, and to what extent blinded us?

Mark Day, a patriot but not a jingo, a pilgrim much more than a traveller, has taken these questions with him all over Australia, asking them everywhere he could reach, on every acreage he could penetrate. The account of his quest will excite and entertain the majority of us whose journeys have never been as extensive or as unified by purpose. I commend this work to the many Australians who will read it.

THOMAS KENEALLY
December 1998

Craig's Hut, Mt Stirling, Victorian High Country.

Preface

We went in search of the essence of Australia: who we are, where we're from, and where we're going in the 21st century. We learned that there is no such thing as the typical Australia, or the typical Australian. For every desert there is a snow-covered mountain; for every towering triumph, a failed dream; for every country town, a thriving metropolis; for every Snowy Mountains Scheme, a hare-brained idea; for every Crocodile Dundee, an ordinary Australian.

For 75,000 kilometres, mostly by road, we pushed and prodded the four corners of the nation in search of what makes us tick, and found what we knew to be true before we began: that we are a complex lot, a polyglot lot, a melting pot of people, ideas, visions and fixations; as diverse a society as any on earth, filled with the paradoxes which are inherent in that diversity. We live in cities by the sea, still yearning for our quarter-acre block, yet we clutch tightly to our self-perception as a rugged, tough, resilient people of the red earth. We pride ourselves on our egalitarianism and tolerance, yet we debate, rather than celebrate, our differences.

There were 18.3 million of us at last count. This, therefore, cannot be the story of every Australian's Australia. It must leave much untouched: whole slabs of Australian life are absent from this work, perhaps awaiting another time. But wherever we went, we applied the eye of the reporter, the conceit of the commentator, and the soul of an Australian to what we saw, to make up this portrait of an ancient land and its people, old and new, on the cusp of a new millennium. We took the pulse of the nation.

MARK DAY
January 1999

Contents

ix

Sunrise at Milikapiti, Melville Island.

chapter one

The heart beats strongly throughout this wide brown land. As we take stock at the end of the millennium, the evidence surrounds us: the economy is growing stronger, we are better educated than ever before, we earn more than any previous generation, more people are working in full or part-time employment than at any time in the past, superannuation contributions are rising by the billions to preserve our futures, we have an enviable national health scheme, we are living longer, more of us own our own homes, we are exporting more, women have emerged in a lifetime to become equal partners in our affairs, more of our land is preserved forever in national parks, we have a solid welfare safety net for the stragglers in our society, and we stand tall among the world's artistic and sporting fraternities as we build for the Sydney 2000 Olympics. Oh, sure, perfection has eluded us, but still we say: this is the greatest country in the world, and we wouldn't live anywhere else.

But there is a murmur in the heart, and it comes from the head. We are unsure of our legitimacy. We are unsure of who we are; and before we can go confidently forward, we must put that question behind us. We have intense pride in the achievements of a little more than two centuries since the beginning of modern Australia, yet we question the very basis on which those achievements were built. Our constant companion is change, and we are introspective, doubtful, confused and uncertain. This is the paradox of Australia 2000.

On the sunburnt, cracked, dry and dusty sweeping plains beside the Darling River in far western New South Wales, we drive from Louth to Tilpa, white bulldust catching our throats. Thunderclouds, purple and flashing, unleash sudden torrents of rain, and the dust turns to glutinous mud. We slip and slide along the ruts called a road, from drought to flooding rains in five minutes and five kilometres.

The land has always been contrary, and it is the land which defines us. A vast, flat land of 7,682,300 square kilometres — into which you could fit most of Europe; most of the mainland United States — stretching 4000 kilometres from Cape York in the north to South-east Cape in Tasmania's south, and about the same from Shark Bay in the west to Byron Bay in the east. A land of deserts, worn down by thousands of millions of years of wind and rain, of low mountains and fertile valleys, contained by 37,000 kilometres of coast, with almost nine out of every ten Australians living within the scent of the sea. Three-quarters of us live in our six state capital cities; 86 per cent of us in urban communities; 94 per cent of us clinging to the coast, cramming

into 4 per cent of our landmass. We are one of the most urbanised countries on earth; we compare our cities and lifestyles to those of London, New York, Los Angeles or Hong Kong — but never Calcutta — and decide, on the evidence of international benchmarks, that we have the most livable cities in the world. We are increasingly a global people, swept up in fashions and fads which know no international boundaries, consuming borderless brands, absorbing a global culture through the relentless eye of television, and following global trendlines which have already made us much the same, and will inevitably further diminish our differences. Yet we say we are different. We say it is because of the land. It is because the land sets us apart from the rest of the world: a unique island continent, without bridges to anywhere; a land of such space, and light, and enormity, and beauty, and paradoxes, that we clutch it and its deep-seated imagery to our breasts claiming that we, too, are unique.

A thousand times as the road stretches ahead to a shimmering horizon of white heat hazes, across the Tanami, across the Nullarbor, across the Top End and through the Gulf, up to The Tip, and over the sandhills of the Strzelecki, I ask myself: why am I drawn here? We live in the cities. This is the bush. Which is the reality of the Australian experience? And I settle on both; you cannot be an Australian, even in a city by the sea, without feeling the call of the red emptiness which has so captured our psyche.

We are all migrants, some more recent than others. No-one knows for certain when the first humans walked across the land bridges from Asia to occupy this remnant of Gondwanaland, drifting north amid tectonic convulsions from its original anchorage at the bottom of the world. Perhaps it was 60,000 years ago; maybe more. Certainly it had happened by 45,000 years ago, but the evidence, like so much of our past and present, is confused and only slowly revealing itself. Our first migrants were the Aboriginal people, who defined their existence by the land; who were its custodians and its historians. Generation after generation, without inventing wheels, sailing ships, farming or writing, they sustained a totemic existence which was *of* the land, and passed on their beliefs, laws, and understanding of the seasons, the cosmos, and flora and fauna through song and dance. Theirs was a gentle way of life, abruptly convulsed by the invasion of Europeans who, in ignorance and arrogance, declared the great southern landmass to be uninhabited. When they found this to be untrue, confronted by the evidence of perhaps 500 tribes of people with complex and sophisticated social structures, they reasoned that if the land were not uninhabited, it was not *owned* in the European way. And so began the legal fiction of *terra nullius*, the empty land, which underpinned two centuries of disease, massacres, poisonings, stolen children, cultural destruction, land dispossession, disadvantage and despair.

Our recognition today of the wrongs of the past — whether or not accompanied by guilt, sorrow, remorse or shame — weighs heavily on our national conscience, and the way in which we come to terms with it will define our future. The lack of a true reconciliation with the country's original occupants will continue to corrode our legitimacy as a nation. The turn of the century beckons as a milestone by which we hope to reach this —

and perhaps we will, in a legal sense. But true reconciliation can come only from our hearts, and it will not come from those unwilling to utter its need.

There is hope. There is more than hope: reconciliation is happening in a thousand ways in a thousand communities across the land. It is happening in spite of those we see on our nightly news arguing, baiting, twisting, looking for the edge in a tortuous search for legal definitions. It is slow, but it *is* happening, because we know the Aboriginal cause is morally and socially just.

We have always been multicultural. We didn't use that word when the First Fleet anchored in Sydney Cove in 1788, nor for a further 190 years, it being an invention of the 1970s. But from the time of the first settlement, people of many nations and hues have made Australia their home. The gold rushes of the 1850s spawned a huge wave of Chinese migration, from which we derived our most Australian expression for truth and value: *fair dinkum* is a corruption of the Chinese *jing kum*, meaning fine gold. Explorers like Strzelecki (a Pole) and Leichhardt (a German) carved out names for themselves as well as lines on our maps; settlements of Germans in the Barossa Valley put down the roots of our wine industry; and many thousands of South Sea Islanders were blackbirded into virtual slavery in the cane fields of the far north.

But it was not until war had reached our doorstep in the early 1940s that the cry went up: 'Populate or Perish', and Australia embarked on an enthusiastic policy of reaching out to attract (and subsidise) migrants in a deliberate program of nation building. But it was a racially selective policy, and blatantly so. Today, in an era when racial slurs, publicly uttered, are against our laws,

Multicultural Australia . . . Salamanca Place, Hobart.

it is inconceivable to think that our Immigration Minister in the late 1940s, Arthur Augustus Calwell, defended the policy on the basis that 'two Wongs don't make a white'. Our postwar migration push was constructed within the White Australia Policy which, as legislation passed in the first months of Federation in 1901, insisted on preserving racial homogeneity, a bulwark against the perception that cheap labour from our northern regions would take jobs from 'real' Australians. Almost a century on, the White Australia Policy is long abandoned, but fears remain about the impact of migrants on jobs.

The first wave of postwar immigrants were predominantly European, with many refugees. It was the turning point — the beginning of the wholesale diminution of Australia's Britishness. Italians, Greeks, Yugoslavs, Poles, Latvians, Estonians and others from dozens of countries poured in, bringing with them their traditions and cultures. It is fanciful to suggest, as is often the case today, that their settlement and absorption into the Australian community was without problems — many had to struggle against insult and slander — but Australians did quickly acknowledge that the contributions of migrants were transparently positive. The great postwar Snowy Mountains Scheme, for instance, could not have been built without them. While some people grumbled about the creation of ghettos in the cities, most came to enjoy the new cafe societies built around cappuccino, latte, macchiato, focaccia, pizza and damned hard work.

In the 1970s and 1980s a second wave of migration began, with a substantial influx of people from the Middle East and Asia. Thousands of Vietnamese refugees made their homes here, along with Chinese from Hong Kong, Taiwan and the mainland. For the first time, migration was plainly visible in the streets, and a period of unease began, spurred along by the recession of the early 1990s. Migration had been a largely politics-free zone because both major parties recognised its value to the nation and agreed with the continuation of a concerted push for new citizens. Debate, therefore, was marginalised among fixated minorities. But the roots of racial fear were deeply embedded in the Australian pysche, and more and more people questioned the value of bringing more workers to a country which could not create enough jobs for those already here. The simplistic cry went up: migrants take jobs. In fact, economists insist, the reverse is true: migration creates jobs as new settlers buy homes, equip them with whitegoods and soft furnishings, and create extra demand in every facet of the economy. But the appealing and jingoistic belief that Australia's interests would be best served by putting up the barricades and creating a Fortress Australia for the express benefit of those already here, took hold, especially in the bush, and the seeds of a damaging and divisive political debate over the 'Asianisation' of Australia were sown. In 1986, 3.4 per cent of Australian citizens were born in Asia; ten years later the figure was 4.8 per cent, and if present policies continue, it is estimated the percentage will rise to 7.5 per cent in 2030. Even if there were cause for concern for any cultural, social or political reason — and there is not — this is hardly a threatening figure, given that we live in the South-east Asian region! In time, when they vacate the low-man-on-the-totem-pole position which inevitably accompanies any new wave of migration, Asian faces in our streets will be no more remarkable than the presence of Chinese restaurants in almost every country town across the nation. In spite of the unease, and by any analysis, Australians have made an extraordinary success of being a migrant nation — a success which can continue into the next century. But first, we will have to wring out of our system the resentment of many voters who believe they have not been consulted about the ethnic future of the nation.

Until the 1990s, annual migration more than doubled the natural increase in population; in the 1990s it slowed to about half the natural rate. Seventy-seven per cent of today's Australian citizens were born here, but 40 per cent have at least one parent who was born overseas. This is a solid base on which to build the bipartisan policy of multiculturalism, which seeks to engage migrants at all levels of Australian life without seeking a repudiation of their cultural heritage. As a word, multiculturalism has been attacked for the blurriness of its meaning and, I suspect, its bureaucratic birthright. It seems to many to be an invitation to migrants to come here, take the benefits of citizenship, vote — but to keep their heart in their homeland, with no incentive or obligation to embrace Australia's cultural values (whatever they may be). Various alternatives, in the form of slogans, have been put forward — many cultures, one Australia; many races, one culture; many origins, one destiny — but the word most Australians seem comfortable with, and take delight in being, is *cosmopolitan*. It is yet another paradox that we embrace the sophistication and 'cool' of being a cosmopolitan people, yet we demand from migrants that they adopt an unspecified Australian monoculture. This has been at the core of our struggle in the 1990s to define our national identity.

On 7 July 1991, I joined a group of about 20 Australians gathered at the Regent Hotel in The Rocks, Sydney, near the site of the first settlement, and called for the establishment of an Australian republic. After a series of rallying speeches, David Hill, the then managing director of the national broadcaster, the ABC, and himself a migrant from Britain, leaned towards me and said: 'This will be easy to sell... it's so bloody logical.'

Selling the republic *hasn't* been easy. It has opened a Pandora's box of consequential questions, challenged our deepest beliefs about who we are — the values of heritage and symbols, our obligations to the past and to the future — and succeeded in undermining the pillars of our self-perception.

Once we defined ourselves by our Britishness — an outpost in a sea of red, on which the sun never set. But the British Empire contracted after the Second World War; Australia fundamentally changed through its migration programs and, as if that were not enough, Britain's entry into the European Community without so much as a 'by your leave' in the early 1970s radically changed the equation at every level except for the kinship felt by many of British descent. Now we are being asked to reject that, in favour of a new Constitution which actually reflects the way we are governed, with our own head of state, a President — one of us — to take the place of the Queen. It is, by any analysis, an unremarkable proposition.

Australians are by nature gradualists. With the brief and quixotic exception of the Eureka uprising in 1854, there have been no insurrections, revolutions or upheavals to bring about instant change. But step-by-step, we have changed our governing arrangements. We were subjected to colonial administration until the mid-1800s, when limited self-government was granted to the states; we federated at the turn of the 20th century but still granted to Britain powers to disallow our laws and to protect us; we changed the status of the Governor-General in 1926 so that he (never a she) became a representative of the Crown rather than the British government; we took on more responsibility, reluctantly, in 1942 with the adoption of the 1931 Statute of Westminster which ended the power of the British Parliament to pass laws over us; but it was not until 1986 that the *Australia Act* ended the colonial status of the states and abolished the Privy Council, in Britain, as the final arbiter of Australian law. The one step yet to be taken is to place the sovereignty of Australian people into their own hands. To me, it is inconceivable that it could be any other way.

But to many — mainly older — Australians, the notion of a republic was seen as a treasonous rejection of past values and past affiliations. They saw no benefits, and argued that our system wasn't broke, and didn't need fixing. The issue became a political tussle and a cause for greater uneasy introspection. We had already challenged our self-perception as the Digger–bushman, tough and lean, carving a life out of the backblocks against all odds; we had overthrown the notion of racial purity embedded in the White Australia Policy; we had been pushed out of the British Empire by its dismantling; we had changed our face through migration; and, in 1992, our High Court had overturned the legal fiction of *terra nullius* and forced us to confront our very legitimacy. Now, we were being asked

World War 1 veterans are greeted by a serving member of the Australian Army during a commemoration ceremony... 80 years on.

to reject our supreme symbol: the Crown. What for? When republicans replied that it was an empowering decision to clearly demonstrate our national independence, to reinvigorate our self-confidence, to stimulate optimism, patriotism and pride, and to assert a new maturity based on Australians as citizens rather than subjects, the monarchists' cry was that it was all a waste of time and money.

The division over the republic is essentially between the old, yearning to hold on to the past, and the young, determined to create a new Australia in their image. Soon, we will decide whether or not to make the change on 1 January 2001. If the answer is 'No', it will merely mean, 'Not yet.' The forces of change, inevitably, cannot be denied.

Since 1988, Australia has indulged in an orgy of nostalgia. Our Bicentenary celebrations glorified the achievements of those who had built the nation since 1788; in 1989 we stopped to remember the Diggers who went off to war half a century earlier in 1939; in 1994 we remembered D-Day in Europe, and in 1995 we marked the 50th anniversary of the end of the war as well as 80 years since our stubborn failure to take Gallipoli; and in 1998 we paused to admire three old Diggers who made a pilgrimage to the killing fields of France to honour their colleagues who never returned, 80 years after the First World War.

There is nothing inherently wrong with nostalgia, but it can be overwhelming and divert us from the realities of today and visions of tomorrow. Who is proselytising the new Australia?

The decade from 1988 can be likened to the Christmas–New Year period, when we slow down, take a holiday, review the year just past, and rest our bones in preparation for the year ahead. Writ large, the Bicentenary was the start of a long period of introspection, and the millennium represents the new year; a new age we are constantly reminded we must prepare for. It has been a period of taking a breather — a national smoko — in which we have looked back, with the 1950s emerging as our favourite period when life was simpler, less stressed, more predictable and more secure. It wasn't, of course, but the mists of time mask the realities of fibro shacks, outside toilets, petrol-guzzling cars, black-and-white TV, twin-sets and pearls, and a Cold War between the superpowers.

We have been confronted with the disappearance of many of our favourite myths. Economic rationalism has taken hold globally, and we have been forced to confront, uncomfortably, the realisation that we are not the Lucky Country; that we no longer ride on the sheep's back; that a mining boom won't save us again. Our postwar manufacturing base has rusted and is long past its competitive use-by date. We can't make the things we used to make here cheaply enough to sell them against the products of newly industrialised nations using their relatively cheap labour. We have a limited infrastructure to make the consumer items of the new age — like electronics. We are computer importers, not makers. Our commodities no longer have guaranteed markets. Our companies have downsized, code for sacking thousands of people who knew no other skills; and we have worried about who will be next.

Also in this period, we have been forced to question many of the pillars of our society's beliefs. Everything we thought we could trust has been shown to be untrustworthy. Our police have been shown to be rotten with entrenched corruption; our judiciary has been brought into question through corruption and aberrant behaviour; our hospital system has been shown to be all too willing to bury its mistakes; some of our members of Parliament have gone to prison and others been fined for rorting the public purse; and even our churches have knowingly harboured people who sexually prey on children. Is it any wonder that we ask: who can we trust? And then provide ourselves with at least part of an answer: certainly not our governments.

In this period of confusion and change heaped on change, we are told we must accept more change as we enter the Age of Information and build a new, rational economy on service industries. We are unsure what that means, or how we are to go about it; we are fearful of the future. This has created a rich vein of discontent in the electorate, mined by political forces which promise to postpone the future. But they offer no solutions, and will surely be seen in time as a democratic expression of our pre-millennium malaise.

Businesses in the 1980s and 1990s embraced new paradigms. The freeing up of global trade restrictions opened new markets and called for new ways of doing business. Companies began their own processes of introspection, involving their employees at all levels in programs to establish with the utmost clarity their reason for existence. What is our vision? What is our mission? What are the critical success factors? What are the strategic action steps we must take? How should we be organised through our job structures, processes and systems, and the competency of our people to achieve our vision?

This is the challenge of leadership in a new millennium. Australians have never been shirkers. We are an educated society, capable, inventive and adaptable. Our society is in good shape, in spite of our insecurities. But all our positives need to be harnessed and focused if we are to make full use of them. In a free society, filled with choices and tolerant of dissent, we cannot dragoon people into Stalinesque five-year plans, but we can offer visions which are exciting, meaningful and attainable.

We have had enough debate about the past, enough finger-pointing and name-calling about elites and battlers, the haves and the have-nots. We live on the doorstep of our greatest future market; we have all the critical success factors at the ready. All we need is the will to do it, and the courage of a leadership willing to take the strategic steps to achieve it.

We all see things through our own prisms. They may be generational, cultural, intellectual, the result of our experiences in life or our political biases; but whatever their basis, they all change and distort our perceptions. I am an optimist and a pragmatist; I cannot say why, other than I grew up on a farm in the bush, so I had to be. I am old enough to have earned the right to cynicism and nostalgia, but young enough to dream of what may be, and naive enough to ask why not. This account of a personal odyssey through my homeland, then, should be seen through those filters.

Failed dreams . . . the ruins of Pondanna station in the Gawler
Ranges, South Australia.

chapter two

My father came to Australia from England in 1923, arriving, he used to tell us, with one-and-thruppence in his pocket. One shilling and three pence: 12 cents these days. It was what remained of his pay after working his passage as a deckhand on a tramp steamer. He was 18. He worked on the land — I don't know where — until the Great Depression, when neither he nor a third of his generation could find work. He survived, living in bush camps, by trapping possums in the high country around Tumbarumba in New South Wales.

In the late 1930s, Dad worked as a carpenter on the locks and barrages which controlled the water flows of the Murray River. At the final barrage at Goolwa, designed to keep the sea water out of Lake Alexandrina, he met and wooed my mother, Alfreda Olive Hardy, daughter of the Victor Harbour chemist. They married in 1938; my brother was born in 1940 and I followed in 1943. My father was with an RAAF construction squadron in New Guinea at the time, and I cried when I first set eyes on him at age 18 months. Or so I'm told.

The barrages at Goolwa, South Australia… where my father met my mother.

After the war, ex-Flight-Lieutenant Cyril Earle Russell Day worked as a carpenter at Leigh Creek, the coal-mining town in northern South Australia. He was an overseer on the house construction program in the early days of the development of the coalfields. By 1949 Dad was working on a property near Edenhope in far western Victoria. He was in the garden of our rented house one afternoon when my mother hurried to him with a letter — confirmation that he had been granted 515 acres at Grassdale, near Digby, near Merino, near Hamilton, in the Western District.

We moved there in late 1949 and lived in a tumbledown 100-year-old weatherboard cottage known as The Glen. It had tiny rooms; we used curtains for doors, and fruit boxes for kitchen cupboards, but if we thought living was pretty basic at The Glen, we had only to look at our fellow Soldier Settlers to count our blessings. They lived in garages, awaiting the construction of their homes. It took about four years, and was the source of much irritation within the small community.

We had a garage, too. It was the only building on a bald hilltop at the Y-junction of the road from Hamilton. Straight ahead took you down a corrugated gravel road, sending clouds of dust over our property, towards the railway station. Veering right took you to Merino, a town which went into shock after the First World War: the shock of losing so many of its young and finest in the muddy horrors of Paschendale and Flanders. The town never recovered.

Ashford, circa 1952. My father rounds up sheep and lambs.

I was six when we went to live in The Glen. Each morning, early, my father would disappear over the brow of the hill in his soft-top Landrover, which doubled as tractor, utility and family car, on to his land. He — and we, at weekends — fenced it with wire netting to keep the rabbits out; then fumigated the burrows, laid poison baits, shot, trapped and wrung the necks of millions of the little bastards, for Dad knew that unless he could eradicate the rabbits, the sheep would go hungry.

My father sweated and slaved over that property, which he called Ashford, after the market-garden town in south-east England where he had lived in his teens. He was determined to turn this block of dirt into a showpiece; 515 acres of pastures fit for the finest-wool merinos he could breed. His proudest moments came when we topped the wool sales in Melbourne and Geelong.

A white-tipped stake in the ground marked the spot where the house would one day be built. And one day it was: small by today's standards; wooden-framed, gleaming white weatherboards, on jarrah blocks and with jarrah front and side porches. Dad fenced off an acre around the house and turned virgin

The sheepyards and woolshed at Ashford.

soil into lawn, a fruit orchard and plantations of hundreds of tiny trees in wooden tubes plugged into crowbar holes, religiously watered through the summer droughts. This was my world; an isolated enclave of buildings — garage, backyard dunny, chook house, dairy and woolshed — clustered around the house. It was a world from which I rarely escaped, except to be bussed to school at Merino, and later Hamilton.

In the mid-1990s I heard that the house at Ashford had been razed. I took the news with a mix of sadness and indifference and I resolved not to bother finding out for sure. I wanted to remember it as it was. But in 1996 I was within striking distance of the old place with my second son, Kenton, who had never seen Ashford, nor his grandfather's grave in

This is where I grew up… I'm standing where my bedroom used to be in the house at Ashford.

the old Hamilton cemetery. So we decided to make a pilgrimage to the old place; to my roots. We drove along my old school bus route; each turn as familiar as it was when I travelled it thousands of times with old Herb Bayley at the wheel. We drove down a slight hill, past the school bus stop, and almost

On the edge of the Nullarbor . . . wilting windmills.

passed the gate before I realised I was at the entrance to Ashford. The mailbox and the name was gone. Two golden cypress which we had planted as seedlings were now towering, their undersides dark and hewn back by men with chainsaws. The garage was gone, but the dairy and chook house was still there, its side patched with rusting corrugated iron. The woolshed and grain shed still stood, and the sheepyards made by my father more than four decades earlier were still there, bent and somewhat bowed. The front fence was gone; nor was there a house any more. The stumps had been removed, but a slab of concrete remained near the back door. The old dunny still stood, crookedly now, and water pipes sprouted from the ground where the kitchen and laundry had been. Only dried grass, cow pats and sheep manure marked the spot where I grew up from six to 16.

Failed dreams. The ruins of the Cadelga station, on the road between Innamincka and Birdsville, are now a roofless, crumbling conjunction of walls and bush-hewn lintel logs. Weeds grow in the rubble, and generations of passers-by have made their marks by carving their initials, stupidly, deep into the lime-rendered walls. There is no sound other than the calls of the birds in the nearby tree-flanked, waterless creek, but the gaping walls echo with the imagined sounds of pioneer families confronting the elements in this remote place.

Why did they come here? This is one of the most arid parts of Australia, yet they drove their sheep in search of slim pickings among the purple gibbers. On the lush grazing plains of the south you count sheep per acre; here it is acres per sheep. It could never be more than marginal country out here near the corner of South Australia and Queensland, yet hardy pioneers believed they could make a living from it. They were wrong. They were driven back by drought and depression, and they left their marks only in their sturdy stone and mud homes.

Failed dreams. A windmill stands crookedly, its remaining steel sails dripping from its rusty head like the petals of a wilted daisy. She loves me. She loves me not. Once this structure sucked life from the unforgiving ground on Colona station on the edge of the Nullarbor Plain. A second, newer windmill is nearby, but it, too, has passed its useful life. It, too, will rust and return eventually to the earth.

Failed dreams. They are everywhere to be seen on the edges of viability. Pondanna in the Gawler Ranges. Arltunga in the East MacDonnell Ranges. Somerset at the tip of Cape York. Farina in the Flinders Ranges. Milparinka in the arid New South Wales north-west. The last remains of a time when we believed we could tame this land by merely scratching its surface. Hope in ruins.

Ashford wasn't a failed dream. My father toiled — and died — to create a showpiece farm. All that yakka; all those hard yards; all that planning; all that pride in achievement, had come from nothing but his determination. Now, with the house gone, it felt forlorn, but the land was still productive, the woolshed and the sheepyards still working, the windmills and troughs still bringing water to the lambs, and the plantations still providing shelter against the cold southerlies. And, I later discovered, the house hadn't been demolished: it had merely been uplifted,

slung on to the back of a low-loader, and trucked to the outskirts of Merino where it now gleams with a new coat of paint and echoes to the cries of another family's children. My father and his family had strut this stage for 15 years. We had come and gone. Times change. Nothing stays the same. It was, after all, almost four decades since I had been in that house and garden, and the world had changed dramatically in that time. So why should Ashford remain in a time warp?

I received an email in May 1997 asking if I would please ring Stuart Aylmer — Stuart Aylmer?... Stuart Aylmer?... — at a telephone area code in the Western District of Victoria. My old stamping ground. Stuart Aylmer... why, yes, of course, we went to school together.

'Hi Stuart, it's Mark Day. It's been a long time. What is it?... I left school at the end of 1959, so that makes it... 37, 38 years?'

'A bit longer than that,' came the chuckling drawl. 'I never went to high school. I want to invite you to the reunion of Grade 6 at the Merino Consolidated School, 1954.'

Nineteen bloody fifty-four! Forty-three years ago! A reunion of kids who were then 11 or 12! I can hardly remember anything about it. Fifty-four: that's seriously stretching the memory. But yes, I'll be there.

Stuart asked if I would say a few words at the reunion dinner. But what? Too many years; so much water under the bridge; so little of it left in my memory; so little in common with those whose paths had never crossed mine since the day I left Ashford. In fact, I thought, the only thing we had in common was that we had survived the years from 1954 to 1997.

The reunion became a stimulus to look back across the decades; to reflect on our

The Class of '54 at Merino Consolidated School: combined Grades 5 and 6. That's me on the far right of the back row.

Forty-three years on: the class of '54 poses in the same spot in front of Merino Consolidated School.

changing times. In my speech, I reminded my classmates that, back in 1954, we were war babies. The first baby boomers were about to start schooling; the great bulk of them yet to come. Our parents were still recovering, economically and emotionally, from the fears of invasion, the pain of death, injury and separation, and the horrors of crimes they wished they didn't have to confront. They spoke little of their traumatic experiences, preferring to wish them away. Yet half a century after their commission, war crimes are still the subject of unresolved debate and the families who have been left to grow old are still trying to learn the truth about events — such as the sinking of HMAS *Sydney* — which took away their loved ones.

There were about nine million of us then. The first waves of postwar migration had begun, but the millionth immigrant wasn't to arrive on our shores until some years later. Wool was selling for a pound a pound in a short burst of super-inflation following the Korean War, and as the young Queen Elizabeth II was crowned the newspapers were full of brimming hope at the coming glories of another great Elizabethan Age. Our school was bussed to Hamilton to stand for hours in wait for a glimpse of Her Majesty as she was carried in an open Landrover between rows of awestruck children. I did but see her passing by...

Atom bombs were being exploded at Maralinga in the 1950s, only to be trumped by hydrogen bombs at Monte Bello. The arms race was on, and we came to appreciate the notion of living today, for tomorrow we may die. Perhaps that is why we were never a thrifty generation, saving for a rainy day. Never did we feel more threatened by the presence of the Russian bear, waiting to

pounce, than when a twinkle in the sky called Sputnik left us slackjawed in amazement as it passed eerily overhead. It never occurred to us that Sputnik and its successors — global communications satellites — would change our lives.

We cheered Our Dawn Fraser when she won gold at the Melbourne Olympics in 1956, but we barely noticed the British Empire crumbling as the African states began to decolonise in Mau Mau blood and endless coups. We stood gobsmacked by the miracle of television as it flickered black and white in shop windows. Migration reached peak levels, and our transformation was under way.

And when the transistor was developed it was greeted as the means by which we could have new, smaller radios to carry around with us, to the beach, to the garden, to the paddocks on the tractor. Little did we understand that transistors were the seminal event of our time; that they would shrink into silicon chips, and then microchips, and now, nanochips, and spawn a computerised, digital world beyond the comprehension of a kid growing up in the fifties.

Our world was Bill Haley and The Comets, Elvis Presley and the evil of swinging hips; of bodgies and widgies and the first signs of a youth revolt. Our parents were worried by this, but they breathed a sigh of relief when the Salk vaccine brought an end to polio.

I entered the work force in 1960, when John Fizgerald Kennedy was elected President of the United States; the beginning of his and Jackie's 'Camelot'; when the generations began to change; when the young challenged the old in the student riots of Paris and Kent State, and the sit-ins on campuses around the globe. We were a generation in revolt, spurred on by Bob Dylan, and entertained by the new sound of the Beatles and the Rolling Stones. We lunged for the levers of power, and our generation hasn't yet let go.

The decade of the sixties was a cultural sea change; when the hippie mantra of making love not war coalesced into Woodstock; when acid trips and psychedelia marked a sexual revolution wrought by the Pill. If the transistor was the wedge to drive a technological chasm between the past and the future, the Pill was the invention which gave women equal sexual rights with men: now they could explore their own sexuality, freely, without fear of pregnancy. And many did, with hardly a murmur of protest from men.

The Pill spawned the emergence of modern feminism and became the platform to launch the drive for equality. The Pill was the trigger for a redefinition of women's roles; a release from the apron strings, the granting of a new status which sent shock waves of confusion through the institution of marriage, the workplace and the male pysche. The Pill was condemned from pulpits, blamed for promiscuity and a breakdown in family life, but it was wolfed down by a female population that was free at last.

The doomsday clock ticked to one second to midnight when Nikita Khrushchev tried to set up missiles in Cuba, and we held our breath as Kennedy faced him down. JFK's 'Camelot' was snuffed out on a grassy knoll in Dallas, and we reeled from the serial horrors of political assassinations: Robert Kennedy, Martin Luther King, Malcolm X; even an attempt on Arthur 'Cocky' Calwell here, in Australia, where political violence didn't happen. It was the way of our time: in Vietnam the killing grew, and we winced at images of children, naked and burning from napalm, running from war, and of police

summarily executing their countrymen for the crime of a different political allegiance. And it came, on TV, into our homes; the first war to do so contemporaneously.

The rights and wrongs of Vietnam challenged and divided us; young against old, father against son, a nation against itself. It seared and tortured our souls. Many a Vietnam veteran today finds it hard to explain why he still doesn't feel part of our society.

In the 1960s we challenged the meaning of our inner souls when a doctor in South Africa transplanted a human heart, dramatically demonstrating that it was just a pump and not the centre of our being. We looked back on ourselves from the moon; the first time we had thrown off our earthly shackles, and rationalised that it was neither blue, nor cheese, nor particularly romantic — just rock. The interdependence of the moon, the romantic and the heart foundered on scientific fact, and today we are blasé about the quest to understand the composition of Mars, Venus, Saturn, Jupiter and the black holes beyond.

In the 1960s we saw the end of Robert Gordon Menzies' reign as Prime Minister and the first jumbo jet ferried passengers from New York to London, shrinking the globe for millions of people who would busily cross-pollinate cultures.

In the 1970s, I reminded my classmates, we were rudely awakened to the economics of the real world when Britain joined the European Common Market. The Mother Country turned her back on us, knocking away a central pillar of our existence, and our resentment grew as European Community citizens walked free through customs at Heathrow while we queued as Austr-aliens. But the Japanese economic miracle had begun, and our enemy of a quarter of a century ago became our vital friend.

Australia II, winner of the Americas Cup in 1983, in trials for the 1985 defence in Fremantle, Western Australia.

The Vietnam War continued to consume us in a way no other firefight — Afghanistan, Angola, the Gulf, or Chechnya — has done. But Gough Whitlam ended 23 years of conservative rule and brought our boys home.

Family law changed, and the rules of divorce — and therefore the structure of marriage — were revolutionised. Depending on your viewpoint, it was the end of family values, or the beginning of a sane acceptance of a different way of life. If the nuclear family teetered, so too did the nuclear structures at Three Mile Island and Chernobyl. Meltdowns in nuclear power plants made us more nervous about nukes — whether designed for destruction or peaceful power generation.

John Kerr sacked Gough Whitlam in an unprecedented constitutional crisis, the essential elements of which remain un-

resolved. The transistor shrank to silicon chips and grew in power. The desktop computer emerged to herald the dawn of the Age of Information, but the Internet wasn't even a dream. Communication satellites opened the window of live TV to any event, anywhere, on or off the globe. Computer technology began to bring changes in every field of human endeavour — a revolution which is still picking up pace, forcing us to confront change as never before, whether we like it or not.

In the 1980s the credo of Gordon Gekko in the movie *Wall Street* took hold: greed is good. Greed creates wealth. Wealth is good. We coined a new word: globalisation, and the economy soared, based on paper trading, asset revaluation, and houses of cards built on impossibly large wads of money handed out by banks desperate to keep market share in a deregulated economy.

We cheered Alan Bond as he snatched the America's Cup from the Yanks after 132 years. He parlayed his fame into a credit card to what seemed to be every bank in the world, and blithely accepted their offers to build his empire on a quicksand of borrowed money. Others, like Skase, Connell and Elliott, competed for the title of Australian superhero of the bourse.

The torrent of money built skyscrapers of glass and marble, but the masters of the business universe fell over in the puffs of wind that followed the 1987 Wall Street crash. The entrepreneurs who had built their temples on the stupidity of the banks faded into oblivion, fled or went to prison.

But we refused to be diverted from our lust for computer-chip-driven electronics. Colour TVs, mobile phones, faxes, CDs, CD-ROMs, the Internet. They were the trophies of the yuppie eighties. Today's cars carry more computing power than Apollo 11 when it flew to the moon.

And John Lennon died in the eighties, and we were left to imagine what might have been.

In the 1990s, we had the recession we had to have. Keating came, saying you get only one shot at it, and flicked the switch to vaudeville in a flurry of excitement. He challenged us to think about our symbols; our definitions of ourselves as Australians rather than British adrift in the south seas. Then he went, consigning himself to oblivion, leaving a growing sense of loss among those who saw his aims as worthy.

China, having stirred and faltered in the blood of Tiananmen Square, began to emerge as a fully fledged economic powerhouse, resuming control over Hong Kong by agreement with the colonial British. We wait to see if it is Hong Kong which infects China with a rampant market economy, or whether China snuffs out the freedoms essential for international trading success.

The wholly unexpected and startling break-up of the Soviet Union left us gasping. Communism, as a theory and a state, was dead at 70, and we struggled to adjust to life without superpower confrontation, but with an arsenal of weapons large enough to destroy us all, many times over.

The Gulf War gave us a front-row seat to the work of smart bombs, and we felt uneasy. But we thrilled as Nelson Mandela and his people triumphed over apartheid. Reconciliation took hold in Australia — too slowly, and with too far to go, but it took hold, nevertheless.

We were gripped with horror and heartache by the actions of a blond man, not wired like you and me, who brought more misery to historic Port Arthur when he massacred 35 people. A car went through the sound barrier. Another sped through a Paris tunnel and Diana, Princess of Wales, died, leaving the House of Windsor trembling at the unprecedented outpouring of grief by people the world over.

And in the 1990s we began the debate about our future in the new millennium — as a monarchy with an absent monarch, or as a truly independent nation where the spirit springs from the people as citizens, not subjects.

Who can imagine the changes yet to come? Within a year of my speech at the reunion, Suharto disappeared into a vortex of Indonesian unrest, and the giants of the subcontinent — India and Pakistan — exploded nuclear weapons. Whatever changes are next, we can be certain they will be no less challenging, no less confronting, and no less inexorable than those we have already lived through.

The sum of man's knowledge is doubling each decade. What products, services, medicines or miracles lie waiting to be discovered in the explosion of knowledge we'll see in the first quarter of the new century?

In early 1998 I visited the world's largest electronics display in Las Vegas. I arrived on the 30th anniversary of the assassination of Martin Luther King. It was with a jolt that I remembered it was, therefore, 30 years and one month since I had arrived in the United States to take up a job as foreign correspondent for News Limited.

Television shows endlessly repeated King's famous speech, delivered the night before his death, testifying that he had been to the mountaintop and seen the vision of the Lord. It rang in my head as I wandered, awed, through the aisles of digital wizardry, watching demonstrations of computer-driven animation software, limited only by the powers of the imagination.

Manly Beach, Sydney… the insouciance of youth, salt spray and sunscreen.

The Corso, Manly… a multi-cultural signature.

OPPOSITE: Sunset at Manly… a restless kaleidoscope of colour.

This convention displayed the pinnacle of technology; the cutting edge — click; show me the weather in Sydney — click; show me the first episode of Mr Ed — click; throw rotten tomatoes or whack a custard pie in Johnny Carson's face — click; let me request a record from a radio station in Boston — click; take me anywhere I want to go, NOW!

'I have been to the mountaintop, and I have seen the vision'... High-definition television. Flat plasma screens. How big would you like it? Video on demand. What's possible? What's real? What's next? What's possible is next.

What's possible for Martin Luther King's people? Without doubt, the American black underclass has made progress in the past 30 years. There is now a large, and growing, black middle class. In the American way, you can pull yourself up by your bootstraps if you really set your mind to it, get an education, and get helped along the way by equal rights rules which demand ethnic balances in employment. But there remains a huge black underclass; homeless, jobless blacks living in povery and declining hope in decaying inner-city ghettos. The more things change, the more they stay the same...

Without doubt, Australia's indigenous people have made progress in the past 30 years. But chronic problems remain — inferior housing, water supplies, educational opportunities, medical services, job availabilities and the despair of cultural dispossession. The more things change...

Leaps in technology can amaze and inspire us, as well as disturb us by driving constant and sometimes overwhelming social change. We can harness bytes, and make them move through cyberspace to do more, better, incredible things which change the way we live. But we have not learned how to harness the spirit of people willing to change the way we are.

I live by the sea now, half a century since we moved to Ashford. Like the great majority of Australians, I cling to the coast, as close as it's possible to get, as if lured by sirens waiting to claim us and take us back to whence we came. My home is Manly, a stone's throw from the entrance to Port Jackson, where modern Australia began in 1788.

From my balcony I see a restless kaleidoscope of colour, of kayaks far offshore, of swimmers pushing out between the flags, of volleyball girls with sand clinging to their sweat, of sunbathers in contorted shapes carefully tanning the shaded recesses of their bodies, of lithe girls on rollerblades swooshing down the cycle track.

I see container ships sink into the horizon, flocks of birds fishing, tots in lurid red neck-to-knee sunsuits squealing as they rush at the waves, purposeful Bayliners idling along the beach, buzzed by bouncing yellow jetskis, waves curling bottle-green, cut by the foaming white wakes of surfboards, spending themselves silver on the sand.

I greet the day with golden sunrises which drift into turquoise and azure afternoons, purple skies etched by flash-blue lightning as heavy dollops of rain announce the late cleansing storms of summer.

I watch strolling families, hand in gritty hand, their images upturned in the wet sand; little angels in Bad Boy caps and teenagers parking their chariots, hitching up their shorts, unloading their triple-finned boards, studying the surf with the insouciance of youth, lemon and sun in their hair.

All around are blazing bougainvilleas and bright hibiscus, the smell of sweet-scented gardenias hanging in the languid air, and pommie-white skins, glistening with salt spray and sunscreen, showering and towelling between the pines on the lawn directly below.

It is undeniably erotic. Coffee-coloured girls baring their breasts in splendid isolation: what is it about the beach which allows this very public form of display to become an essentially private act? If they took off their tops in Pitt Street, arrests would follow; here, beach protocol demands that the observer must grant space to the sunbaker, and must not be seen to be admiring, let alone perving.

I stroll down the beachfront to The Corso and watch a busking clown amid the colour and movement of saris, sarongs, turbans, T-shirts and thongs, marvelling at what we have become. The evidence is on the awnings: Copenhagen ice-cream, Urcan kebabs, Dian Chinese, Red Gum Australian fare, Manly kebab house, Dong Dong noodles, McDonald's, Cristal's seafoods, Delifrance, Asian soup noodles, Paradiso Pizza, Burger King, Pizza Hut, Nando's Portuguese chicken. I am told there are 47 restaurants within 500 metres of my place. What do we feel like tonight? Japanese, Italian, Malay, French, Lebanese, Chinese, Moroccan, Thai, Indian, Tex-Mex?

This is multicultural Manly. Surf, sun, sand and sex. It is a Sydney signature we take for granted, and it is the envy of the world. Yet I am drawn to the bush.

The Blue Mountains at Katoomba, New South Wales.

chapter three

As Wendy and I punched the Pajero over the Blue Mountains, headed for Perth, we left behind multiple cries of envy. Many of our friends and acquaintances told us they had always wanted to drive around Australia; to see their homeland in all its red-earth richness; to experience first-hand the sights and sensations they had only glimpsed on television. This was the stuff of their dreams.

Demographers will define us by age and sex, by marital status and family form, by our dwellings and by our socioeconomic standing. They can put us in little boxes and define us by acronyms like YUPPIES (Young Upwardly Mobile Professionals, which I once was), DINKS (Double Income, No Kids, which we now are), or whatever. But when we hit the road, we joined the GGs — the Geriatric Gypsies.

There is a huge, largely unmeasured, floating population on the roads. Its make-up is varied, covering the spectrum from backpacking kids in beaten-up old bombs to retirees in lumbering caravans and mobile homes. But, from our observations, the largest single group is of liberated 50-plus-somethings: retirees and the retrenched. This is a symptom of our times. As companies pare their work forces in the global trend euphemistically known as downsizing, thousands of middle-aged, productive workers have got their marching orders. With their pink slips have come handsome 'piss-off' payments. Some have paid off mortgages and sought re-employment. Others have simply seen opportunity in adversity and taken to the road to follow, at last, the dream which had lurked within them, unfulfilled, while they wrestled within the corporate jungle.

One evening, the motel rooms adjoining ours were suddenly filled by three couples travelling in a convoy of muddy 4WD vehicles. Two of the men were retrenched bank managers; another a retrenched supermarket manager; together they had confronted the harsh economic facts of their lives by taking to the roads and challenging themselves on the Canning stock route.

The Geriatric Gypsies have cut the ties that have bound them to their homes and extended families; detached themselves from their neighbourhoods and communities; and abandoned the routines of their previous lives. They no longer participate in local debates or volunteer for school tuckshop duties. They have cancelled their newspaper deliveries, and watch the television news only when they find themselves in a motel room or front bar where luck, rather than management, makes their visit coincide with news time. Even then, they find it difficult to engage with the news: unfamiliar faces recount unfamiliar events about unfamiliar people and unfamiliar places. There is little

point in trying to absorb the nuances of council politics in, say, Bunbury, when by tomorrow night you'll be in Albany. And, from their perspective, who cares if the Russian government is in meltdown? What possible impact could that have on tomorrow's visit to the tall timbers of the tingle forests?

The Geriatric Gypsies have become a disconnected generation; insular drop-outs from the realities of their past lives, and the realities of the lives of those who continue to toil in the cities. But that doesn't mean they abandon all contact. They learn, quite easily, to do without regular infusions of news, but when the opportunity presents itself they can be voracious consumers of information. I took a copy of *The Weekend Australian* to a resort at Punsand Bay at the tip of Cape York, where it was leapt upon, divided and devoured by dozens of guests over the course of a week. It represented precious contact with the outside world.

As we drove further and further from home, we found that the issues which had previously weighed on our minds became less and less relevant. The grip of previous connections loosened. What mattered now was fuel (how far to the next service station?), food (grab a hamburger, or sit down for a plate of grey steak and soggy chips?), distances (where shall we stay the night, and how far does that mean we have to travel tomorrow?), and the sights and sensations of the country we were travelling through.

Gradually, we learned the many protocols of life on the road. And some simple, incontrovertible formulas, such as: the greater the distance from the capital cities, the more essential is The Wave. This can be the slight wave of a hand, glimpsed through the windscreen of an oncoming vehicle, or even just the lifting of a finger from the ten-past-ten position on the steering wheel. It is an acknowledgment, not merely of two individuals passing in the middle of nowhere, but also of a shared state of adventure. It is the mobile equivalent of 'G'day'. On the Nullarbor, The Wave is discretionary east of Port Augusta and west of Kalgoorlie; in between, it is de rigueur. To fail to give The Wave is to insult the flashing passer-by.

At the service stations which provide the only stopping places across the Nullarbor, a conversational protocol is followed. It requires mandatory observation and a little logic. For example, if I were at Yalata, heading west, filling up beside a West Australian-registered sedan facing east, I would say: 'G'day. Where you from?'

'Perth.'

'We're heading there. What's the road like ahead?'

'Good. Make sure you fill up before the border. Petrol's more expensive in WA.'

'Thanks. You'll find the cheapest this side is at Penong.'

'Thanks. Good luck, then. See yer.' Which, of course, we wouldn't.

The protocol has within it a little more excitement when you spot a registration plate from your home state.

'G'day. Where you from?'

'Sydney.'

'So are we. Whereabouts in Sydney?'

'Curl Curl.'

'Oh, we're from Manly.' And then follows a chat about the beaches; how long they've been on the road, how long you've been on the road; where you're going, where you've been, what you've seen; and helpful bits of advice, like: 'Make sure you spend an hour or so at the Wadlata Centre at Port Augusta — it's terrific.'

In this way the disconnected generation of travellers pick up tips and information specifically tailored to their needs, and quickly absorb a sense of what is worthwhile ahead and what isn't. It's a kind of sharing that is both unnecessary and unlikely to take place at your hometown corner service station, and the information exchanged is so rarely available in newspapers, or on the radio or television, that they are rendered superfluous.

It's wise not to push the Sydney bit too hard on these bush encounters. There is a suspicion about Sydney and its people: too smart-arse, too pushy, too up-themselves, too much glitter to be taken seriously; not like the rest of us.

There is statistical evidence to support the contention that Sydney isn't like the rest of Australia. It has the highest proportion of migrants — 35 per cent of people who live there were born overseas — and it's an accelerating trend. Since 1991, Sydney has attracted 36 per cent of all migrants to Australia. The migrant mix is also different — and visually so — in Sydney, where 20 per cent are from Asia — well above the national average.

Sydney has developed into a global city. Its geographic location, its natural beauty built around a dazzling harbour, its labour sources and skills (including Asian languages), and its communications infrastructure have made it the first choice for thousands of local and multinational companies which have established their national or regional headquarters there. Sydney-based companies dominate the banking and financial sectors.

It's also the first port of call for a majority of visitors to Australia; it has a thriving artistic and cultural community, and its 'who cares?' insouciance towards its substantial gay and

Nullarbor coast… the cliffs of the Great Australian Bight.

lesbian community is witnessed through the success of its annual Gay and Lesbian Mardi Gras.

Sydney's position as the communications capital of Australia — like London and New York — also contributes to misgivings. All the newspaper, radio and television networks have their headquarters there, and programming decisions which impact around the nation are taken with the Sydney market at the forefront of the mind. While most TV stations have capital city or regional newsrooms, almost all current affairs and entertainment programs show a distinct Sydney bias.

These elements coalesce into a suspicious envy, articulated most frequently in Melbourne, but felt around the land. There's no crime in coming from Sydney, but hey, don't brag about it.

When this project was in its formative stages I did what any normal bloke would do: I discussed it with my wife. Wendy and I had just passed our 20th wedding anniversary, so I had a fair idea of her reaction: doubt, bordering on disbelief. Why, she asked, would we contemplate leaving our lovely home in Sydney, with its views over Middle Harbour, for a life roughing it in the bush, away from our friends, barbecue mates, drinking buddies, and the girls' Friday lunch club? And what would we do with our dog, Claudie, whose sweetness and nuzzling companionship had so much to do with making our house a home?

I proffered the thought that it wouldn't be all bad. We would still have some comforts. We would stay in motels where available — even resorts; and where such luxuries weren't available, it would be, well, an adventure.

Wendy wasn't immediately convinced. Behind her buoyant, bubbling personality and her ability to make people laugh lurks a mind geared to disaster. Where I assume things will be all right, she assumes everything will go wrong. She says I am too optimistic; that I take too much for granted. She is the devil's advocate, identifying all the things that may get in the way. The morning after I proposed that we move to an apartment and rent out our house, she came downstairs irritable after a sleepless night and demanded to know what we would do with the food in the freezer. I said: 'Eat it,' which seemed to settle that for the moment.

We eventually resolved the problems and moved, jettisoning ten years of accumulated junk, and arranging for Claudie to share a friend's home with a jaunty black bitzer named Bundy. No sooner had we shoe-horned ourselves into our beachside apartment than we were packing the Pajero to leave for Perth.

We stayed the first night in a motel in Orange which smelled like a dead dingo's donga, and planned to spend the next night at Ivanhoe, in the arid central west of New South Wales. But the Ivanhoe pub had burned down and no accommodation was available, so a solution lay in the shearers' quarters at the old Willandra station, now a national park. For $25 each we could bunk down on the old beds which used to accommodate the shearers and roustabouts on their annual pilgrimage through the outback. But, the ranger warned, it was best not to leave the back door light switched on. The door led to the outside toilets, but the light was activated by a movement sensor, and because the kangaroos come in each night to feed on the lawn grass, 'their movement will keep the light going on and off and you won't be able to sleep'.

The thought of sharing her nocturnal missions of relief with a bunch of kangaroos didn't appeal greatly to Wendy. I ventured the thought that they were probably only little ones, not killers, and would move away if she said 'Shoo', but from her point of view the trip was rapidly descending into a farcical disaster. She was by now believing a friend's comment that, in agreeing to this whole barmy project, she must be brave, loyal and stupid.

Neither of us was confronted by boxing kangaroos that night, but they served to vividly illustrate Wendy's pessimistic view of the world next morning. Shortly after sun-up we headed out of Willandra and were treated to one of the quintessential Australian sights: a mob of roos — 30 to 40 of them — in full flight across the desert, accompanied by a dozen of so emus. They had been feeding on a flat and sparse plain near the Willandra Creek when we disturbed them, and they took off, stirring puffs of dust at every leap, tails up, bounding in unison towards the north, lit by the early morning sun. The emus were at full stretch, too, kicking up dust which glowed in the oblique light. It was a sight I imagine very few Australians have seen, except on film or television. I felt privileged and awed, but Wendy saw it differently. To her, the sight of a kangaroo evokes the image of it splattered on our windscreen; of a bent and broken Pajero upside down in a ditch; of black crows and wedge-tailed eagles picking at our bones until there remains no trace of us: lost and forgotten victims of the interminable conflict between Man, the Desert and its Beasts. As we idled forward, Wendy held her hands up to her eyes, twittering with dismay at our impending doom. When the animals hopped away and we resumed our drive, she reflected with breathless relief on her lucky escape from certain death.

But kangaroos, and the danger they represented on the road, didn't leave us. On the few occasions we travelled after dusk, Wendy maintained a non-stop 'roo watch, bolt upright in her seat, eyes peeled. If we saw one, she spluttered in fearful anticipation, throwing her hands up to her eyes, instinctively crouching and curling up her body, preparing for impact. She offered to drive, from time to time, but admitted if she had to react quickly to a kangaroo — or any other potential roadkill for that matter — she would be more likely to panic than to take avoiding action.

So I drove, and in the near 14,000 kilometres we travelled on this first trip we didn't hit a roo, a wombat, a camel, a bird, a rabbit, a feral cat, a fox, a dingo, an emu, a sheep, a cow, or even a snake, although we spotted them all on or beside the road, dead; victims of roadkill.

When I was growing up at Ashford I travelled to and from school in a bus driven by a stuttering, roly-poly First World War veteran named Herb Bayley. His favourite trick was to yell out 'Hang on, kids!' as he swerved to sideswipe a rabbit scurrying across the road.

Happiness was when he succeeded in merely knocking the bunny senseless. He'd scamper out the door, pick it up, wring its neck, and return to the bus with a grin, saying: 'Underground mutton! Dinner for Mrs Bayley tonight.'

Unhappiness was when he ran over the poor blighter. Its bones being no match for a bus, the bunny was just a feed for his dog.

We have become a trifle more sophisticated in our eating habits since those days. The food and wine trails of Australia are attracting more and more visitors. They take us through the Hunter Valley to award-winning restaurants like Roberts; into the Barossa Valley to sample the sublime fare of Maggie Beer; down the Yarra Valley, and into the bucolic backblocks of Tasmania.

On a blistering hot January day I found myself at a food and wine festival on the Mornington Peninsula, south of Melbourne, where 70-odd stallholders vied to titillate our tastebuds with homemade goodies like strawberry and curaçao jam, kiwifruit conserve with melon liqueur, yabby and green peppercorn pâtés, garlic and mint jelly, hot and spicy tomato relish, fig and ginger chutney, black olive and herb paste… plus some sublime pinot noir and sauvignon blanc wines.

It was about as far as you could get from rabbit stew, or the tins of IXL apricot or strawberry jam of my youth.

But what's this? One of the stalls was doing a roaring trade. People were queued ten deep to get their hands on — I don't believe it — Outback Jack's Road Kill Grill! This is a food stall with attitude. It's a contraption of rusty corrugated iron, supported by twisted gum branches and shattered floorboards. Handpainted, or daubed, signs promise fresh road meat ('We get it before the buzzards'), and behind the servery (an old dunny door) is a bloke with a floppy hat and bobbing corks.

Off the griller come succulent steaks covered in bell peppers, yellow squash, tomatoes and eggplants sautéed in their own juices and wrapped in pita bread. Plus chicken Sydney (plucked and headless, thank goodness), shrimps on the barbie, and a 'rather large butt on a bun', or, if you wish, a sausage in a bun.

The odd thing about this quintessential Aussie Outback Jack's Road Kill Grill is that… it's American! Well, sort of. Twenty-three years ago, Jack Williams of Adelaide, fresh out of the Australian Army after a stint in Vietnam, married his sweetheart, Penny, from Melbourne. They took off on a three-month honeymoon overseas.

Somehow they got sidetracked, and stayed. About ten years ago, in Washington state, they were roped in by friends to help at a charity fair. They cobbled together some old wood and corrugated iron, called it Outback Jack's, and sold out of food by lunchtime.

They were invited to set up stalls at other fairs. Word spread about the zany Jack and his cork-rimmed Aussie hat, and suddenly he was a hit. He built 27 Road Kill Grills of various shapes, sizes and permanence, and hawked his wares at fairs and festivals across the United States. He never quite challenged McDonald's or Pizza Hut, but he made a motza along the way.

In late 1995, Jack and Penny came home. They heard of the Mornington Peninsula food and wine festival and signed up for stall space. Jack's first thought was to convert his concept to Texas Jack's Road Kill Grill. He reasoned that the Americans liked the exotic Australiana of Outback Jack; ergo, Australians would respond to the exotica of Texas. But Jack was persuaded he was wrong. And why not? The great majority of us are city dwellers, for all the world a branch office of America, surrounded by Big Macs, KFC, Pizza Huts, Hungry Jacks, Coke, Pepsi, Baywatch and Beverly Hills 90210. We, too, thrill to the lure of our outback. It might be on our doorstep, but how many of us actually go there?

Odd, isn't it? Here's an expat Aussie importing an Aussie idea to his native land, instinctively believing he had to make it American to bolster its character.

On one stretch of road between Yalata and the Nullarbor — shortly before we reached the Treeless Plain — we counted 16 dead animals, mostly kangaroos, in two kilometres. Wendy cowered at the sight of flesh and blood, and was particularly put off by the sight of large wedge-tailed eagles lumbering into the air to escape us as we

Outback Jack's Road Kill Grill . . . Jack Williams' gimmick.

approached. She hated the concept of flying carnivores tearing at red-raw meat, and wouldn't be placated by the fact that the eagles, and other animals, do much to clean up the roadside carnage.

When I suggested a stop to try to get a long-lens photograph of an eagle with its roadkill, Wendy agreed readily. She was tired of being cooped up in the vehicle, and a good, brisk walk would get the circulation moving again. I also wanted to make some calls on the satphone. So Wendy strode ahead.

Some minutes later I noticed that a small yellow car which had passed me had stopped beside Wendy. After a few moments, it drove off again. I hurried to catch up with her.

'He thought I was bonkers,' she said. 'He asked if I was all right; if I needed any assistance, and when I said, "No thanks, I'm just having my morning walk while my husband makes some phone calls," he looked at me as if I were barking mad. Well, you would, wouldn't you? Who goes walking alone out here? Who makes phone calls out here?' By nightfall Wendy was telling the story as if she had escaped the clutches of a serial killer in the middle of the desert, while I marvelled at the technology which allowed roadside phone calls by satellite.

When the first satphones were developed, a trailer was required to transport the complex electronics. Later, they were scaled down to suitcase size. The Mini-Sat unit, supplied for our travels by Telstra, was no larger than a laptop computer, with its antenna in the hinged lid. Aimed north-east at about 45 degrees, the antenna fired its signal 35,000 kilometres into space, to one of four Inmarsat satellites in geostationary orbit around Earth. The signal was then retransmitted to Telstra's Land Earth Station in Perth's northern suburbs, where it was fed into the terrestrial system.

I explained to Wendy that my roadside conversations to a connection in Sydney were travelling about 70,000 kilometres through space before whizzing through an optic-fibre link buried beside the Eyre Highway, just metres from where she walked. If she was impressed, it was lost in the speculation of what might have been with the 'serial killer', but the phone was to be our great comfort for the remainder of our travels. Occasionally, meeting other travellers in the outback, I would get doubtful looks and questions about the absence of bristling radio antennas on the Pajero until I produced the phone from its dusty carrying case, when rebukes about a cavalier attitude to safety dissolved into envy.

The Nullarbor is home to many a myth, but none more vivid than that of the Nullarbor Nymph. In the welcoming and cool front bar of the Eucla Motel in early January 1972, sometime journalist and public relations man Geoff Pearce shared a few beers with locals Ron Sells and Laurie Scott. Together they dreamed up the story of the Nullarbor Nymph — a woman who roamed the plains stark naked, feeding kangaroos.

It was the silly season, and the story went around the world, enhanced by a deliberately blurry photograph of motel waitress Fiona Campbell running starkers through the scrub.

Ron and Laurie made a film to 'prove' the story to TV audiences. They caught a kangaroo, doped it, and filmed Laurie's wife feeding it. Nude, of course. It was enough to put Eucla, and the Nullarbor, on the map.

The Nullarbor has a special place in the psyche of Australians. It symbolises our vastness, our battles against the elements, our harsh heat and endless plains. Across it lies one of the longest desert highways in the world, a white-stripped ribbon of grey through a red-earth desert of gibber and saltbush.

The Transcontinental railway goes to the core of our national existence. The railway lines are the ties which first bound east to west: the promise to build a rail link from Kalgoorlie to Port Augusta was a critical factor in the decision by westerners to join in the Australian federation in 1901.

Buttheroadis the challenge. Thousands are drawn to it from around the world, just to say: 'I've done it.' Just to wear the rear window sticker saying 'I crossed the Nullarbor' or the $25 T-shirt saying 'I survived the Nullarbor.'

Survival is relative. Edward John Eyre, who made the first east–west crossing in 1841 in an unparalleled feat of endurance and tenacity, spiced with treachery and death, would have laughed at the notion that a 1200-kilometre airconditioned car trip from Ceduna to Norseman somehow equated with survival. Not on his terms, anyway.

Eyre had left Adelaide in 1840 to find a route through to the north coast. He pushed and prodded at the desert, but each time was forced back. Rather than return to Adelaide a failure, he looked west and decided to become the first person to complete a western crossing.

It was a death-or-glory venture, and he took with him four volunteers — a white overseer named John Baxter, two New South Wales Aborigines, and a West Australian Aborigine named Wylie. They are remembered by today's names of the Baxter Cliffs and the Wylie Scarp (escarpment).

Eyre and his party left Fowlers Bay in February 1841, following the coast to Eucla. What takes six hours by car today took them 15 days, but it wasn't hard going. The clifftops are flat and support only low scrub in the shallow soil above the limestone.

But after Eucla the cliffs recede inland, and Eyre followed the coast, battling mountainous sandhills which continue to move to this day, all but burying the old Eucla telegraph station.

Unable to find water, and low on stores, the party survived on boiled horsemeat, rotten stingrays found on the beach and eagle stews. They licked the morning dew off the leaves of shrubs for water.

They scaled the cliffs for an easier passage, but Baxter and the New South Wales guides wanted to turn back. Eyre wouldn't have a bar of it. Baxter was killed by the New South Wales Aborigines who absconded, never to be heard of again.

Eyre and Wylie pressed on, travelling seven days without water. Sick and near death, they lay to rest on an idyllic beach with squeaking white sand from where they spotted a French whaling vessel, the Mississippi. They were taken on board, rested for two weeks, and then continued west, arriving in Albany in July 1841, having covered 1650 kilometres in 132 days. They were greeted by the amazed populace as men returned from the dead.

Eyre had blazed a trail through some of the most inhospitable land imaginable. His feat later inspired those who dreamed of an east–west telegraph link which was established in 1876, but it was to be 100 years before a proper road crossed the Nullarbor.

Until the Second World War a few hardy souls battled a rough limestone and sand track from east to west. The sharp limestone ripped their

tyres to shreds; the narrow treads of Model-T Fords sank into the sand.

The needs of national defence saw a gravel road formed by army engineers in 1941, and the crossing became easier. Even until 1976, when the road was finally sealed, the Nullarbor was a challenge.

For most people in a relatively modern vehicle, the Nullarbor is just an interminably long drive; one to be taken in a single, huge, keep-the-wheels-moving gulp, or in smaller bites, with stops at the spots on the map which indicate towns but are, in reality, just food-and-fuel roadhouses. They exist for no reason other than to service travellers — about 1000 a day on average, but up to 3000 a day in holiday times.

Today, this gruelling stretch of road acts as a magnet to adventurers, and misadventurers, from around the world. On the longest straight stretch of road in Australia — 146.6 kilometres from Balladonia to Caiguna — we stopped to talk to Koichiro Tachibana, 22, from Yokohama, who was riding his bicycle from Sydney to Perth.

The Nullarbor has a special attraction to the Japanese. Many companies encourage their executives to challenge themselves, and to increase their 'face' by overcoming the difficulties of the challenge.

'You see them go past on motorised skate-boards, mopeds, circus bikes — even pushing a wheelie bin,' said Peter de Leuw, a roly-poly cook at the Eucla Motel. 'The more unusual, or difficult, the crossing, the more "face" they have when they go back to their jobs.'

Lindsay Coates searching for his lost sidecar on the Nullarbor... like an extra from the set of *Mad Max.*

Koichiro Tachibana, from Yokohama, riding his bike across Australia . . . a burning ambition to succeed.

Koichiro wasn't doing his crossing for his company, but for himself. He had long nursed a dream to conquer the desert and see Australia, slowly. His bike was equipped with more saddlebags than Gene Autry, carrying his tent, sleeping bag, clothes, camera and tripod (so that he could take pictures of himself in his isolation) and food for 20 days.

His journey began in Sydney and took him via the coast roads of New South Wales and Victoria. Near Millicent in South Australia he was burned in a campfire accident, and spent a month in an Adelaide hospital. Recovered, he pressed on, each day spending eight hours in the saddle. For 24 consecutive nights before we met him, Koichiro pitched his tiny tent by the roadside, boiled some rice

or noodles, and opened a small tin of vegetables; enough of a ration to fuel a burning ambition to succeed.

A little further on were Mariko Sakamoto and Koji Sekine, from Osaka, who called themselves 'Team K & M, the Journey Run Club'. Mariko, a tiny, wiry 49-year-old, is a sports instructor and her partner Koji, a writer and coach. Together they were on what a hand-drawn banner stuck to the front of their Tarago van announced as the 'Trans-Australia Journey Run Indian–Pacific Ocean to Ocean Run'.

When we met, the Tarago had been their home for the past 28 days, and at their average 60 kilometres a day, they figured Sydney was 85 days away. Mariko was running into the face of a bitterly cold easterly with light rain falling, the antithesis of the sweltering sun and parched landscape we imagine the Nullarbor to be. But she was unfazed by the elements: for her, it is cold only when she stops.

'It is the ultra-runner's dream to cross a continent on foot — just using our own energy,' said Mariko. 'We are experiencing some wonderful adventures, learning a lot, and communicating with nature. It certainly looks desolate out here, but we enjoy it very much. It is very good to see so much, so closely. This sort of challenge renews our faith in the joys of running. Our mutual theme is to go as far as we can, and as long as we can. We want to run around the world, so Australia is just the first leg.'

If Koichiro and Mariko were adventurers, Lindsay Coates and David Cummings were quintessential misadventurers. Their tale of woe was almost unbelievable and certainly embarrassing.

Not for them the search for inner peace by challenging the desert. Their trip across the

Mariko Sakamoto and Koji Sekine, from Osaka, running across Australia . . . a bleak day on the Nullarbor.

Nullarbor was a transcontinental search for work. They were both chefs, and had left Cairns to ride their motorbike and sidecar to Perth on the promise of jobs.

I found Lindsay, 44, walking listlessly along the highway. David, 42, was about three kilometres ahead, sitting disconsolately beside the road, dazed and disoriented. Both were wearing army-style greatcoats, and were unshaven and jaded. They looked as if they might have been extras on a *Mad Max* set.

'I feel ashamed to admit this,' said Lindsay, 'but we've lost our sidecar.'

It wasn't a bad opening line.

He explained further: 'We came through here four days ago, and got a puncture in the wheel of the sidecar. We unhooked it, and because it contained all our possessions

— our clothes, chef's uniforms, knives, years of references, even my adoption papers — we didn't want to leave it on the side of the road where someone might have stolen it. So we pushed it about 100 metres off the road; but because it was silver we could still see it, so we put a green tarpaulin over it, and then added some tree branches. We then rode the bike into Balladonia to get the puncture fixed. Now we can't find the sidecar! It's too well hidden. We put a piece of orange-coloured tape on a tree to mark the spot, but we can't find that, either. Perhaps it blew off in the wake of a passing truck.'

Talk about finding a needle in a haystack! The guys had failed to accurately record their odometer readings, and when we found

The Nullarbor… a magnet for adventurers.

them they were on foot, searching a 30-kilometre stretch of highway. They had been at it for three days, and every tree, every bush, every stretch of saltbush plain looked the same.

They were out of money and were relying on the kindness of the owners of the Balladonia Motel for accommodation. I racked my brains: how could we help? 'Maybe, just maybe,' I said to Lindsay, 'someone has seen the sidecar and picked it up... or saw it being picked up.' I set up the satphone and called the west's leading radio talkback personality, Howard Sattler, at radio 6PR, Perth. I explained the situation and — not unnaturally — it appealed to him. It's not every day a radio host gets a satphone

call from the middle of the Nullarbor asking, 'Has anyone seen my sidecar?'

Lindsay explained his predicament to Howard. It must have made funny radio. Interview over, we wished Lindsay and David well and drove off. For months, we told the story without knowing the outcome.

Listening to Sattler that day was John Gracey, a former RAAF officer and Cathay Pacific flight engineer who had left Hong Kong to retire to Perth in 1995. He was still chuckling about it that evening when his wife, Babs, came home. He told her about Lindsay and David's predicament, and she said: 'Well, why don't you go and help them?'

'You're joking,' said John.

'No.'

'When?'

'There's no time like the present.'

It wasn't, John reasoned, a silly idea. In his 20 years in the RAAF he had learned a lot about search and rescue operations in our trusty Hercules aircraft; he knew the logic of establishing search patterns; he was familiar with maps and compasses, and he was at a loose end. So at 9.30 pm he jumped into his Nissan Patrol and headed east. By mid-afternoon the following day he was in Balladonia.

'They were in a mess,' John said. 'They had lost all perspective. Their memories were like scrambled eggs. I sat them down and we went through it minute by minute. What had they remembered?

'We drove 225 kilometres back up the highway to Cocklebiddy where they had last filled up with petrol. Then we retraced our steps. They remembered vaguely a slight cleared area between two stands of trees, which wasn't much to go on. But we established a kind of grid pattern and for two days we kept at it.'

Then, near the end of the seventh day of Lindsay and David's search, Eureka! They found it! Well off the highway, near a Telstra service track, behind a tree, well-covered with the tarpaulin and tree branches.

'They had done a good job on it,' said John. 'But they were delirious, and I felt we had won the world championship of something. I was very pleased for them, and they were profuse with thanks.'

Richard Swanson, proprietor of the Balladonia Motel, said: 'We get lots of sad stories here. We run the local ambulance service, and we have to deal with rollovers; sometimes fatalities… lots of cracked heads. The story of these two fellows with their missing sidecar went up and down the highway for months — and no-one's been able to beat it yet! But at least it had a happy ending.'

Lindsay and David sharpened their kitchen knives and put in a couple of days' work at the motel in appreciation of their free accommodation and meals. Then they hopped on the motorbike and sidecar, and faded into the western horizon.

changing times in the old port city.

four chapter

It's always a pleasure to be in Perth. It's an open, welcoming city; smart, clean and assertive. Perhaps because it boasts the most hours of sunlight each year of any Australian capital, its people seem to amply meet the description of sunny, too.

Perth people have a lot going for them, and they know it. The tall glass towers reflecting in the wide and placid waters of the Swan River, surrounded by well-groomed river-bank parks, give off an air of affluence and caring. It is a distinct signature. Stroll through the parks and this mood is underscored by the frequent presence of the symbol of Western Australia — black swans.

Perth is fast-growing. Its population doubled between the 1960s and the 1980s, and by 1996 had reached 1,295,000. This represents almost three-quarters of the total population of Western Australia. Yet growth has been orderly. They take their planning seriously in the west, and have largely avoided the hotch-potch planning muddles which have accompanied the sprawling of

Perth, Western Australia… smart, clean, assertive… and sunny people.

Perth architecture . . . assertive and affluent. This house faces Sunset Beach near Scarborough.

cities in the east. Perth may indeed sprawl in a giant coastal ribbon from Joondalup in the north to Rockingham — and on to Mandurah — in the south, contained to the east by the Darling Ranges, but transport corridors make the journey fast and easy.

The moneyed, well-to-do feel of Perth now extends to this once down-at-heel historic precinct, and a Sunday morning in the sidewalk cafes of Freo offers an interesting blend of old and new; old facades and strikingly modern and architecturally adventurous interiors; old faces of pensioned-off wharfies clutching a glass of stout while young trendies sip their café lattes and nibble croissants.

At Peppermint Grove and Dalkeith, the moneyed heart of the booming west, giant, often excessive, mansions mingle with other, less ostentatious but nevertheless sedately rich homes along the fabled Jutland Parade, where the mining and financial entre-preneurs of the eighties staked their claims to images of success. Alas, most were just that: images. The home-building follies of the heroes of the west are today relics of a time of excess.

Yet, while the visitor may feel confronted by such symbols, the locals seem not to notice. There is an attitude here that it is to be expected. After all, this is the west. This is the land of opportunity. This is the state, the locals will sometimes belligerently tell you, where 79 per cent of Australia's mineral wealth is derived. This is an oft-quoted but spurious statistic — Western Australia contributes about 30 per cent of the mineral wealth of the nation — roughly equivalent to its 33 per cent of the Australian landmass. The bragging arrogance of westerners, particularly in the company of a visitor from the east, is deep-seated. It is also, in many respects, well justified, for Western Australians have much to be proud of. But there is an unstated though underlying inference that all of this has been achieved on their own and in spite of the people, politicians and corporations of the east. There is a mistrust of the east, the result of Perth's isolation. It is the deeply rooted driver of frequent calls — and one successful referendum, ignored by the national government — for secession from the Commonwealth.

Isolation is a double-edged sword for the people of Perth. It promotes the self-sufficiency for which the west is famous, but it's a burden for those who need to integrate their businesses with the rest of the nation. Transport costs, by air or road, can alone obliterate a business's bottom line. The mind doesn't easily grasp the size of the state. A Melburnian can jump in a car and drive interstate in less than three hours; a Brisbane resident can be in New South Wales in less than two hours; but a drive from Perth to Adelaide takes almost 30 hours. Set out from Perth to travel north along the coast, and in just over 40 hours non-stop you'll reach Kununurra — and still be in Western Australia. But distance does have its compensations: many national companies feel the need to have a presence in Western Australia and establish offices in Perth, while cities such as Adelaide and Brisbane miss out because they can be adequately serviced from Sydney or Melbourne.

The isolationist subtext of western thinking manifests itself clearly in the emerging trend of building walled housing estates in the developing outer suburbs. There was a time when a new subdivision would be given a name, and For Sale billboards would presage the rise of cheek-by-jowl bungalows and triple-fronters on barren quarter-acre blocks. Not any more. The affluent demand today is for integrated estates, often surrounded by verdant golf courses and self-flushing waterways, and almost always hemmed in by sturdy high walls built from the region's signature cream limestone blocks. The walls, often kilometres long, reek of exclusivity — and security. If they could speak, they would surely say: 'We've made it in here — and we're gonna keep it!' It is cocooning on a large scale, where buyers can assume they are entering a club-like sanctuary to find new friends among like-minded people of a social status equal to theirs. Like the bulwarks around medieval castles and the great trading cities of Europe, the suburban housing estate walls serve as a barrier to the perceived dangers of the outside world, and calm the inner fear that whispers, 'Although we're isolated, clinging to our sandy patch of the western seaboard, we're safe in here.'

On 24 April 1997, we drove into Kings Park for the obligatory tourist's view of the

Perth skyline. The scenic vantage point is adjacent to the war memorial, and on that day preparations were taking place for the next morning's Anzac Day dawn service.

Kings Park is an expansive bushland reserve, melding into the Perth Botanic Gardens as it overlooks the city. It is the lungs of the city, a conveniently close place for a peaceful stroll or a lunch-hour jog. Through the park wind avenues of honour named May Drive and Lovekin Drive, and we mooched along these boulevards, quietly reading and reflecting on the names on plaques under each of 1104 trees. In preparation for Anzac Day, poppies and other flowers had been placed on each plaque: Corporal D. N. Kennedy Smith, killed in action, New Guinea, aged 21; H. G. Dix, war correspondent, killed in an accident in Queensland, aged 26; Leonard A. Green, missing, Germany, aged 24; Private J. Hodder, killed in action, Gona, aged 30; killed in action, Timor, aged 21; killed in Borneo, aged 20; killed in Flanders, aged 18... names, places, regiments; dead at 19, dead at 23, dead at 22, dead at 21... The names don't grip you. It's the ages. The flower of Australian youth, plucked, uselessly, before their time. A litany of sacrifice and waste. Endless rows of trees and plaques of kids — 686 of them in May Drive recognising the West Australian victims of the First World War, and 418 of them in Lovekin Drive, remembering the Second. One thousand, one hundred and four trees; 1104 young lives.

My father used to say that Anzac Day wasn't something we should make too much fuss over. He came back from the war wanting to put it behind him. I don't think this was because of a desire to forget all about it, but rather that it was part of his life, a job that had to be done, now done. Let's get on with it.

He didn't march when we were at Ashford, probably because there were none of his RAAF mates within cooee. But occasionally we would have visits from old comrades like Don Hackett, who spent much of his war in Singapore's Changi prison camp. The Cooper's Ale would flow, with a bottle or two of Stout to put a cap on the night, and along with it Dad and Don would remind each other of their escapades, chortling, chuckling and reminiscing in a way which was, to this pair of childish ears long sent to bed, so unlike Dad. He could be pretty dour at times, but not when Don Hackett came to visit.

My mother says the war changed Dad. He was, she said, such a dashing chap when they met. He had an A-model Ford, and she was the envy of the local lasses when they married in 1938. But the honeymoon was short-lived, because Dad soon left to go to war.

In later years, my mother suggested that the change in Dad was a result of his officer status. He became used to the military way of giving orders; of having underlings to do things for him with a 'Yes, sir!' and no questions asked. When he came back into married life, the habit was hard to kick. As a kid, I remember his propensity to give orders, and woe betide you if they were questioned!

But my brother and I would occasionally quiz him about his wartime experiences. He had, in the garage, a compass souvenired from a shot-down Japanese Zero. He also had souvenirs taken from the pilot — if I remember rightly, a silk scarf and identification papers. There was also the aluminium nose cone of a wingtip fuel tank which was used as a plant pot. And sometimes he would rummage through his brown envelopes of pictures; tiny contact snaps of men toiling over bomb holes on remote

The sun sets across Leschenault Inlet, near Australind, en route to the Margaret River region of Western Australia.

We made friends with a playful seal in Geographe Bay, near Cape Naturaliste.

Papua New Guinea strips, Dad in front of the barracks, men on water trucks, unknown faces with peaked caps and bare chests.

To a lad with his nose in Biggles books, this was exciting stuff. After one session of hearing adventure stories from the old man in a rare mood for reminiscing, I said I hoped there would be another war when I grew up. 'Boy,' he snapped, 'I fervently hope there will not. It wasn't a picnic, you know.' End of subject.

What struck me in the pre-dawn of Anzac Day wasn't the number of old codgers shuffling, medals jingling, towards the memorial; not the number of people my age, the sons and daughters of those who died or came home forever changed; but the number of kids. The word is used loosely: some were infants, propped on their pop's shoulders, in prams, or toddling along hand in hand with their parents. But more were teenagers, or young folk in their twenties. At least half the quiet, reflective audience at that service was at least two generations removed from those who fought. This was reflected at Anzac services around the nation; crowds were up, and increasing numbers of young people were attending.

Anzac is taking on a new meaning. Each year, fewer gather to remember what it was like to put their lives on the line for the sake of their country, and to pay homage to their departed comrades-in-arms. But the crowds are growing, rather than dwindling; the places of participants being taken by those who never knew war, but feel the urge to pay their respects to those who did, and to remember what they fought and died for. Their parents and grandparents answered the call to uphold, preserve and protect the central pillars of our life today: freedom, tolerance and fairness to all people.

In these uncertain times, there is strength to be gained from reminding ourselves of those ideals, for many would now feel they have been abandoned, or are at least threatened, by the greed, individualism and separatism of modern economically rational societies. The common good has given way to the grasping chance; I'm all right, Jack — bugger you. The discipline of military training and wartime restrictions has given way to the me-me-me elbowing aside of our fellows who are too slow, or unable, to grab an opportunity or a bag of money. The unity which springs from a common cause has dissipated into the disharmony of individuals jostling for position in the name of their individual freedoms.

We no longer pull together as a nation. We fight and bicker within our communities, arguing the toss about this council development, or that council spending proposal. We have a sense that we are Victorians, or Queenslanders or South Australians, or whatever, but it stops short of marching in step because we wear that label. As Australians, we wear our nationality with pride, but we don't respond to calls to put the national good before our individual whims. The forces of war were fearsome, but they were also unifying.

We confuse our notions of freedom with our rights to dissent. The pressures of change — largely driven by economic rationalism which puts market forces and the bottom line ahead of our traditional values of human fulfilment and a fair go for all — fuels an uncertainty; an insecurity. Restructuring is code for job-shedding. Who will be next?

Into this jittery time come apostles of extremism, encouraging the insecure to look for scapegoats. Politicians. Asian migrants. Aborigines on welfare, for God's sake — the most downtrodden element of our society — targeted in a myopic and pathetic attempt to portray the victims as the problems. Politicians who encourage people to look for scapegoats rather than solutions produce the very thing we stood up and fought against in Europe; horrors which led to the near-extermination of a whole race.

Why do we allow such cancerous division among ourselves? Why do we not demand of those who exercise their freedom of speech the responsibilities which come with it? The responsibility to truth. The knee-jerk creation of scapegoats puts the cohesion of our society at risk, creates hatreds and erodes the fraternal good-naturedness of being Australian.

To visit the avenues of honour in Perth's Kings Park is to be starkly reminded by name, age and location of the personal sacrifices of those who died. How would they feel about the unwillingness of today's society to make individual sacrifices for the common good?

We hit the tourist trail after Perth — a relaxed few days, exploring the nooks and crannies of the fabled Margaret River district of the lush south-west. This is food and wine heaven, an Antipodean Provence stretching little more than 100 kilometres cape-to-cape — Cape Naturaliste to the north, and Cape Leeuwin to the south. It is an area steeped in history. This coast was charted by Dutch navigators blown to it by the fresh winds of the Indian Ocean as early as 1622 — well before the arrival, further north, of the British buccaneer William Dampier in 1688. As we stood watching the awesome power of the waves crashing on the rocks of Cape Naturaliste, their swells uninterrupted since southern Africa, we could imagine the isolation felt by early sailors searching here for fresh water, or those hardy souls who made up the crews of the 300-strong whaling fleet which 150 years ago sought protected bays along the entire coast from Bunbury to Esperance.

We made our first base at Dunsborough, a trendy weekender town for Perth's middle-ranking affluent, and wound our way through a matrix of roads in and out of forests to find vineyards, dairy farms, caves, galleries, potteries, wineries, restaurants, sawmills, a lavender farm, and — well, I'll be blowed — a boutique brewery among the wineries.

It's so well coiffed. The people here have an obvious pride in their region. It's smart. Clean. Environmentally aware. I took a stroll through Bunbury's Big Swamp, a low-lying lake system which separates the main business section of the city from its southern dormitory areas. If this had been on the Gold Coast the wetlands would have been dredged into a canal-plus-marina residential development, its mud reshaped and sculptured, a boat in every front yard, a golf course, and a fancy name. Bunbury Quays. Retire here!

But no. To their very great credit the citizens of Bunbury have protected their swamp, and now delight in it being a haven for 100 species of waterbirds. Treated timber walkways wind through fine stands of wetland melaleucas, reeds and grasses, and bird hides allow visitors to observe the wildlife at close range. It is nature untouched in the middle of their little city.

Throughout the region there are many signs of environmental awareness. I remarked on this in a pub in Augusta. 'Yeah,' said a local fisherman. 'We've gotta look after the joint. It's the only one we've got.'

For many years the quality of the wines of the Margaret River region was a well-kept secret in the east, but by the early 1980s the reputation of the sublime, herbaceous sauvignon blancs, and the earthy, rich cabernet sauvignon varietals took them from

Cape Leeuwin, Western Australia . . . side by side, oceans apart.

the palates of the cognoscenti on to the wine lists of any self-respecting eastern restaurant. Most winemakers in the region also produce a skilfully and consistently blended semillon, chardonnay and sauvignon blancs known as the Classic Dry White.

The boom in wine sales sparked an amazing rush to invest. Hundreds of millions of dollars have been poured into wineries, and many more into a contest to build the biggest, classiest, and most dramatic cellar door sales and restaurant facilities. Even tiny hideways such as Woody Nook have eating — inside or out — facilities. Chefs in the kitchens of Vasse Felix produce food to rival that in the best up-market restaurants of Sydney or Melbourne, and additions to the stone and hewn-wood Driftwood complex have the shape and form of a Greek amphitheatre to enhance the ambience of distinction and permanence. Ask the locals and many will say the boom is driven in part by ego — many of Perth's entrepreneurs have palates and aspirations to match the size of their bank accounts — and partly by confidence in the future of the region. I doubt that the latter is misplaced.

But the arrival of the nouveau riche, with their attendant cockiness and willingness to compete for bigger, better, best, titles, has divided the Margaret River community. This was once the preserve of farmers and young surfers drawn to the challenging beaches which lace the western coast. Many of the surfies now run galleries and potteries; others make a living as plumbing, electrical or carpentry tradesmen. They joke about it — sometimes not too lightly — saying it's impossible to find a tradesman when the surf is up. Simmering rivalry exists between the long-term, laid-back hippy brigade and the newly arrived, up-market winery and tourism operators. In a typically Australian way, it's the workers versus the wankers. To the former, Margaret River has become, dismissively, Maggot Creek.

But to the casual visitor, the tourist facilities of the region are first class. Indeed, this extends throughout the entire south-west, where the wineries of Pemberton and Mt Barker vie for patronage with the national park forests and tall timbers. This is the kingdom of the giant karri, jarrah and tingle trees, awesome in height and girth. The new Valley of the Giants facility is a worthy example of modern tourist management; for years, travellers on the South Coast Highway made an almost obligatory stop near Nornalup to photograph their cars parked *inside* the trunk of a giant tingle tree. As visitor numbers grew to 100,000 a year, the entire valley area came to resemble a gravel car park, and dozens of walking tracks compacted the earth and destroyed nourishing humus, while exploring hands polished the trunks of the trees and robbed invertebrate relics of the supercontinent Gondwanaland of the environments in which they had survived for millions of years. The wheels of vehicles and the feet of

Reaching for the sky . . . and plentiful supplies of free wind power at Esperance, Western Australia.

The beach near Ten Mile Lagoon, Esperance . . . windswept and beautiful.

hundreds of thousands of visitors strangled the nutrient supply of the star attraction — the giant drive-through tree — and in 1990 it fell over. The valley was being loved to death. The solution was to build a suspended walkway of 60-metre spans of slim steel through the tops of another nearby stand of tingle and karri trees. Walking along the shuddering spans 40 metres above the valley floor is an experience not to be missed, and a lesson in catering for the demands of both the tourist and the forest's sustainability.

From the major city of Albany we pushed on towards Esperance, diverting to the fishing village of Bremer Bay and poking our way back to the highway among the wildflowers of the Fitzgerald River National Park. Esperance was named by the French explorer D'Entrecasteaux, who sheltered from storms here in 1792 with his two ships, *Esperance* and *Recherche*. The archipelago of hundreds of islands dotted along the coastline was named after the *Recherche*, and at the height of the American whaling boom in the early 1800s, Middle Island was home to the pirate Black Jack Anderson. He was, by all accounts, Australia's only pirate, and for ten years he ruled his fiefdom with harsh cruelty, killing intruders, kidnapping women, plundering sealing and whaling ships, and allegedly burying his treasure somewhere on the island. Black Jack suffered the fate of many rogues in that period: he was shot dead by disgruntled gang members while he slept. His treasure has never been found.

We enjoyed Esperance, with its wild and windy coasts, a lake turned pink by algae, and a museum of intriguing old farm machinery displayed side by side with remains of the US Skylab space station which crashed to earth between Esperance and

Balladonia. But the sight which stopped us in our tracks was the Ten Mile Lagoon wind farm. Here, on nine 30-metre towers, huge three-bladed rotors swish and swoosh through the air, powered by the ceaseless winds which blow across the Southern Ocean, generating electricity. It's an incongruous scene: desolate rolling hills, covered by low scrub, with these giant windmills standing as modern white symbols of sustainable energy. The $6 million Ten Mile Lagoon farm contributes less than 20 per cent of the region's total power use, but is estimated to save 1.5 million litres of diesel fuel a year. Along this coast, wind is plentiful — and it's free!

By now I was getting twitchy. My promise to Wendy — to introduce her slowly to the joys of discovery of out-of-the-way places, to four-wheel driving and bush camping — was being well met. Dammit, we hadn't seen a dirt road since Broken Hill. We never booked motels, but we never missed out on a bed with clean sheets. We had eaten well — too well — in the up-market nosheries of the south-west. It was time to get off the beaten track.

Wendy sensed this and schemed a 'suck it and see' diversion off the Vasse Highway near Pemberton to visit Lake Jasper, a delightful hideaway spot 14 kilometres off the bitumen. This took us over some washed-out gravel roads, and through some deeply rutted sandtracks over dozens of low sandhills. She survived without complaint and her confidence rose.

From Esperance we drove along the beach to Cape Le Grand — 25 kilometres of firm sand and sensational beach sights. Wendy was delighted. This was easy. So she voted that we should push on along the track towards Israelite Bay. We made for

We met fishermen in Sandy Bight who suggested we bait a hook to catch a salmon . . . then wait for a shark to take the salmon! We didn't get the shark because we didn't get the salmon.

Cape Arid, where we bumped into some fishos from Kalgoorlie who told tall, but inspiring, tales of catching salmon on the beach in Sandy Bight. The idea, they said, was to ganghook a pilchard — known locally as muellies — on to your line, catch a five-kilogram salmon... and wait for it to be taken by a bronze whaler shark. Then watch your rod bend!

It seemed a fair enough proposition to me, so we took to the beach, but first had to pass over a rock outcrop. Wendy believed the drive was impossible, irresponsible, stupid, unnecessary and dangerous. It looked OK to me, so she got out and I picked a path over the rocks. Alas, I propped the Pajero on a rock on the left-hand side, bending the

aluminium running board. I backed off, took a wider turn, and drove safely up the beach as if nothing had happened. Wendy came storming after me, pointing at the damage, dramatically sweeping her hand over it. Sarah Bernhardt couldn't have done it better: 'See what you've done!' she cried. Whack! Ouch!

What she didn't see was a sliver of aluminium peeled back by the rock. It deeply sliced two fingers of her right hand, and immediately blood flowed freely on the pristine white sand and her bluster was replaced by blubbering. This was my chance to redeem myself, for my stupidity had been supplanted by hers. Out came the first aid kit and a jerrycan of water; we washed and

The Torndirrup National Park, near Albany, Western Australia, has some of the most spectacular scenery in the south-west, including this natural rock bridge carved out of granite by the sea.

The islands of the Recherche Archipelago, seen from the wind-swept coast near Esperance.

tightly bound the wound, sprinkled it with antiseptic, and plastered the fingers. Wendy sat sullenly as I fished. No talkies. No fish, either.

Israelite Bay was still 65 kilometres away, and it was getting late. As any traveller knows, 100 kilometres is about one hour on ordinary roads. But this 65 kilometres was two hours away, through rough, undulating, sandy tracks which eventually gave way to the muddy shores of Daringdella Lake. Here, any semblance of a road also gave way, with tracks in and out of mud patches and low-lying scrub.

It was dusk before we made the camp site. This was to be the first time we had erected

our tent. An onshore wind was blowing as I pegged the groundsheet and flung the top over the igloo-style poles. Out of the tent's bag of tricks came flimsy pegs which had no chance of holding in the sand, and a bird's nest of ropes to tie down the tent cover. As I banged in the sand pegs, Wendy tried, with bloodied, fumbling fingers, to unpick the tie-down ropes. Together we performed St Vitus's dance in the wind, and eventually succeeded, only to realise *we had the bloody thing back to front!* The wind was screaming right down the throat of the tent! But the sand pegs held long enough for me to reposition the Pajero as a wind break, and we settled into a stew of double chilli sausages — double, because the lid had rattled off the top of a jar of chilli pickled onions and *everything* in the fridge was chilled! As we faced a frigid night of stinging rain, I said: 'Welcome to the joys of camping.'

We were the only people at Israelite Bay that night. Fishermen come and go, using their semi-permanent camps near the object of attraction to me — the old telegraph station. This was an extraordinarily large and imposing structure, brought ashore stone by stone more than a century ago from ships anchored in the shallow bay, and built to the design of post offices of that era. It was, by any standards, over the top and out of character. I could imagine this building gracing the main street of a thriving country town in western New South Wales, but it made no sense here, almost 200 kilometres east of Esperance and 400 kilometres south-east of Kalgoorlie. Beside the front entrance were slots for posting letters. Why? There was no-one here to post letters, except for the dozen or so men who manned the telegraph repeater station. For them, mail services were restricted to the monthly supply vessels. To me, the Israelite Bay telegraph station represented bureaucracy gone mad: I could imagine 120 or so years ago a post office architect in Melbourne dusting off plans for a building, insisting, regardless of where it was to be constructed, that 'this is how we build post offices'.

The next day the rain continued as we inched our way through 185 kilometres of rough limestone tracks, often so narrow we could scarcely fit through, up the Wylie Scarp, past Mt Ragged, through scrub infected with the dieback fungus, and on to a muddy, slippery gravel road into Balladonia. Wendy was fearful throughout,

and when we checked into the Balladonia Motel, civilisation never felt quite so good.

My yearning to get off the beaten track was undiminished. As we gobbled up the bitumen of the Nullarbor, I hatched a plot to head north, to the railway line, to watch the sun set on the true Nullarbor, and wave at a train.

The true Nullarbor — with its endless, treeless plains, lies north of the Eyre Highway. It is a vast limestone escarpment, riddled with caves and underground rivers which have been traced more than 30 kilometres from their ground openings. This vast nothingness is punctured only by the Transcontinental railway. It winds through the Gawler Ranges north-west from Port Augusta, skirts the salt lakes Torrens and Gairdner, passes through Pimba, Kingoonya and Tarcoola, and straightens up at Ooldea — home of the legendary Daisy Bates — for the 744-kilometre unbending run to Nurina. From there the railway rolls on to Perth, about 550 kilometres further on.

I was enchanted by the thought of camping in the middle of nowhere, watching the trains go by. Why? Well, it just seemed *odd*. To be utterly alone in the desert, where a 360-degree pirouette revealed the sameness of saltbush from the foreground to the dead-flat horizon, and nothing else; then to be interrupted by a roaring stream of commerce for a minute or two, only to see the desert quickly return to its silent emptiness.

This seemed to me to starkly juxtapose something about us and our land. For all our endeavours out here in the bush, we don't seem to have done more than interrupt it for a flash before it reasserts itself. I know we have conquered it in the sense that we have put snaking steel lines on concrete sleepers right through its heart. We haul vast loads of economic benefit from east to west and west

Here comes the train… out of a fiery sunset comes a pin-prick of light, and the distant throb of diesel motors becomes a roar which overwhelms the Nullarbor.

to east; we drive through it with our iron horses. But it still drives us back by its inhospitable harshness.

So we turned north off the Eyre Highway and headed for Cook, one of the few remaining points on the Transcontinental rail line where a name on the map means a town. Most people would look at a map, see a dot and a name, and assume it amounted to something. Not out here.

Many of the old fettlers camps and water stations, spaced about 50 kilometres apart for the needs of steam trains, are named after Federation politicians: Lyons, Barton, Watson, Fisher, O'Malley, Cook, Hughes, Deakin, Forrest, Reid. How they would be disappointed today to see what the settlements carrying their names have come to: modern trains no longer need regular drinks of water;

concrete sleepers have replaced the old jarrah wood carved from the forests of Manjimup and no longer need constant servicing; and today most of the place names are just that — a sign, and nothing more. (Mind you, the ghosts of the old pollies would probably be satisfied with the fact that most are also honoured as suburbs of Canberra.)

Cook (population 55) is actually a rail siding. There is a railway station, with a sign proudly proclaiming 'Cook, Queen City of the Nullarbor' and another inviting donations to its hospital — 'Our hospital needs help — get sick,' and 'If you're crook, come to Cook.' There is also a store, run by Australian National, the railway operators, and helpful advice is available from Graeme and Julie Schwartz at the store. Graeme's timetables indicated two trains would be

through that night: one at 11.30 pm and another at 5.15 am.

From Cook we drove east along the track for 25 kilometres before pitching our tent in the gathering dusk just 20 metres off the line. Cloud covered the sky, much to our disappointment (no stars tonight) and we could see rain squalls to the north and west of us. But incredibly, as the sun sank below the horizon, it illuminated the underside of the cloud and the squalls, in a gobsmacking display of swirling crimson, scarlet and gold. It was an amazing light show, utterly unexpected, and as I photographed the moment I spotted a prick of light on the horizon.

A train! What a bonus! Camera ready, I stood at the side of the line and watched the light grow brighter. And then I heard it: first through the rail lines, a low hum, rising in pitch; higher, higher... until it was a whirring

sound; and above that sound came out of the desert the throbbing of the diesel motors; throbbing, thunk-thunk-thunking until that sound was merged and then overwhelmed by the roar of the entire colossus bearing down on us. Sparks flew from the wheels as steel gripped steel, and the driver klaxoned a 'G'day' from his cabin, adding a cheery wave as I reeled back in astonishment at the power, speed and enormity of it all.

I was tremendously excited by the experience. I cracked a beer Wendy had a brandy. We cooked a stew, with a fine Margaret River sauvignon blanc for openers, followed by a Cape Mentelle shiraz. We played cards under the lantern, alone, super-relaxed, waiting for the 11.30 train. It became quite cold, so I put on my multicoloured harlequin-patterned woolly jumper — and dug out another fine red wine. After all, this was to be our last camp before

Camping in the middle of nowhere… utterly alone.

we hit the big smoke again. Not to put too fine a point on it, we had a party.

By ten o'clock Wendy was ready for bed. But not me. A cleansing ale seemed to be the go; perhaps another, who knows? Who cares? I put Handel's *Music for the Royal Fireworks* on the car CD player and turned it up loud. I retreated to the desert, perhaps 200 metres from the camp, listening to the music roll over our wilderness, conducting (as you do in such a mood) the orchestra, revelling in the sounds and sensations of it all, searching for a line in the blackness which delineated earth from sky.

And then I saw it: first, a smudge of light below the horizon which soon became a pin-prick. 'Here comes the train,' I cheered. The light grew and the rails began to join the orchestra, adding their well-modulated low hum, then their high pitch,

and as Handel's trumpets blared to herald the royal fireworks, I waved my arms in frenzied conducting as the diesels chimed in with their throb-throb-throb-thunk-thunk-thunk until the whole cacophony merged into one roaring, cataclysmic crescendo of sound.

And then it was gone. The roar gave way to a diminuendo of containers clackety-clacking away into the night, and Handel returned to reclaim the desert. I stumbled to bed and fell immediately into the sleep of the dead.

An hour or so later I was prodded awake, blearily, by a terrified wife. 'Mark! . . . Mark!' she exclaimed in what she hoped was a whisper, but sounded like a panicked shriek. 'There are men outside!'

It was true. Through the fog of my mind I could hear the tink-tink-tink of an idling diesel motor, and I could make out voices.

'Did you check the car?' 'They must be in the tent then. . . ' 'Can you find the front of the tent?' Wendy was having conniptions.

'It was scary enough just being out there,' she said. 'Where would we get help if we needed it? But when I heard the men's voices, I panicked. They have to be here for a reason… they're not just passing by. I was absolutely convinced they were going to murder us. Maybe Ivan Milat has escaped. My heart was pounding… in my mind I knew I was going to die and the only question was how. Did they have guns? Knives? Would I be raped before I was killed?'

'Hello,' I shouted through the tent.

'Oh, g'day,' said the voice. 'We're from Australian National in Cook. Did you wave at a train?'

'Yes, I waved at the train.'

'The driver thought by the way you were waving there might be something wrong, so he radioed us in Cook to report it. Is everything all right?'

'Yeah, thankyou… everything is fine. I was just having a good time watching the trains go by.'

'OK, mate. Sorry to disturb you.'

And with that the diesel picked up revs and the tink-tink-tink faded into the night.

I went back to sleep, and Wendy listened to the raindrops on the tent, imagining what might have been, until dawn — and the 5.15 am train — came.

I felt guilty about this incident all the way back to Adelaide. I was mightily impressed, of course, that these guys would get out of their beds in the middle of the night, pick their way along a rocky track for an hour or more and search for a silver and lavender tent in the middle of the desert on the off-chance that someone was in trouble. The great Australian tradition of helping a mate is far from dead. But we weren't mates in the accepted sense; they didn't know us from a bar of soap. But still they came to check on us. It was, and is, the code of the bush; the Anzac DNA which shapes us and defines us and causes us to share the pride of our navy lads and lasses when, impossibly, they pluck lone sailors from upturned yachts in the icy Roaring Forties far from our southern shores. We will never let a bloke down.

But my gratitude at being, for the first time, a recipient of this laudable Australian trait was overcome by guilt. What would they be saying about us? Some stupid city-slicker yahoo, probably pissed, putting on an act like that! What an idiot! What an irresponsible ning-nong! And the bastard didn't even get out of his tent to offer us a cup of coffee, or a beer, to thank us for our trouble.

Back in Adelaide, I summoned up the courage to phone Graeme Schwartz at the Cook store. I asked him to pass on our thanks to the guys who had come out to check on us. I apologised for my slow thinking in not getting out of the tent to say thanks, or how about a beer? I explained, as best I could, that the madman in a harlequin jumper the driver had seen waving his frenzied arms was in fact conducting *Music for the Royal Fireworks, plus Train,* in ebrious excitement at the wondrous incongruity of it all. I ventured that I could well understand how annoying idiots such as myself must be to those who make unnecessary mercy dashes into the desert in the middle of the night, and for that I would like my abject apologies recorded.

'No worries,' said Graeme. 'No need to apologise. There's not much to do out here, and the blokes rather enjoy things like that.'

Sustainable energy at work in the Strzelecki Desert . . . an old
windmill and a newer solar-powered pump suck water from a soak.

chapter five

We were camped by a billabong, Jolly Jumbuck and I, under the shade of a coolabah tree. We were 1210 kilometres from Sydney, as the crow flies, and 1207 kilometres from Melbourne, on the banks of Cooper Creek, amid ghosts.

We were in what amounts to a sacred site of Australian folklore. If we had to select one spot to represent the challenges, hardships, fortitude, heroism and blind ignorance of the battle to tame this land, this would be my choice. For it was here that the triumph of the first north–south crossing of the continent by Europeans foundered in tragic death. A few kilometres to the east of our camp, Robert O'Hara Burke perished in 1861. A short way to the west, a cairn marks the spot where his second-in-command, William John Wills, died of malnutrition. And around the corner is the spot where the sole survivor of the crossing, 23-year-old John King, was found — a rescue hailed as a miracle.

For the first quarter-century after the arrival of the First Fleet, the European settlement clung to the narrow strip of land north and south of Sydney Town. Pastoral expansion to the west was blocked by the Blue Mountains, which many believed to be impenetrable. The successful crossing by Blaxland, Wentworth and Lawson in 1813 opened up the New South Wales western plains to grazing, but the push beyond, into the arid interior, was slow and repeatedly marked by failure. It was to be almost another half-century before the continent was crossed from north to south.

The feats of the early explorers, and the hardships endured by those who followed in their wake, contributed greatly to the perception of Australians as tough, resourceful, resilient and self-reliant. It was in the bush, alone, against the elements, that the spirit of mateship was born.

Today, the interior is open and accessible — roads follow droving routes, towns mark the spots where they intersect, airstrips beside homesteads provide an umbrella of safety — but it is impossible to drive through it — to be there — without reflecting on the bravery and the daring of those who challenged it without a clue as to what lay before them.

Jolly and I were heading for Alice Springs, via the Simpson Desert, but rain had made the desert track impassable. So we, like Charles Sturt in 1845, and the Burke and Wills expedition in 1861, waited beside the creek in the company of myriads of chirping corellas, whistling kites and galahs. The yellowbelly were biting, the beer in the fridge was cold, the Innamincka pub's roast night was on, and Birdsville was just nine hours up the track.

Jolly is Jolyon Ernest Hardisty Simpson, Jolly Jumbuck to his mates, a builder from the New South Wales Central Coast, and a friend for 20 years. It seemed right and proper that he should be my travelling companion to tackle the eponymous Simpson Desert.

We had survived a few adventures in our time, Jolly and I: hunting feral goats at Mudgee, getting skinned by the crew of the *Empress of Tasmania* playing crown and anchor on a wild Bass Strait crossing, dodging crocodiles on the King River, escaping a sinking boat on Brisbane Water. He had twice driven me to hospital — once with a broken ankle after falling from a motorbike, and once with a split head after falling from a mountaintop. I returned the favour when he injured himself on a building site. But throughout, he remained the cool, laconic, easy-going, she'll-be-right, quintessential Aussie.

And, remarkably, our friendship has survived the greatest test of all: twice Jolly has built houses for me. Anyone who knows how tensions can arise between clients, architects and builders will appreciate the point. Jolly's forte is building pole frame houses on the mountain-goat hills around the Central Coast. Jolly's Pollies: no slope too steep; no risk too great. She'll be right, mate.

But she wasn't right, mate. On the banks of the creek where Burke and Wills poisoned themselves, Jolly was unknowingly suffering from chronic arsenic poisoning.

We put 1000 kilometres of bitumen behind us on the first day out of Sydney, sweeping across New South Wales to Wilcannia. Our first objective was to be the Red Centre — Alice Springs — where Jolly would swap with Wendy and we would resume our north-west crossing to the Kimberley. We wanted to travel right through the heart of Australia, in as straight a line as possible.

Our route took us through Dubbo, and on to Nyngan, through a virtual snowstorm of fluffy cotton balls caught in the grass or on roadside fences. Huge bales of cotton, sometimes stacked three high, lined the road for kilometres. This is a multi-billion dollar industry on the flat blacksoil plains, but it's not one without controversy, especially in areas such as the Macquarie Marshes to our north.

The marshes are part of nature's filtering system. But out here, man-made channels divert water to thirsty cotton crops, annually requiring 200 megalitres of water for each hectare. Irrigators are allocated more than twice the amount of water directed through the marshes, resulting in drying marshes, reduced bird breeding, and a disturbingly high level of chemical nutrients draining into the river systems.

In 1991 farm nutrients contributed to a 1400-kilometre-long blue–green toxic algae bloom in the Darling River. It was an environmental disaster. The Murray–Darling river system drains more than one-third of Australia, reaches into four states, and sustains life and agriculture in areas which would otherwise be desert. In 1991, when much of New South Wales was in drought: the rivers slowed, or stopped flowing; and the combination of sluggish water, heat and nutrients provided the perfect breeding ground for the algae.

In that sense it was a natural phenomenon, and it was overcome just as naturally — by big rains which eventually came and flushed it away. But the event spurred research on ways to reduce the problem in the future — and one way is to create artificial drainage areas which replicate the work of the marshes. At dams near Blayney and Tamworth, artificial wetlands are being constructed, forming huge ponds where

nutrients and other pollutants can drop out of the water and nourish wetland grasses and other vegetation. Only clear water will feed into the rivers and water storages, and the wetlands will encourage birds and other aquatic life to return.

These total catchment management plans are being developed as part of the realisation that we have blindly, unthinkingly, gone too far in shaping the environment to our perceived needs. We now know that we have to return to nature to solve the problems we have created. It will be a long, slow process, but if we fail to start the journey we will consign our river lifelines to the role of sewers.

From Wilcannia, we struck north, through the opal-mining town of White Cliffs, towards Tibooburra. On the way, we dropped in to Milparinka, once a bustling gold-mining town boasting three hotels, four stores, several boarding houses, its own newspaper, a photographic studio, a blacksmith, a saddler and two butchers. Today, only one pub remains open for a cool beer or petrol.

Milparinka is the gateway to Depot Glen where Charles Sturt was marooned beside a dwindling waterhole during the drought-stricken summer of 1844. Like most explorers of his time, Sturt was intent on finding a way to cross the continent. He had been mapping the Darling, Murray and Murrumbidgee rivers for more than a decade, and during his frequent surveys had noticed water birds flying northwards. He plotted their courses — north-west from a point near Bourke, and north from Adelaide. He was convinced an inland sea lay where the plot lines intersected.

Sturt left Adelaide with 16 officers and men, 11 horses, 30 bullocks, one horse dray, one spring cart, three bullock drays, 200 sheep,

Sunrise over Innamincka, South Australia . . . the isolation sears the soul.

two sheep dogs, four kangaroo dogs — and a wooden boat on a boat carriage. What a sight they must have made crossing the low, undulating hills towards the unknown. It's easy for us, in our airconditioned Pajero, kicking up a cloud of dust as we put 80 or 90 kilometres behind us each hour on these graded roads, silently absorbing the majesty of the landscape. It's not the kind of majesty which comes from soaring mountains cleft with ravines filled with robust rainforests: quite the reverse. These dry plains of far western New South Wales are as arid as anything to be found in Australia; often featureless except for the occasional jump-up, or low mesa, and vast expanses of purple–red gibber stones. There is a serenity in its inhospitableness, and the mind's eye imagines the scene as teams of horses, bullocks and grumbling Poms tortuously lugged their hare-brained boat into the desert.

Sturt established his base camp at Depot Glen, west of Milparinka, where he found the only permanent water for 100 kilometres.

It is believed the boat was abandoned here, but it has never been found. As the summer of 1844 wore on, he was trapped, afraid to go back into the waterless wilderness, and daring not to strike out for his northern destination. Parties made forays in various directions from Depot Glen, but he was beaten back each time. Scurvy struck down his men, but he was able to establish a forward camp and corral at Fort Grey, just east of what is now known as Cameron Corner, where the borders of South Australia, New South Wales and Queensland meet.

From there Sturt took four men, ten horses and a dray, and crossed the Strzelecki Creek and the watercourse he named Cooper Creek near Innamincka. Given the drought conditions and the depleted waterholes, there is little wonder he took this mighty drain to be nothing more than a creek. It's the only creek in Australia to be fed by two rivers: the Thomson and the Barcoo. When the monsoons turn the channel country into impassable swamps, the Cooper

Cameron Corner, where South Australia, New South Wales and Queensland meet . . . and the dingo fence protects livestock.

carries enormous volumes of water which would qualify it as the mightiest of rivers, but they rarely reach the natural destination of Lake Eyre.

Sturt finally gave up on the edge of the Simpson Desert, at the bone-dry Eyre Creek. His men were exhausted and his horses lame. 'I have to admit I have given up hope of finding any body of water,' he wrote. He was worried the waterholes behind him were drying up, cutting off his retreat. He wrote: 'It is impossible to find words to describe the terrible nature of this dreadful desert in a country so dry all efforts are abortive, and it remains to be proved whether or not my retreat is altogether cut off.' Another entry reads: 'The deathlike stillness of these solitudes is awful and oppressive. We have not seen a single living creature since we left Cooper Creek.' And: 'The scene was awfully fearful. A kind of dread came over me as I gazed upon it. It looked like the entrance to hell.'

It is a gated entrance, these days. And you could cop a $1000 fine if you leave it open.

The gate just before Cameron Corner passes through a remarkable, if largely unrecognised, Australian achievement — the dingo fence. Almost 5300 kilometres long — more than twice the length of the Great Wall of China — the dingo fence was built to put a barrier between Australia's wild dogs and its then most important export — wool. Construction began 100 years ago, and bit by bit the fence grew — through the northern pastoral backblocks of South Australia, across the north-west of New South Wales and into Queensland, where it stops about 100 kilometres west of Brisbane. All the sections were joined in the late 1950s.

Australia has more than 120 million sheep, and an estimated one million dingoes. But those dogs which do get through holes in the fence — caused by the erosions of time, flash floods, falling trees or attack by animals — wreak havoc with sheep and lambs. Queensland alone estimates the loss of $50 million worth of sheep to dingoes each year. Attempts to minimise this loss mean the fence must be constantly patrolled and repaired.

It shouldn't be necessary to plaster warning signs over the gate at Cameron Corner because the first rule of travel through pastoral properties is: *always leave a gate as you found it*. It's a rule which founders only when some idiot breaks it, so I suppose the threatening warnings are necessary.

Suddenly, out of the desert, the towers of the Moomba gas field appear.

As Jolly and I swept through Cameron Corner into the Strzelecki Desert, through endless clay-capped sandhills on a corrugated, roller-coaster road, we felt Sturt's dread. Frequently stopping for photographs, we played the tortoise and the hare with a grandmother in her seventies, alone in a 2WD Nissan Urvan she called home. We were amazed at her courage, because this was country not to be trifled with. We had our spare wheels, long-range fuel tank and emergency gear; we had our satphone where help was just a call away, but we felt a vulnerability here which could only have been magnified a thousand times in the fretful minds of those daring explorers a century and a half ago.

Past Merty Merty station, we came across an incongruous wreck of a double-decker bus, marking a soak from which a windmill and a solar-powered pump sucked water —

two examples of sustainable energy at work. Our road soon joined the Strzelecki Track. This has a fearsome reputation as a challenging outback throughway, so we were surprised when we turned on to a clay-topped, well-graded road as smooth as a billiard table sweeping its wide way through voluptuous red sandhills, spotted with saltbush-grey shrubbery. The reason for this quantum leap in road conditions became apparent as we rounded a corner past a sandhill to be confronted with a very different desert vista: the mighty Moomba oil and gas field.

I had been here 30 years ago, scooping a hole in the sand for my hip as I bedded down under a billion sparkling stars in the desert while reporting on the search for gas at Gidgealpa. These were early, exploratory wells, sunk when geosurvey mapping gave cause for no more than a hopeful dream that the Cooper Basin may one day yield more than enough gas to supply all of Sydney and Adelaide. Today, a massive infrastructure of towers, pipes and flaming burn-off outlets spreads across the desert sands and signs say 'Keep Out'. It was quite unexpected — but it explained the improvement in road conditions. Heavy equipment requires more than a sandy desert track.

As we pulled into Innamincka we resolved to rest a while: a cold was becoming a chest infection, and I felt a certain simpatico with Sturt and his scurvy-struck men.

The isolation sears into your soul under the DIG tree. Sit a moment. Observe the spreading coolabahs; listen to the birds; watch the eddies and boils in the turbid, buff-green water, and spare a thought for William Brahe.

For four months in 1860–61 Brahe sat here, fearing an attack by Aborigines, waiting for Burke and Wills to return from the Gulf of Carpentaria. Eventually, he pulled out and trekked south. Nine hours after he departed, Burke and Wills staggered from the desert, stranded, unable to follow, unable to signal a single soul, unknowing of the laws of survival.

For two months they survived along the creek before they perished, victims of their own ignorance. By any standards, this spot is the epicentre of an epic and moving saga of endurance. But it is laced, from its ill-conceived beginning to its tragic end, with foolishness to the point of stupidity, ineptitude and incompetence.

In the particularly Australian way which compels us to revere valiant failures like the invasion at Anzac Cove, or Ned Kelly, this spot on Cooper Creek is as close as we come to a white man's sacred site. More than a century on, its importance in Australia's development can be palpably felt: it has assumed a sanctity in White Man's Dreamtime, not only for the magnificence of its failure, but also because of the accidental impacts in its wake.

The dream in the cloistered clubs of Melbourne and Adelaide was to unlock the vast, unknown hinterlands beyond the Darling River. Burke and Wills succeeded in becoming the first white men to cross the continent from south to north. They perished, but the far more capable explorers who crisscrossed the region in search and rescue missions succeeded in opening up more pastoral country than had been dreamed imaginable.

Cooper Creek runs in a series of waterholes from Burke and Wills' Camp 65 at the DIG tree east of Innamincka: Bullah Bullah, Nappaoonie, Cullyamurra, Mulkonbar, Tilcha and Minkie are just some of the exotically named permanent or semi-permanent water sources in this 100-kilometre oasis straddling the Queensland–South Australian border. For eons, this had been home to wandering Aboriginal tribes. To them it was a boundless source of food. So how could Burke and Wills have perished? Stupidity, blinkered vision; shoddy thinking.

In 1860 the South Australian government offered a £2000 prize for the first crossing of the continent. Its challenge was accepted by the Royal Society of Victoria, who appointed police inspector Robert O'Hara Burke as leader of the expedition. It was the largest and most elaborate yet seen in the colonies, and it left Melbourne with great fanfare, with 21 tonnes of supplies and equipment, including 26 camels.

The choice of Burke was staggering. He had no scientific background as an explorer

The DIG tree, a majestic coolabah, where members of the Burke and Wills expedition played their macabre game of tag almost a century and a half ago.

or surveyor; he had never set foot outside Victoria; he had no bush training, and had never led an expedition of any kind. His second-in-command, William John Wills, was at least an astronomer and surveyor.

In spite of early mishaps, the party reached the outer limits of settlement at Menindee, on the Darling, in October 1860, where a supply camp was established. Burke divided his party and set off with eight men for Cooper Creek, where Camp 65 was set up. Then he divided the party again: Brahe was left in charge of the camp, and told to wait at least three months — four, if he could — for their return. Then, on 16 December, Burke, Wills, Charles Grey and John King trudged north in

the heat of summer, 1100 kilometres across the searing, inhospitable plains to the Gulf. It was a feat of superhuman endurance. They never actually wet their toes in the waters of the Gulf, finding their way barred by thick mangroves. But they left evidence of their visit on 11 February 1861 at Camp 119, south-west of Normanton, on the Bynoe River.

Their return journey was a race against time. Grey died a few days before Burke, Wills and King staggered from the desert at sunset on 21 April, only to find that Brahe had pulled out that very morning.

Weakened and dispirited, they followed Brahe's instructions cut into the tree: 'DIG —

A white brumby near the spot where Burke died beside Cooper Creek.

The remains of King's Tree — where John King was found alive.

3ft NW April 21 1861' — and recovered rations. Exhausted, they couldn't follow Brahe south to Menindee, and formed a plan to head west to Mt Hopeless for help. But that failed in the face of the same desolation and lack of water which had forced Sturt back 20 years earlier.

A macabre game of tag centred on Camp 65. Recovering their buried supplies, Burke left a note reporting his return and intentions, and buried it. Brahe, heading south, had met members of the Menindee party trying to make their way north to Cooper Creek.

He doubled back to Camp 65, but saw no signs of any disturbance. He didn't, therefore, dig for supplies, or discover the note which would have pinpointed Burke's party to the west. So Brahe headed south again, leaving no trace of his second visit!

At this point, one of the great conundrums of early exploring came into play. Why didn't the marooned men seek help from the Aborigines? Just as Blaxland, Wentworth and Lawson could have crossed the Blue Mountains on any one of four well-known and well-travelled crossings used by the Aborigines, Burke and Wills could have employed local guides to lead them from waterhole to waterhole on their crossing.

Back at Cooper Creek, stranded, they could have sought help to get to Menindee. Or, at the very least, to unlock the food sources which drew the Aborigines to this oasis in the first place. But they didn't. They merely 'observed' the Aborigines plucking berries from the nardoo plants which grew in profusion in the area, and grinding them into a damper-like flour which they cooked on their campfires. But what they didn't observe was the critical act of soaking the berries overnight in water to remove toxins.

Burke, Wills and King ate their nardoo cakes, and slowly poisoned themselves as the toxins attacked their thyroids. Wills died alone, downstream from Innamincka, on 27 June 1861. The site of Burke's death is marked by a cairn; a peaceful spot, about as placid as you could find, shaded by rivergums filled with trilling birds.

John King was sustained by Aborigines until a rescue party sent from Melbourne arrived on 13 September 1861, and found him two days later, demented by his ordeal. He was 22. He died in Melbourne after spending the next ten years in a mental asylum; poignant proof that the difference between triumph and tragedy in the Australian outback often lay in preparation and experience.

But if the Burke and Wills expedition was, in itself, a failure, its aftermath was not. Several search parties, led by bushmen far more experienced than Burke, surveyed good-quality grazing land in the regions east of Camp 65, and provided the basis for another, inexorable push by pastoralists into the interior. The next year, John McDouall Stuart blazed a far more viable trail across the nation, from Adelaide to a point near what is now Darwin.

As we absorbed the Burke and Wills saga, I kept coughing and spluttering, like death warmed up. More than once I muttered to Jolly: 'I know how they felt,' as an infection gripped my head, lungs and aching muscles.

Jolly was his normal, soothing self. Plucking another yellowbelly from the creek, he said: 'You'll be right, mate.' Early on our second morning in Innamincka, I struggled from my sweaty bed behind the Innamincka pub and went in search of Mick Davies, the licensee. My medical kit could offer no more than aspirin or throat lozenges; maybe he had something to help.

I knew that outback places like pubs, roadhouses and many stations carried Royal Flying Doctor Service (RFDS) medical kits. I had picked up that piece of knowledge at the Wadlata Centre in Port Augusta where the history of the South Australian outback is displayed in a gripping and informative way. One section of the display dealt with the RFDS, and visitors were encouraged to listen in to live RFDS radio action.

When I picked up the handset to listen, I eavesdropped on a legitimate drama. The doctor was talking to a station owner about an employee who had been gored by a bull. He had suffered a deep wound from a horn in the groin; he was bleeding, but was otherwise conscious and alert. The doctor gave instructions about the administration of immediate first aid, including looking in the medical kit for painkillers. The plane would soon be on the way to pick up the patient.

Not for a moment did I think my flu could compete with a horn in the groin. But I knew there were medical kits tucked away, ready to meet any emergency.

Mick looked doubtful. He quizzed me about my condition, and I felt he was disinclined to help. I was testy. I explained, in as precise a manner as I could, that I had recently had a similar bout with a cold or the flu, and it had infected my lungs. I'd had to see a doctor, and it was fixed up, but now it's back, and I'm not a doctor so I don't know how to fix it, and I'm trying to find out how to get the help of a doctor out here.

Mick, I gather, didn't like my tone of voice. He said he had to make a judgment about the use of precious RFDS resources because they weren't meant for malingerers and hypochondriacs. He offered me a pad of paper and curtly suggested I write down my symptoms.

By this time I didn't like Mick's attitude. He didn't actually accuse me of being a malingerer or a hypochondriac, but the message seemed pretty clear. So, thinking of my friends from Cook and their dead-of-night mercy mission after I waved at a train, I shot back: 'I thought people in the outback were famous for helping those in need.'

'Help!' he exploded. 'I'll give you bloody help. I've been out to road crashes in the middle of the night. I've battled floods and I've pulled people from plane crashes, and put their bits in body bags! Don't say I don't help!'

We glared at each other. With hindsight, I think I had presumed too much. Believing medical help would be available, I had asked for it, and assumed it would be forthcoming. Out here, help is willingly given — as an act of generosity delivered freely by the giver, rather than as a response to a request or demand from the recipient. This stand-off between us was a culture clash: the city versus the bush.

Mick jabbed his finger on the pad and repeated that I should write down my symptoms. I did, while he busied himself with his cleaning chores. He then took the pad away and I could hear him on the phone. He spoke to a doctor called Helen in Port Augusta. He quoted my symptoms, then called me into his office. 'The doctor would like to talk to you,' he grumbled, thrusting the phone at me. I went through the whole rigmarole again, including the past experience, and Dr Helen hummed and hawed. Then she said: 'I'm going to give you some augmentin…' The penny dropped: that was the antibiotic I had been given by my doctor in Sydney last time.

I thanked her, and handed the phone back to Mick. He took notes, rummaged for a box of pills, and proffered a release form for me to sign. By now his attitude had softened. I surmised it was because the doctor had decided I did qualify for help, and therefore I wasn't a malingerer or a hypochondriac. I, too, felt the heat pass from the exchange, and we parted, me clutching my precious medicine.

For the rest of our stay Mick was pleasant, helpful and relaxed, and I was eternally grateful to Dr Helen and the Royal Flying Doctor Service.

I had grown used to Wendy's panicky approach to outback driving, but I hadn't reckoned on her fertile imagination working overtime back home as I travelled with Jolly. From time to time on dirt roads we would come to washaways which were hard to see, but deep enough to cause a bang-thunk! from our heavily laden suspension as we careered over them. Wendy took a particular dislike to

The gibber plains of the Sturt Stony Desert… so big, so dry, so desolate.

Good rains gave the desert a brush of green… but the heat shimmering on the horizon will soon return it to barren red.

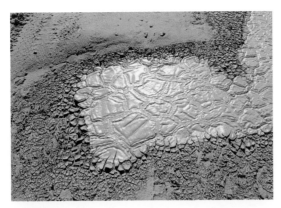

The desert cycle… rain turns dust to mud, and the sun bakes it back to dust.

The sun sets over a billabong near Birdsville, Queensland, as Jolly plucks a yellowbelly from the water.

these unexpected bumps, fearing we would smash nose-first into them, roll over end on end, and end our lives as carrion for the wedgies. I pooh-poohed her fears, but as she described her experiences to friends, the washaways became deeper, wider and more rugged with every telling. Soon, these bumps were ravines.

I kept in touch from Innamincka. She could hear the flu and chest congestion in my voice. As always, she feared the worst and worried to her friends, canvassing outlandish what ifs. What if he has to go to hospital? What if his lungs collapse? What if he dies out there like Burke and Wills?

When I told her I had some medicine from the Flying Doctor she was quick to relay — and ramp up — the news. My telephone consultation with Dr Helen became, in her vivid reports to others, a mercy mission — a desert rescue, where life had been plucked from the jaws of death! When one friend offered sympathy over my illness, he sounded disappointed when I shrugged and said it was only the flu.

We drove out of Innamincka, over the gently flowing causeway, and into the Sturt Stony Desert. This was the vista of barren misery which drove back Sturt in despair and dismay. For hours we plugged on north, the road at times sandy, threaded through low sandhills a stone's throw from the Queensland border; at times a mere scar through horizon-to-horizon rust-red gibber.

Jolly was silent. Occasionally I would speak, pointing out a mirage, or perhaps a small tree. Such was the desolation; a lone tree became an object of interest. I wrestled, and failed, to find a word to describe the immensity of the desert. Jolly's responses were slow and most often in monosyllables. From time to time I sneaked a glance to see his eyelids drooping, so I zipped my lip while he dozed fitfully.

This wasn't the bright, drily witty mate I knew.

'You bored, mate?'

'Yeah. A bit,' he replied, so we stopped to stretch our legs and demolish a cold can. He went to sleep again soon after. It took more than nine hours to make it to Birdsville, with short stops at the historic Cordillo Downs station, and the ruins of Cadelga station a few kilometres south of the Queensland border. At one point, Jolly volunteered that his comment about being bored wasn't intended to be insulting to the stark grandeur of this mighty desert we were invading.

'There's not much to see here,' he said, 'but what we do see is incredible. Amazing. I never thought it would be as big, as dry, as desolate, or so remote.'

On that drive of 700-odd kilometres we didn't see another person or vehicle. I was puzzled by Jolly's unusually taciturn demeanour, but rationalised it by thinking he was probably put off by my sniffling, grizzling and generally crook behaviour. If I weren't too much fun to be with, why should he be?

Only months later did it fall into place with news of his poisoning. Shortly before we left Sydney, Jolly completed a pole home and in the process gave himself a mighty dose of arsenic from the copper arsenate impregnated into the Koppers logs he was using. Plus, he admitted, he might have sloshed some more on himself when he was painting arsenic treatment on the exposed sawn ends of logs and beams. He was losing weight from a lean and wiry body with not much to lose, and in the two months after our trip he lost a further six kilograms until, as his wife put it, 'He was just a bag of bones.' She insisted he go to a doctor, who identified the problem and urgently set about remedying it. I gasped at the revelation and hurried to the medical dictionary:

ARSENIC: Arsenic has been used intentionally to murder, particularly in fiction, but most poisoning occurs through accidental ingestion, particularly in rural areas where arsenic is an important constituent of some pesticides. Arsenic poisoning may be acute or chronic. Chronic

Conquerers of the Desert… the adventurers who crossed the Simpson Desert — in a flood — whoop it up outside the Birdsville Hotel.

Jolly Jol Simpson

poisoning is usually first noticeable as weakness, tiredness, scaly skin, thickening of the skin, a raindrop pigmentation of the skin, and a swelling of the lining of the mouth. Degeneration of the nerves then sets in, producing tingling and numbness in the hands and feet.

The treatment is simple: stop ingesting the poison, and allow it to flush away. Jolly is still building pole homes, but he now wears protective masks and clothing. We might say that Burke and Wills were bumbling fools in a fearsomely hostile environment, ignorantly poisoning themselves beside Cooper Creek. But so were we.

The news in Birdsville was bleak: the way to the Simpson Desert crossing was still barred by Eyre Creek. Where Sturt had despaired of finding water and turned back, we were blocked by water. That's the way, out here: mud and dust; boom and bust. And the locals said it would take at least three weeks to dry out. So we went to the fabled Birdsville pub to discuss our next move. North, via Bedourie and Boulia, or south, via the Birdsville Track, before swinging up through Oodnadatta to the Alice?

At sundown the bar began to fill. Men in leathers, riding boots caked with mud, removing helmets and gloves, pressing the bar, urgently ordering beers, talking among themselves, joined from time to time by other groups of twos and threes, all sporting a week's stubble and carrying an air of furtive triumph. What did they know that we weren't to be allowed to know?

'You come up the Track?' I asked. It seemed logical: we hadn't seen any bikers on our way through from Innamincka, and the

We made it to the top of the Big Red sandhill, but couldn't cross the Simpson because of floods.

only other way into this former border tax collecting town was from the north.

'Nah,' said the kid. He rejoined his mates.

'Talkative bastard,' said Jolly. By now there were ten of them. We took the hint and called for another can.

A short time later the kid sidled up. His name was Mick Mawson; he was 21 and came from Macedon in Victoria. 'We came across the desert,' he confided.

'But it's flooded.'

'Yeah, I know. And we're the first to get through since the rains. Bloody hard, though. We're a bit lucky to make it.'

Mick was hesitant about telling the story. The group was worried they might have broken a law. Perhaps the desert track had been declared closed, and maybe they would be prosecuted. But still, bit by bit, they told of the six tortuous days in which they became

the Conquerors of the Desert. With four 4WD vehicles and five motorbikes, they had taken on 500 kilometres of sandhills and desert, at times hopelessly bogged, sucked by glutinous mud beyond their axles, remote from all help, battling breakdowns, river torrents, hypothermia and a dwindling supply of beer.

But they out-thought and out-fought the elements and that night in the Birdsville bar, as a cosy fire warmed their bones and the booze warmed their spirits, they celebrated in triumphant exclamations of how they beat the odds. The spirit of adventure is alive and well, if not sometimes misplaced, in Australia.

Mick's father, Bill, explained how the group of family and friends from Victoria and South Australia set out in convoy to follow the Finke-to-Alice Springs desert

Eyre Creek, near Birdsville, in flood. The explorer Sturt had been unable to penetrate further inland because of a lack of water!

motorcycle race. They then trekked across the desert to Mt Dare and Dalhousie Springs to cross the Simpson Desert along the French Line — an oil search route blasted through 1300 sandhills in the early 1970s.

No-one had told them the desert was closed and that they would face 15-kilometre-wide floods at Eyre Creek. Fear of official condemnation explained their initial tight-lipped attitude, but they needn't have worried. Desert track closures are an advisory service, not a law.

The first problem for the group came not with floods, but mechanical failure. Bill Mawson's Landcruiser sheared a harmonic balance key — a vital component to run the water pump, alternator, fan and air-conditioner. Good old Aussie bush engineering came to the rescue. They chopped off the side of a spanner with an axe and hammer, shaped it with a file, and fitted it into

the slot. The slack around a worn pulley was taken up with a piece of beer can, cut and shaped. It worked, just like a bought one!

Mick Mawson's bike dropped a screw into its gearbox, and it was half a day before they had it stripped and the offending article fished out with a bit of wire, and Dean Chamberlain's tailshaft dropped off over a dune. But these were minor matters. Eyre Creek was yet to come.

The official term 'creek' is a misnomer. It appears on maps as a single blue line, not even linking into the Diamantina. But in flood it is seen from the air as a myriad of waterways, flood plains, lakes, sumps, marshes and billabongs stretching in an incredible maze up to ten kilometres each side of its main channel. It was at the first of these muddy floodways that Bill Mawson's Landcruiser sank to its floor. For 24 hours it stayed there, resisting all efforts to move it. Eight-tonne snatch straps broke, countless logs were busted, and the team trudged endlessly through knee-deep mud as they scratched their heads to invent a way to get the vehicle out.

Paul Koczak and Paul Donaldson took to their bikes on a rescue mission, hoping to break through the flood plains to Birdsville to get a 100-metre steel rope to winch the Landcruiser out. They pushed their bikes through chest-deep creeks, rode 175 kilometres north in search of a viable crossing of the main river, shared a packet of chips and a can of cold spaghetti for dinner, slept on a sandhill in wet clothes on a night so cold they kept their helmets on their heads for warmth, and made it to Birdsville.

But while they were battling the mud and slush, the guys around the campfire had an idea. They took the drop-side panels off the Landcruiser's tray, jacked it up, and put them under the wheels.

'We got two other vehicles around the swamp ahead of the Landcruiser,' Bill said, 'and chained them together. Then we winched like hell, and all of a sudden it popped out of the mud and slid forward as if it were on waterskis. Easy.'

It took another day for the party to find a way through the muddy maze to the relative safety of Big Red, the last major sand dune before Birdsville. And then it was downhill all the way to the bar.

Jolly and I had to make do with Big Red. We careered up it, and sat longingly on its ridge 90 metres above the desert floor, looking disconsolately at the dead-straight track west into the Simpson Desert. So near, and yet so far. Then we turned around and headed north into the Channel Country towards Bedourie and Boulia.

Just out of Birdsville we passed through a stand of Waddi trees — a stunted acacia which takes 150 years to reach its full height of about ten metres, and is known to grow in only three places in the world. Here, perhaps 100 of them were scattered across a gibber-strewn claypan. Then, abruptly, there were no more, and we entered a moonscape — horizon to horizon of rusty gibber plains with not a blade of grass to be seen.

But further north, rain had fallen and given these fabled beef lands a green pick, especially in the shallow valleys. We stopped by an artesian bore which had been pouring its 95°C water into the desert uninterrupted for 100 years. Too hot to drink, the water flowed through a channel for a kilometre or so before settling into an oasis-like lagoon. Beside the bore was the rusting hulk of a steam engine, carried here in pieces by bullock drays in the 1890s. Its drilling job complete, it was uneconomical to try to dismantle the engine and freight it out.

The rain had turned the track into an impassable mudbath west of Lake Machattie, forcing us on to a lengthy detour to the east, where, incongruously, we encountered kilometres of deep, invasive bulldust which caked our windows and crippled my throat.

We stopped at the little Bedourie pub to wash down the dust. This is a settlement with one main street, no more than a dozen buildings, a petrol bowser and the pub, its old, daubed walls painted grey and pink, topped by a satellite dish.

Behind the bar, in front of the XXXX signs, sat a stout woman. On stools at the bar were four or five locals; men in singlets and shorts, women in thin floral cotton dresses. It was a typical bush pub, except for one thing — the locals were singularly uninterested in our arrival.

Normally when a stranger wanders into a pub like this, drinks are served and either the

Mustering cattle on the plains of far western Queensland... prime grazing land.

publican or the patrons start up a conversation. Where yer from? Where yer headin'? The chat usually ends up with the observation that things are different out here. Not like in the cities.

But not today. The attention of every soul present was entirely taken by *The Bold and The Beautiful* on the television hung above the bar. The woman behind the bar allowed herself to be distracted for only a moment as she passed us our cans. Drawn to the screen, we saw chisel-faced Hollywood hunks woodenly acting out a vacuous script with pneumatic, collagen-lipped, Hollywood bimbos. The communications revolution has brought wondrous change to the outback, but, I wondered, is this a benefit? To vicariously transport the good folk of Bedourie to Beverly Hills?

I obligingly waited for a commercial break to ask the bar lady what the road was like to Boulia. Without taking her eyes off the screen, she said: 'Some say it's OK; some say it's pretty bad.'

It was OK. So, too, was the Donovan Highway which took us west from Boulia towards the Northern Territory. But 'highway' is a laughable misnomer. At times it was nothing more than two wheel ruts in the dirt. In wet weather it can quickly become impassable. This is prime grazing country, with good growths of Mitchell grass which give way to low brigalow scrub closer to the Northern Territory border. The Boulia shire boasts 60,000 square kilometres, with 250,000 sheep, 75,000 cattle — and about 600 people! After crossing into the Northern Territory at Tobermorey station, the road became the well-graded gravel Plenty Highway, and we settled into a relaxed run towards Alice Springs.

The beautiful Barossa Valley, South Australia.

chapter six

In our travels to date, at times remote, we had felt we were in 'our' country. We were free to choose where we went, and when we went. Our contact was almost exclusively with white Australians, at service stations, pubs and motels along the way. But now we were entering another realm: Aboriginal territory, where the vivid landscapes were often available to us only by permit, and where our interaction with the people took on the demeanour and obligations of being a guest. We expected the issues of coexistence between black and white, pastoralist and native title owner, city and the bush, would be very real. From the Centre to the Kimberley, across the Top End and through the Gulf of Carpentaria, we aimed to set ourselves apart from those who so readily thumped the table and proffered their views at fine city dinner parties: we wanted to arm ourselves with some facts.

I was gloomy about the course of reconciliation between black and white, having just come from the Reconciliation

Convention in Melbourne where I had delivered a paper about the media's role in redressing the wrongs of the past two centuries. I not only wore my heart on my sleeve, but also wore my convention cap on my head until I realised no-one had noticed it. My mission was to learn more; to see if I could picture reconciliation as a way of life, rather than a concept.

I could sense, but not explain, the notion of Aboriginal spirituality and attachment to the land. It's a palpable thing. I have felt it in Arnhem Land, on the banks of the King River and the Goomadeer; I have felt it in the majestic canyons of the Kimberley, and I was to feel it again as we camped beside the Wailbri Ranges, near Yuendumu. It is well-nigh impossible to define, but it has to do with the timelessness of these places. They have been here, untouched, for millions of years. They are nature's reality. We are mere interlopers for a moment in the time of this land. We are visitors from another place. We bring our customs, our cultures, our names and our laws, but somehow, we don't fit here in the way the spirits of the people who have been here for at least 45,000 years before us, do. They are enshrined in the land around us; in the Dreaming.

Look up at the stars in the cold, clear night, away from the flickering glow of the campfire where they sparkle so breath-takingly bright. What are they? How did they get there? Our ancestors asked those questions, and before they had science to help with the answers they assigned the unanswerable to the unseen hand of their gods. The early Aborigines posed the same questions and invented equally plausible Dreamtime stories, then passed them down through generations of oral history. They became linked to a complex social structure where age, gender, totemic and land affiliations provided important guideposts. Are their stories of their spirits any less valid than our stories of the virgin birth, Lot's wife or the parting of the Red Sea? Why are so many of us so ready to accept the truth of Noah's Ark while rejecting as baseless the Rainbow Serpent?

Because it's not our culture, and even today, very few of us understand, or seek to understand, it. In this sense we aren't much advanced on our ancestor Europeans. They brought cultural arrogance and a superior determination to reshape the land in their own image. They didn't wish, and didn't attempt, to learn or to know of any existing culture. They saw the indigenous people as savages who lived impermanently on the land, making no attempt to do anything — like farming — with it.

They saw the convenience of this. If the Aboriginal people didn't work the land, how could they have property rights? And so the doctrine of *terra nullius* became the foundation of a very shady legal framework for colonisation. The empty land. No prior ownership. In a sense, they were right, because the notion of ownership hadn't occurred to the Aborigines. They didn't *own* the land; they were *of* it. It nurtured and nourished them; it gave them their place in the cosmology defined by their Dreaming stories, and generations of children learned the complexities of their place, and their strict marriage laws, through their various relationships with the land.

The Europeans came here under instruction to negotiate with the owners of the land, the British explorer Cook being told: 'You are also with the Consent of the Natives to take possession of Convenient Situations in the Country in the Name of the

King of Great Britain.' But in 1770 he didn't bother with such niceties. He simply declared unilateral possession, judging the east coast to be thinly populated and assuming the interior would be uninhabited. It was a breathtakingly arrogant assumption, given that he had no knowledge whatsoever of the interior.

The First Fleet of convicts and marines followed Cook in 1788, and Governor Arthur Phillip was under instruction to 'endeavour by every possible means to open an intercourse with the natives, and to conciliate their affections, enjoining all our subjects to live in amity and kindness with them'. It was a policy made to be ignored. Phillip and his successors simply appropriated whatever land they wished and cruelly, ruthlessly, quelled any opposition or unrest by musket and axe. As the invaders spread out of the confines of the plains surrounding Port Jackson, they took possession of the Hunter region, the Bathurst plains, and the fertile valleys of the northern rivers. Tens of thousands of Aborigines died in unequal battles with colonial settlers, and diseases like smallpox further ravaged their population. It was a pattern which continued for a century; a hidden war of massacres, poisoned waterholes and wholesale slaughters, where British law was ignored in order that British law could be fearfully imposed on a people. It was an illegitimate, unjust and concerted campaign of dispossession; an invasion followed by conquest. Its legacy was fear, suffering and dependency.

The popular acceptance of social doctrines such as Darwin's theory of the survival of the fittest gave solace to those who were uneasy about the plight of Australia's Aboriginal people. The superior

Camped under an awesome ridge of rocks in the Wailbri Ranges, near Yuendumu… feel the Dreamtime.

Europeans saw themselves as far more advanced than the black savage stereotype and, turning a blind eye to their hand in a genocide, they consoled themselves that the Aborigines were a dying race, anyway. How convenient. Soon, they argued, the problem would disappear. It was their job to smooth the pillow. Government policy was to hasten the process, removing children from their families, breaking down any remains of tribal law and structures, and herding the survivors into missions and reserves. It was of no consequence that the people didn't want to leave their land — they were simply removed by trickery or force, or both.

I ask myself, do I feel guilty about this? Is my view of the tragedy which casts a shadow over the very legitimacy of our nation reasonably called a 'black armband' view of history? Should we all feel guilt, or do we dismiss our history by saying we had no part in it, and therefore it is of no consequence to us?

Yes, I feel guilty. I don't accept the blame for the massacres and the heartless killings of more than a century ago — or even in the 1920s and 1930s. I'm not guilty of those crimes. But I am part of a community which continues to prefer ignorance over knowledge; which continues the policies of repression while denying it; which now recognises prior ownership and tries to suppress it; and which prefers to fear difference rather than celebrate it. That is my shame. I feel guilty that we cannot seem to find the generosity in our hearts to say sorry.

The opening of the Reconciliation Convention was marked by speeches of goodwill inviting us to aspire to the loftiest ideals of inclusion, fairness, dignity and decency. There was hope that Prime Minister John Howard would use the occasion to deliver an official apology for the actions of past government agencies in removing the children of Aboriginal families — now known as the Stolen Generation.

The full impact of these terribly misguided policies was outlined in the 1997 report *Bringing Them Home* which had been released just prior to the convention. The report told of a great national shame, documenting in harrowing testimony the stories of Australians still living, and still suffering. Much as we might not like to hear it, the report details a systematic violation of human rights which our government would be the first to condemn — if it had happened in Africa, the Balkans or Afghanistan. But the Prime Minister baulked at the opportunity to deliver a formal apology — one of the first recommendations of the report. Undoubtedly goaded and insulted by a section of the audience which turned its back on him, the Prime Minister aggressively hectored his audience about his proposals to amend the *Native Title Act* after a High Court judgment ruled, in the *Wik* decision, that native title and pastoral titles could coexist. By so doing, I felt he instantly negated his personal apology over the Stolen Generation, and redefined the gulf between black and white. I felt diminished and ashamed by his actions. After his speech, gloom descended. It seemed impossible that any good could come of the convention.

Both sides are frustrated. The white community is frustrated that so much effort over so many years — including a billion-dollar annual budget — has amounted to so little. The black community is frustrated at the legal roadblocks erected by squabbling politicians, and by the damaging impact of some of their own hot-heads who apparently don't want to give reconciliation a chance. There are elements of truth in both points of view. Both communities are divided within themselves. Just as there is no one white point of view, there is no single black point of view. White politics cover the spectrum from the bleeding heart left to the redneck right; what's not always understood within the white community is that black politics — and cultures — are just as diverse. The difficulty is to find the common ground, and build on it.

That takes leadership, and that is precisely what wasn't forthcoming from the government. The numbers men had done their counting and had decided there were no votes in an apology. There would be no

Cheryl Kernot and John Howard receive greetings from elders of the Kulin nation at the opening of the Reconciliation Convention in Melbourne, May 1997, as the former chair of the Council for Aboriginal Reconciliation, Patrick Dodson, looks on.

electoral backlash from refusing this decent, but essentially symbolic, gesture. So principles and compassion were jettisoned at a time when they were most demanded. How, then, can we avoid responsibility for a deliberate step back from any notion of human justice? We will be seen by historians as no better, and no more enlightened, than those who, in the past, committed shameful and tragic deeds against the original inhabitants.

Paradoxically, though, public opinion surveys show there is a community desire for reconciliation almost as strong as the 1967 referendum vote which finally made Aboriginal and Torres Strait Islanders citizens in their own land. If you dig deeply into the core values of Australians there is a strong demand for egalitarianism, good citizenship and a fair go for all. Most of us say we would rather have a harmonious, inclusive society over the bitterly divided, exclusionary alternative. But as social researcher Hugh Mackay told the convention, that view often doesn't extend to including the indigenous. It is still the Shame of Australia.

In spite of its shaky start, the convention continued for three days. Gradually the gloom lifted and by the time of the closing speeches there was a feeling that perhaps the event would make a difference. It ended

Todd Mall, Alice Springs… saddened by the sights.

with high hopes, lofty communiqués, and a five-volume report of proceedings and recommendations for the way ahead. Whether we embrace them and implement them, or reject them on a scrapheap of indifference, will define us as a nation.

After weeks on the road, Alice Springs was like an oasis to us. Wendy flew in from Sydney and we roamed the souvenir and Aboriginal art shops of Todd Mall. This is a magnet for tourists from around the world, but goodness knows how they separate the tourist junk from the few items of true value. Perhaps they don't. Perhaps it's enough for them to be in the Red Centre, experiencing the difference at places like the fine Red Ochre grill restaurant which features Australian bush tucker ingredients such as bush tomatoes, wild limes,

pepper leaves, wattleseed, quandongs and vegetables in paperbark. They make an interesting difference to the flavours of beef, kangaroo or emu meat, but so far have failed to ignite the culinary imagination of the great chefs of Europe.

The Alice Springs economy is built on tourism, and the city has a strong, positive air about it. But it also has a racial tension within it, and it's not possible simply to avert one's eyes and wish it away. On a grassed area in Todd Mall a group of Aborigines were whiling away the day, accosting passers-by and asking for handouts of money, occasionally shouting abuse at those who refused. Several of the group were clearly affected by alcohol, swaying and stumbling. Others appeared to be sleeping it off. This was the stereotypical image of the drunken Aborigine which does so much harm to their cause. This is the image which is thrown up by those who argue that the Aborigine is slothful, lazy and good for nothing.

Part of the problem, we were told, is that so many Aboriginal communities have outlawed alcohol. They are dry communities, and proudly so. The decisions to ban grog have been taken by the communities because they recognise the harm it has done to them. A walk through the shopping malls in the Alice underlines the point strongly — we saw a display of school projects where the children had produced heartfelt posters featuring slogans like 'Dad — Don't Drink' and 'No Grog — Please' among drawings depicting home violence and ruination. It was a powerful and moving display, but I wondered sadly how long it would be before some of the kids who had produced these messages would be sniffing petrol or swigging booze themselves.

But while alcohol is banned in many of the communities, there is no law against its consumption in cities or towns like Alice Springs. Many people leave their communities and head for the Alice for a few days of partying. This has so offended many of the white — governing — population that the Northern Territory government has called for wet canteens to be established in the communities. In other words, the government is saying: 'If you're going to get drunk and lay about, do it in your own backyards, not in our towns.' This is a heartless and knee-jerk response from white politicians who want to sweep the problem under the carpet, rather than seeking to resolve it. But it's true: I was confronted by the sad sights in Todd Mall.

No visit to Alice Springs is complete without a look at the old telegraph station. This is the Alice's reason for being. A town grew around the telegraph station. Originally there was just one building — now known as the barracks, which was built with gun slits high in its walls so that it could be defended against hostile Aborigines — but expansion came with a new telegraph office, station master's residence, and a battery room established before 1900.

As Burke and Wills were battling the deserts further east, the Scottish surveyor John McDouall Stuart set out to find a viable north–south crossing of the continent in 1860. The limits of South Australian settlement at that time reached only a little north of what is now the Leigh Creek coalfield, but good water supplies had been found among the mound strings which dot the landscape south of Lake Eyre. Three times Stuart pushed north, only to be beaten back, but in July 1862 he reached the Arafura Sea east of Darwin.

His success fired the imagination of the South Australian government. Intense lobbying began for an overland telegraph line to link Australia to the rest of the world. The telegraph had, by then, found its way from London to India, and would soon be in Java. The British-Australian Telegraph Company undertook in 1870 to bring the line to Darwin — if the South Australian government would guarantee to construct a 3000-kilometre line from Darwin to Adelaide by 1 January 1872. This gave the government 19 months to supply 36,000 poles and to plant them, 12 to a kilometre, across the harsh interior. Amazingly, the southern and central sections were completed on time, but rough going and monsoons delayed the northern 600 kilometres between Tennant Creek and the King River. The telegraph company demanded compensation for this delay, but the government instituted a pony express to carry messages over the gap, and the demands ended in embarrassed silence when the overseas cable broke down.

The line was completed in August 1872. A public holiday was declared and the *South Australian Advertiser* editorialised:

> Of course the cost of the line far exceeded the original estimate, but that has arisen from circumstances which human foresight could not control. The cost however, compared to the advantages which the colony will reap from the construction of the line, is a mere bagatelle. We have, by the telegraph, given an impetus for the settlement of the Northern Territory. Already a large quantity of land has been taken up for pastoral purposes in the interior, the rent from which will do something to pay the interest on the expenditure on the line. But above all, a highway has been formed across the very heart of Australia, the future benefits of which at present no man can estimate.

The benefits were immediate. Messages which used to take months by sea now travelled to and from London in hours. Suddenly, the isolation of Australia was dramatically reduced. And the inexorable march of communications began to reduce isolation within Australia.

Yuendumu, on the southern fringes of the Tanami Desert, is home to a remarkable experiment in communications. Called the Tanami Network, it is an antidote to the virus of Hollywood cultural imperialism, a means of delivering government services, and a proven weapon in the battle against Aboriginal deaths

in custody. It also turns on its head the notion that digital communications technology requires mass audiences. As the world waits for the inevitable arrival of video phones, a videoconferencing system brings together ancient cultures in one of the most sparsely populated areas of the earth, and gives them access to global communications.

To understand the impact of the Tanami Network we need to absorb the scale: Yuendumu is the hub, the main centre for the Warlpiri people who have wandered the Tanami Desert area for eons. It is linked with other Warlpiri communities at Walungurru, or Kintore, 250 kilometres as the crow flies to the south-west, Willowra, 150 kilometres to the north-east, and Lajamanu, 460 kilometres to the north-west. Other links are to the main government service centres of Alice Springs, 250 kilometres to the south-east, Katherine, 850 kilometres due north, and Darwin, 1100 kilometres to the north. It therefore spans almost the entire length of the Northern Territory, and half its breadth, bringing together the major Warlpiri communities of between 300 and 600 people each. It is the largest network of its type in the world.

Putting together a communications network on this scale — vast distances, tiny populations — had never been considered before the Tanami Network. Conventional wisdom prophesied that high-capacity broadband or narrowband applications would be the exclusive preserve of city folk, where high-density populations would provide the mass to make the investment viable.

The launch of Australia's Aussat (now Cables & Wireless Optus) satellites in the 1980s provided both an opportunity and a threat. The opportunity was for remote area television services beamed directly from space. The threat was that those services might be no more than a relay of capital city television fare — essentially, light entertainment, American sitcoms and Hollywood movies. Aboriginal cultural guardians argued they had a hard enough time trying to maintain their languages and cultures without increasing the pressure via a never-ending diet of Hollywood shoot-'em-ups and re-runs of *Married With Children*. The Central Australian Aboriginal Media Association won the rights to the central Australian satellite TV footprint and launched its Imparja service with a promise to tailor its programming to suit the cultural interests of its audiences. It was a promise largely overwhelmed by the harsh economics of running a TV channel on a very limited advertising base. Imparja's programs, particularly during prime time, generally replicate those of its major supplier, the Nine Network. Cultural preservation is mainly confined to a limited news service and community service advertising aimed at health issues.

One of the main proposers of a dedicated communications network for the Warlpiri people was Northern Territory politician Peter Toyne who told me: 'Remote area TV was held up as a great benefit for isolated communities, but the truth is it was envisaged as something for the white communities — the homesteaders. No-one gave much thought to its potential to help preserve cultural enclaves which are quite vulnerable to being swamped by mainstream language and world views. We realised that if you wanted to preserve your culture and language, you can't just sit there and let it hit you from the outside — you've got to put up some counterbalancing media activity.'

So the Warlpiri Media Association was born, and a low-powered radio station was established at Yuendumu. That was soon followed by a TV transmitter which sent out a tiny signal which travelled just three kilometres. The problem was that the broadcasting rules and regulations, designed for the populated areas of the nation, didn't allow for the Warlpiri moves. They were unlicensed pirate transmissions, and the regulatory authorities took a dim view of them in spite of the fact they couldn't be heard outside the immediate confines of Yuendumu. A solution was found by the tail wagging the dog — a new licence category for open narrowcast broadcasting was established, and the Yuendumu model became available for any community throughout Australia.

According to Peter Toyne, there was nothing new in this. 'Out here, we have a long history going right back to the Overland Telegraph of communications technology actually appearing here first, and having it more extensively used, because the imperatives driving it are here, not there,' he said. That's exactly what happened last century when remote station owners found they could order plant, equipment, food and clothing by telegram and have it delivered months earlier than if they had used horse-and-buggy mail services.

After the radio and TV services were established at Yuendumu, the Warlpiri Media Association began looking sideways at other technologies. A series of workshops were organised and the value of videoconferencing was immediately apparent. 'Everyone jumped on it,' said Peter Toyne. 'All age groups could see its value. On the first day of a three-day workshop and demonstration of videoconferencing between Lajamanu, Yuendumu and Sydney an old man had died in one of the communities, so the elders got on the system and arranged sorry business, which was a stunning use of a technology they had seen for the first time only that day. They didn't give a bugger *how* it worked — they simply asked "What does it do?", and used it. It was a very unselfconscious uptake at the grassroots level.'

Today videoconferencing is used in classrooms, bringing children together for lessons about their culture in their own language, to provide support for case management services for various government agencies, taking witness statements (although not yet as a way of giving evidence in a law court), and to provide vital contact between families broken up by imprisonment. This has led to a marked decline in deaths in custody. A Royal Commission into the disproportionately high rate of prison suicide among Aborigines found that isolation from families was a major contributing cause. Today, the Tanami Network provides the facility for a mother in, say, Kintore, to talk to and see her son in Katherine or Darwin gaol on a weekly basis. The fees for this are paid by the Correctional Services Department.

The network hasn't limited its activities to local contact. An indigenous art community thrives at Yuendumu and a major fire dreaming work was consigned to London to be the centrepiece at an exhibition. The artists who made the painting were connected by videoconference to London and explained to an audience of 400 what the painting meant, and how its component parts related to the dances and songs of the land of its origin. In this way the artists were able to avoid the usual European reconstruction of what the eye of the beholder *thinks* it means.

What will come of this? The Tanami Network has already created a media-savvy community, and a demand for radio and TV production skills. Local men and women have undertaken media training courses, and have produced many hundreds of hours of TV for broadcast via the tiny transmitter. A CD-ROM has been produced, and others are under way.

It is unlikely that all those participating and learning media skills here will spend the rest of their days in Yuendumu. Many will surely leave and take up jobs in large regional centres and capital cities. They will take with them their cultural heritage and sensitivities, and slowly they will cross-pollinate their knowledge with their workmates'. They will promote a greater understanding between black and white, bush and city. Some may rise to become decision-makers in national media markets, and find themselves in a position to influence the outcomes of future debates.

Given that a major criticism of the (white) media among Aboriginal communities is its lack of knowledge, interest, care or concern for cultural matters, and its generally negative portrayal of Aboriginal issues, the young trainees of the Tanami Desert have the potential to bring about a major correction. In time, their influence could contribute hugely towards the creation of a national mind-set that the only true path to reconciliation is a willingness to walk together, each recognising and respecting the others' differences.

From a tiny acorn does the oak tree grow.

The coordinator of the Warlpiri Media Association (WMA) is Tom Kantor, 32, a tousle-haired graduate of media studies at the Royal Melbourne Institute of Technology. We had arranged a permit to visit Yuendumu and were told to report to Tom for details of the conditions covering our visit. These included a signed undertaking to submit a copy of any writing before publication, and a restriction on photography. A media-savvy community, indeed, but why?

The people of Yuendumu have a long history of being pried upon, prodded and dissected by researchers and the media. A web site lists 229 linguistic texts, 171 other writings and 36 films made about the Warlpiri since 1931. Not all have been complimentary. WMA researcher Melinda Hinkson says the reasons for Yuendumu's favour as a destination for researchers, film-makers and media groups are multiple and complex, but include relatively easy access and a large population. 'Accordingly, [it] is a favoured destination on politicians' itineraries, and for footage to cover stories on the "Third World" conditions in which Australia's indigenous people continue to live today,' she wrote in a 1996 paper.

A number of negative incidents and the presence in the community of 'outside crews' led to the development of a comprehensive and legally binding Agreement to Film which all film-makers and media groups must sign prior to arriving to shoot. Accompanying this agreement is a well-formulated briefing and set of rules which crews must abide by, designed to protect the privacy of

Tom Kantor and Valerie Napaljarri Martin at the Warlpiri Media Association's edit suite at Yuendumu, Northern Territory.

Tom Kantor, coordinator of the Warlpiri Media Association, outside Yuendumu's tiny radio and TV station.

community members and more generally to give the community some control over the kinds of representations constructed and circulated to wider Australia. These rules include the need for a local liaison to accompany the crew at all times; that no Warlpiri person can be filmed without their permission; that copies of all footage shot must be returned to the community for archival purposes; and that once edited to broadcast format, a copy of the program must be sent to the WMA to be vetted by relevant people. In

the event that the program contains material of a culturally offensive nature (secret or sacred material in particular) WMA reserves the right to have that material edited out prior to it being broadcast.

These are stringent conditions which many film-makers and editors find rankling because they argue that editorial control must rest with them, and anything less is to compromise their journalistic integrity. But, no signature, no filming.

In spite of this attempt to manage the portrayal of the Warlpiri culture, problems do occur. Melinda Hinkson details an encounter with a crew from CNN subsidiary Global TV, where the prospect of an audience of 170 million across America, Europe and Asia for a seven-minute 'human interest' segment seemed too good to refuse. In her account of the visit, titled 'The Circus Comes to Yuendumu (Again)', she alleges friction between the locals and the film producer, and an incident where a 'cameraman [was] shooting footage of nearby humpy camps — a definite no-no in terms of the community's wishes'. A local elder had also been filmed, without permission. The crew eventually departed with ten tapes of footage. But, Melinda Hinkson wrote:

… a level of unease accompanies the send-off given to every media crew and writer at the end of their stay; a suspicion of the unseeable contents of their video tapes, notebooks and heads. What might come to be constructed from materials taken, where that material might end up, and what ramifications might come to pass as a result.

The development of indigenous media associations across remote Australia has been seen as a contribution to the tipping of the scales in favour of indigenous representation of indigenous affairs, both for local consumption and to present to the outside world. Dubbed as a way to 'fight fire with fire', commentators have argued that through their own media activity, groups such as the Warlpiri can themselves have some control over the way in which they are represented in the public realm. Moreover, this development is part of a much wider political process which has irrevocably shifted the relationship between those traditionally represented and those who represent. Who can speak for whom and about what is now a highly contested area both in political and academic arenas.

Warlpiri from Yuendumu will continue to give access to cultural commentators from 'outside'. They will do so out of pride, generosity, and out of a desire to be known and thus 'exist' in the wider society, and in hope that a greater understanding of [their] aspirations may be communicated as a result. They will do so at the same time as knowing and attempting to minimise the risks involved. Moreover [they] will continue to participate because they know that any form of self-determination necessarily entails knowing how to play the game.

OK, so I've got to play by the rules, or I don't get a game at all. Fair enough. I'm a guest in their community. But does that mean I must shut my eyes and my mind to all I see and hear?

A report on the 1995 sports weekend — an open day at Yuendumu; no permits required — appeared in *Quadrant* in October 1995. Written by Dr John Carroll, it compared what he called shocking living conditions — delapidated housing, rubbish, lack of hygiene, mangy dogs — with the heavenliness of football played by barefoot kids on the dusty oval. It caused an uproar. A group of Yuendumu teachers and WMA representatives responded fiercely, saying Dr Carroll had done no more than enforce the most common stereotypes about Aboriginal people — they are either savage, demoralised and lacking in self-esteem, or they are romanticised as spirit-like, mysterious, ancient and other-worldly.

But equally interesting was their proposition that the rubbish which litters the streets of Yuendumu has a cultural basis, if not justification. In a response to *Quadrant*, the group argued:

> Warlpiri people live publicly. Nothing is hidden. In a sense Yuendumu leaves open to public view what so-called civilised society hides under the surface of the clean city. For any visitor to Yuendumu, this is the first and most superficial level of engagement with the community. Western capitalism has left its mark in remote Aboriginal Australia in the form of waste that did not exist prior to contact with Europeans. It is only 50 years ago that Yuendumu was established as a reserve, and more recently still that people became dependent on shop-bought foods. The outcomes of this colonial process make themselves apparent as an eyesore.

This is a novel proposition. An outsider is immediately struck by what is, by general community standards, a litter problem throughout the town. The instinctive reaction is to assume a lack of care or a lack of pride in the residents' surroundings. There is nothing here a good working bee couldn't fix in a weekend. But no: it is explained away as a Western (read white) capitalist plot. In the days of nomadic hunting and gathering there was no mess; a kangaroo came wrapped in its skin alone, not off a supermarket shelf in slices, cling-wrapped on a white polystyrene tray; a yam dug from beneath a eucalypt was not pre-cooked and packaged in freezer-resistant cardboard. But 'shop-bought foods' today do come in packages. Surely it requires no great cultural shift to properly dispose of this modern detritus. If the community of Yuendumu is so concerned about the way it

is portrayed that if feels it necessary to legally bind the hands of those who write about it or film it, and if it genuinely seeks wider understanding of its aspirations, it might decide to do something cosmetic about those first impressions, specifically to avoid the kind of stereotypical reporting about which they complain.

I find myself thinking that, while my sympathy for the Aboriginal cause is in no way diminished by the rubbish in the streets of Yuendumu (or any other community), there must be a mutual obligation to seek the path of cultural understanding. Have your legally binding agreements to film, by all means, but do us a favour: don't blame your rubbish on us.

Tom Kantor was co-producing a film on behalf of the Warlpiri Media Association when we arrived. It was for the ABC, one of eight half-hour documentaries made by indigenous film-makers. The film was about the Yuendumu Night Patrol, a community self-help scheme established by volunteer women who patrolled the streets in an effort to break the heart-rending habit of petrol-sniffing among young Aborigines.

This puts the Night Patrol in a gap between Northern Territory law and what the kids see as the insufferable boredom of a small, remote community. Incredibly, petrol-sniffing is not outlawed in the territory. Police, who tell of finding kids whacked out of their brains, are powerless to act. But the Night Patrol women can — and do, armed with metre-long nulla-nulla sticks and sharp tongues.

I thought it strange that the WMA would make a film which highlights a problem in their community. Given the sensitivity to the way they are portrayed in the wider media, a film about petrol-sniffing could be seen as

First Class Constable Chantal Parsons talks with Judy Nampijinpa Granites and Lucky Nampijinpa Langdon before setting off on the Yuendumu Night Patrol.

negative. But when it was shown some months later, it had a positive slant.

'The Warlpiri are a fascinating, gentle people with much to teach us,' Tom said. 'There's no doubt there are community problems, but what community doesn't have its stresses and strains? In that sense, Yuendumu is no different from many other small Australian towns. What is interesting here is the way the local people are dealing with the problems, and this is what we want to show through the Night Patrol documentary.'

The women have no powers other than the moral authority of tribal elders. But they work closely with Yuendumu's three-person police force, and receive high praise from First Class Constable Chantal Parsons, 32. A striking woman with a diamond stud in her nose, Constable Parsons is a popular figure with the children of Yuendumu.

'They are little angels when they're very young,' she said. 'But often the problems come later. It breaks your heart to see some of them take to petrol-sniffing. It is addictive, and it slowly destroys the brain function. You can't reason with them when they're out of it, just as you can't reason with a drunk. Sometimes they think it's a bit of sport — they want you to chase them, but it does them terrible harm. I have seen 16-year-olds in nappies and wheelchairs in Alice Springs institutions, wrecked by petrol. Among the kids, sniffing is a bigger problem than alcohol is with the adults. Alcohol is banned here, but sniffing petrol isn't against the law in the Northern Territory, as it is in Western Australia. Therefore, we're powerless to act, but the

Night Patrol can roust the kids out and send them home. If they need us to help, we're there; but sometimes jobs such as solving domestic disputes, or finding a woman a refuge for the night, or getting the kids off the streets are better done by the community.'

As we talked, Constable Parsons took a phone call. The community recreation centre was closed through the unavailability of staff, and 200 kids had to make their own fun that Saturday afternoon — highlighting the problem of boredom. But suddenly, there was a dash for the airstrip, because the army had just dropped in. Two Iriquois helicopters, having taken part in military exercises in the Northern Territory, were en route to their base in Queensland and landed to refuel. By the time we got to the strip, dozens of excited children were swarming all over them, taking turns to climb into the pilot's seat, wide white smiles breaking their faces in unbridled delight. The crew happily assisted until it was time for all to stand back and watch them take off into a setting sun. The choppers rose, swirling dust over all below, flew west for a few moments, cartwheeled and made a low pass over the crowd of kids, silhouetted arms waving goodbye through open windows on each side of the aircraft. It was like a scene from *Apocalypse Now*, and the kids loved it.

We retired to our camp in a creek under an awesome ridge of rock and reflected on our visit. The arrival of the choppers seemed a metaphor for the cultural tensions at play in this ancient desert; no matter how remote, and no matter how determined the push to preserve the Warlpiri cultures, influences

The army helicopter takes off after dropping in to Yuendumu.

First Class Constable Chantal Parsons with the children of Yuendumu… 'They are little angels . . .'

from other worlds can just drop in. Satellite TV is just another sort of helicopter.

The cry is to preserve the culture, so they establish a high-tech communications system, both as a way to foster their own languages and customs, and as a shield to ward off the corrosive influences of Hollywood. They like their culture — but the evidence is that they don't want to live it, particularly the younger ones. Generations ago they caught their kangaroos on the hop; then it became easier to use a .303 rifle, but today, no-one bothers about that — they go to the supermarket instead. Is that a rejection of their culture, or merely the inevitable embrace of an unstoppable, global way of living?

The desert had been drenched with rain two months before we crossed the Tanami. Gratefully, the spinifex grasses leapt away, and in places were eye-high beside the road. It didn't look like a desert to me. There was enough feed here to fatten all the cattle in the nation — but very few cattle to enjoy it. This is the cruel irony of the outback: with regular water it can be made lush and productive, but the rains refuse to be regular. Any attempt to increase the size of the herd to take advantage of the growth we saw would founder next season when the grass gave way to bare, windswept soil.

Out of this horizon-to-horizon flatness rise the new mileposts of the desert: slender Telstra towers, guyed and solar-powered, which catch and boost microwave signals each 50 kilometres or so. And beneath them, termite mounds; millions of them; skyscrapers of mud, cooling towers for billions of busy ants. The profusion; the sheer number of these mounds provokes mind-boggling speculation as we gobble up the 400-plus kilometres to the West Australian border — speculation which increases in bizarre complexity as we travel further through the Top End and see many different varieties of mounds. What are the secrets of these insects? How many of them are there? What gene within them pre-programs the shape of each mound? Why are some designs angular red-earth towers, while others look like grey, melting ice-cream? Why does a Tanami termite build to about two metres, while the Cape York termite reaches for the sky with a four-metre tower?

There are so few signs of people out here. The Granites goldmine, with a chequered history of stop–start operations over the past century, is currently being worked, but is firmly off-limits to the passer-by. Sixty kilometres further on is the Rabbit Flat roadhouse, a fortress-like pile of concrete bricks and barred windows reflecting the fact it is the only place within hundreds of kilometres where alcohol may be obtained. It's a strangely forbidding and unwelcoming place, where ordering a hamburger involves talking through a small opening in a concrete wall, speakeasy style. It was here we encountered the most expensive petrol in the nation — $1.25 a litre. A semi-apologetic sign noted that transport costs alone to this remote outpost amounted to 14 cents a litre, but hey, why bother to explain when the traveller has no alternative?

Over the border into Western Australia the track is officially called Maguires Track, named after a Catholic priest who established the Billiluna Aboriginal Community on Sturt

Creek, a serene camping site where the road leaves the desert and turns north into the undulating rises of the outer Kimberley region. Twenty kilometres off the highway is the Wolf Creek Crater, a giant pock-mark in the desert created by a meteorite which crashed to earth somewhere between 500,000 and two million years ago.

This is an extraordinary sight. Approached from the desert it appears as a low range of hills in an otherwise flat landscape. But once you climb the rocky path to the lip of the crater a giant circle appears, almost a kilometre across, with near-sheer sides dropping 70 metres to the crater floor. The meteor which made this second-largest crater in the world struck in a spectacular column of flame and gases at a speed of 900 kilometres a minute, deeply penetrating the earth's crust and pulverising rock to a depth of 200 metres. But time and winds have partially filled the crater, and today rain flows towards the centre, allowing the comparatively recent growth of wattles and melaleucas which, from the air, give the impression of a pupil within an eye.

On the lonely track to Wolf Creek Crater we met a cyclist making his bone-jarring way over the corrugations. This is a much tougher proposition than crossing the bitumen Nullarbor, but Matt Likar, 35, from Adelaide, insisted he was maintaining a great Australian tradition as he pushed himself day after day along the highways and bush tracks of the Never-Never. 'This is how people travelled from job to job in the pioneering days,' he told us. 'And during the Depression, the bike was the main form of transport for people looking for work.'

Ask Matt Likar where he has been, and he'll tell you: 'Everywhere, man.' He'll also volunteer that he hasn't had a wash in 11 days, but who cares? He's only got himself to live with.

'I'm addicted to this,' said Matt. 'I couldn't give it up even if I wanted to.' His addiction began in 1993 when he and his wife both bought bikes to ride to work. Matt decided on a one-week ride to the state's north, then a four-week adventure via the Victorian coast road. 'And then it snowballed…'

Perhaps because of his increasing absences, Matt's marriage failed. 'I had no place to live, so I said, "What the hell", and took to the road.' With a vengeance. He set out from Adelaide for the Flinders Ranges, doubled back to Mildura (for a spot of fruit picking to raise some funds), then rode north through Broken Hill, up the dog fence to Queensland, and on to the Gulf of Carpentaria.

There he received a message that a mate was getting married, so he pedalled back to Melbourne to be best man, picked some more fruit in the Goulburn Valley, and tackled the mountain ranges of Victoria and Southern New South Wales before heading north again to Alice Springs en route to Broome. In the past two years he has covered 19,000 kilometres on his 21-gear bike.

Larry Nolan, 51, a former vet from the Sydney suburb of Ryde, is another outback cyclist we encountered on the Plenty Highway, north-east of Alice Springs. Larry, who said he made enough from his veterinary

Outback cyclist Matt Likar, on his way to the Wolf Creek Crater.

practice to retire 18 years ago, has crossed Australia — north–south, east–west, and diagonally — seven times. On this trip he planned to cross the Gunbarrel Highway to Perth which was then five weeks away.

'I've done the Eyre Highway each way, followed the Transcontinental railway line across the Nullarbor, taken the tar road to Fitzroy Crossing, the Gibb River road through the Kimberley; I've ridden from Melbourne to Cape York, done the Birdsville and Strzelecki and Oodnadatta tracks, and the Tanami Desert track,' he told us. 'I dunno where I'll go next, but I'll find somewhere.'

Larry said he averaged 100 kilometres a day, and carried food and water for two or three days. Deeply tanned, he wore a light singlet and shorts — and no helmet. 'I put it on when I go through towns,' he said with a laugh. 'Out here, who cares about anything?

Cooinda (Yellow Waters), Kakadu National Park, Northern Territory.

chapter
seven

At first bark, you could be forgiven for feeling a little apprehensive about Roy Walker's bite. Bush poet, stockman, horse-breaker, saddler and latter-day squatter, Roy Walker is a legend around the wild and majestic Kimberley region of Western Australia.

And with good reason. He is an increasingly rare link with a tough but romantic cattle-droving past; an outspoken advocate of a return to the old values which he insists served Australia so well, and a fierce protector of the land he has claimed as his own. Roy is a great Australian character. He calls a spade a spade; my colonial oath he does. But beneath the rough, tough exterior lurks a well-hidden tender soul, as soft as butter.

We met Roy when my eldest sons, Scott and Kenton, sought to expand their Kununurra backpacker hostel business by establishing a canoe adventure down the Ord River. The plan was to drop off their customers at the base of the Argyle Dam and let them go with the flow downriver, through mighty gorges and stunning sunsets, to Kununurra. It would be an easy three-day paddle, but it required the establishment of two semi-permanent overnight camps along the way.

Kenton figured a likely spot would be near the junction of the Ord and Spillway Creek. Roy's land. Permission would be required. 'They say he's an irascible old bugger,' Kenton said. 'There's a story going around that he got so angry at noise from low-flying sightseeing planes that he once shot at one. I don't know if it's true, but I don't think I'll be giving him any cheek.'

Roy met us, barefoot in the dust, his blue eyes all but disappearing behind bushy eyebrows into the squint lines of 68 years in the sun; his high-peaked Akubra covering thinning hair tied loosely into a scraggy ponytail; a broad white moustache shading his top lip. He was slim and wiry; not much meat on him at all, and certainly not an ounce of excess. 'All prick'n'ribs,' said Kenton. His upper arms were partly covered by torn strips of a cotton shirt; his leathery skin lined with bulging blue veins. He bade us g'day, and listened to Kenton explain his mission.

'You'd better have a cuppa tea, then,' he said.

Roy's house was small — one bedroom and a kitchen/dining area. It was built out of polished timber logs holding up an unlined corrugated iron roof, with hessian stretched over cyclone wire to allow light to filter in while filtering out dust and flies. Pots, pans, ladles and kitchen paraphernalia hung on the inside of the wire, and gas fuelled the stove and refrigerator. We sat at a sturdy wooden table and met Roy's wife, a 39-year-old Swiss artist named Barbara Straub. At various points around this rustic home she had carved patterns into the logs — a kind of quaint scrimshaw more at home in an alpine

B&B than the hot and dusty outback of Australia.

The house is new, replacing Roy's original stone-and-logs home 200 metres away, closer to the permanent rocky waterholes of Spillway Creek. It burned down a couple of years ago, but Barbara plans to rebuild it as an art gallery. The entire encampment, with its cattleyards, barbecue areas, store shed and building sites, covers several hectares enclosed by a bend in the creek to the north and a huge buttress of red rock, stained black where monsoonal waterfalls cascade in the Wet, to the south. Long grasses and straggly gums cover the drier areas, with more substantial eucalypts closer to the creek.

'This is my land,' Roy told us emphatically. 'I first camped here in 1960 when I was head stockman for the Duracks over there at Argyle Downs. It's all gone now, of course, flooded by the dam. But this is mine, and I'll shoot any bugger who comes on to it or tries to take it away from me. My colonial oath I will.' I am at first puzzled by this fierce insistence on Roy's legitimacy as a Kimberley landowner, but a somewhat cloudy explanation emerges in time: it seems he squatted on his favourite plot of land in 1987, and only after years of pestering and haranguing council and government bureaucrats did he succeed in getting a valid lease over 1400 hectares of it.

But his battles with authority over his frontier attitudes are far from over. He has joined battle with the local shire over the non-payment of $6259.68 in rates, asking in an open letter published in the *Kimberley Echo* newspaper: 'What have you people done for me? You never helped me maintain my road, not once, and you never helped me keep the roadway clean of beer cans, cartons and other sorts of rubbish — not *my* end anyway. The car licence pays for the use of the road and we also pay tax out of our pension. So tell me, what are you doing for us?

'You government people are the cause of my illness. I have had four strokes so far fighting with you. I know you won't be satisfied till the old bastard is gone at last. That means you can have a go at taking this land what I now lease (sic). But I am sorry, you will have my wife to fight then and I can tell you today she will give you the fight of a bloody lifetime, that's for sure.

'You get no $6259.68 off Roy Walker, even if it means gaol or a fine, which I could never pay and will not pay.'

Over tea and fruitcake — made by Roy — he told how he ran away from home in Bunbury when he was 13 and headed north to the Kimberley, arriving in 1942; how he worked as a stockman on various stations and outposts; how he broke horses, built cattleyards, made his own saddles, and became the head stockman for the Duracks. Throughout, it was clear he yearned for those days to return; emphatically so when the subject turned to the place of Aborigines in today's Kimberley.

'The problems began when they got their citizenship, back in 1967, after the referendum,' he said. 'They got their rights, but their rights were nothing more than a passport to the pub. When we used to go droving with the bullocks, we had half black and half white teams — or mostly black — and they were the best horsemen on earth — the smartest stockmen you'd ever see. Nothing could come near them. And we'd drop off our bullocks at the meatworks and ride down to the pub in Wyndham, step off the horse and go straight into the pub. Now, at that time the [black] boys weren't allowed to touch grog or anything. They'd

wait on the other side of the street. They watched the whitefellas go to the pub and they'd think, "One day we're gunna do that," which they did — because we'd set the example. They thought that's what life was all about — and it was, for us, too: work, work, bloody hard work, then down to the pub. There were no women up here then, only the gins, and they were damn good wives, too. There were no white women up here — none — and the gins held the men in the country. My oath they did.

'It was good going, back then. You weren't allowed to talk to the blackfella in the street — oh, no — that was called co-habiting. My colonial oath, they'd whack you in gaol. So you don't talk to the blackfellas 'coz you'd spoil 'em; they get cheeky. You give 'em a cigarette — that's the worst thing you can do, 'coz in the end they're taking cigarettes out of your pocket. And it buggers them up. Don't do any of that and they'll respect you. And I'll respect them. Bloody good stockmen. But in their place. They've got their camp, and I've got mine. The tucker is put out there; they come and get it. I'd go into their camp to check if they had too much meat, but they wouldn't come into my camp. No. I'd meet them halfway. It was spot on. The stock camps were like army camps.'

Like army camps. Officers and men. Orders. Total, unquestioning control. This appalling old coot represents everything old, every overpowering evil, about our relationships with our indigenous people. We invaded their place and demanded no less than total obedience. Step out of line, sonny, and you'll get busted. Know your place. Salute as we pass. Kiss my arse! And if you're good, we'll throw you some damper, some sugar and some bakky. I listened to Roy, tape conspicuously running by prior

Roy Walker… a Kimberley legend.

agreement on the table between us and was fascinated by this tub-thumping diatribe of dinosaur attitudes. Appalled, I couldn't help but interrupt.

'But surely it's not an unreasonable proposition that they should be citizens in their own country?'

'Look,' Roy shot back, 'they're entitled to all the rights we've got. But why should they try to live the way we do? They can't live our way; we can't live their way. But we win, because we're ruining them, and we've ruined them now, and they'll die. The only Australian Aboriginal is the black man, not the half-caste. He's not a blackfella, definitely not, but he's a stirrer. You never hear the blackfella spruikin' the way the half-caste does. We've buggered them, and now we've got a problem.

'We could have given them their money a different way. They gave 'em millions of dollars in their hands like givin' a little boy a bag of lollies. He sits down and eats the lot and gets sick. Then he comes back and asks for more. That's exactly what these people have done. They sat down and drank the lot and asked for more. They're dependent on us. We've babysat them, wet-nursed them; they've got stations out there — beautiful country — but they don't want to go out there anymore. They want to be in the town, with TV and pubs and gambling. It's very sad, because I've seen these people at their best. It'll never be the way it used to be. The young people have lost all their respect for their elders; there is no more of their heritage…'

Roy with kangaroo: Roy Walker . . . a real softie.

Roy shook his head and gulped his tea. We are all, to a degree, products of our times. This nation was federated partly because of fear of cheap labour from our north, and racial exclusion through the White Australia Policy was a foundation on which it was built. I judged Roy to have failed to move with the times. He was rooted in his own nostalgia for a simpler time when God was in heaven, Menzies was in the Lodge and the blacks knew their place. He was unwilling to accept the compelling realities of today's world. There can be no turning back. The omelette cannot be unscrambled.

I said, 'You pine for the past, but you can't return to it. So what now?'

He quietly replied, 'We've got to learn to live together.'

It would have been easy to dismiss Roy Walker as a ranting relic of a happily bygone era of outback apartheid. But he is more complex than that, as we were to learn. Tea finished, Roy and Kenton moved outside for discussions about Kenton's camp proposal for the canoe trippers. Soon I could hear Roy's raised voice: 'If they come on my land, I'll shoot 'em. I will. I've hunted people off my land before, and I'll do it again!' Kenton later told me he had tried to point out to Roy that the river banks at the junction with the Ord were Crown land, but Roy wouldn't have a bar of it. He wanted a share of the revenue to allow the campers anywhere in his vicinity.

It was impossible to tell if Roy were genuinely hot under the collar or just posturing, but he soon quietened down. He took us for a walk to his favourite spot — a grotto within the towering outcrop of rock behind his camp. As we walked, him still barefoot, picking his way through tussocks of grass and prickles without so much as a

wince, I asked if it were true he had shot at a low-flying aircraft.

'So they say.'

'Well, that's enigmatic enough. Did you?'

'Might have; might not have.'

We reached the grotto by walking through a natural rock arch. Roy squatted on a rock, the evening light filtering dimly down on us through a canopy of trees, and told how he had married Barbara here, carrying her through the arch on the back of a white stallion. At this, Wendy laughingly accused this weatherbeaten old ruffian of harbouring the soul of a hopeless romantic. He didn't deny it, but began to recite a poem:

> Oh Lord, give me a job mustering in
> paradise
> Won't you please answer my prayer
> They say the grass is like a green carpet
> and all the cattle are quiet up there.
> I've got me swag with me roll,
> Lord and I'll bring me billycan too
> Then we can all have a good drink of
> billy tea
> Just like we always used to do
> We could muster the Milky Way, mate
> From here I see mobs of dust up there
> Guess it's some of me mates already
> mustering
> Means you've already answered their
> prayer
> It would be wonderful to muster the
> valleys in paradise and to camp with
> my old mates again and to ride the
> winged horses like Pegasus
> No drought, no flies — only rain
> So Lord, now I'm ready to join you
> down here I've done more than
> my share
> And it's not too much to ask you

What about a job ringin' up there?
So drop me down a set of wings, Lord
And I'll buckle 'em on while it's still light
And I'll pack up my gear and saddle
And I'll fly straight up there tonight.

We left the grotto with Roy telling of his plans — a yearning desire to give back something before he flies up there. 'I want to help the Aboriginal kids. They have no purpose any more. They have most of the best stations under their ownership, but hardly any of them want to work them.

'I want to train them — train them to be stockmen, 'coz they can be the smartest stockmen in the business; I want to teach them discipline; teach them the things they've forgotten, like bushcraft, like how to make saddles; how to work leather.

'I've had some naughty kids referred to me by the juvenile justice people, and I get them out here, and I get to know them, and they're just starting to get to know me and then they'd go back to the cities. I want to build a big shed out here as a mess and recreational centre. All they need is a clean home, clean swags, good tucker, and I'll show them what they can do. Once they start, they won't want to stop.'

As we prepared to leave, Roy and Barbara invited us back a few days later when they would be holding a camp for 75 children from the Kimberley region. 'And me mother-in-law's arriving from Zurich,' he added.

It was about as preposterous a proposition as you could invent: 80-year-old Judy Straub leaves her picture-postcard home in the snow-clad outskirts of Zurich, and flies with

Roy Walker with (*l to r*) wife Barbara, niece Sandra Straub, and mother-in-law Judy Straub.

Judy Straub inspects her bath . . . 'It is very nice, *ja?'*

her niece halfway around the world to Kununurra, to meet her 68-year-old son-in-law for the first time, and to see her daughter's home among the gum trees — Roy's Retreat: Walker's Youth Training and Accommodation Centre.

On arrival, she finds 75 at-risk Aboriginal kids learning to ride horses, abseiling, canoeing and taking traditional-art classes. A brumby strolls among the kids, sprawled across a tarpaulin, making their dot paintings under the watchful eye of noted Kimberley artists Alan and Peggy Griffiths. A pet kangaroo eases by, nibbling, and a flock of geese gather by the ruins of the old cottage.

'It is very difficult for a European to imagine this,' Mrs Straub said. 'It is so big, so

dusty, and so red. The difference between our way of living and this is like night and day.'

I asked, 'Have you seen your bath?'

'No.'

'Come with me.' As we walked towards the shed where Roy had set up his visitors' swags, I explained that Barbara and Roy took regular skinny-dips in the creek. Their toilets were rudimentary bush long-drops, but their home didn't have a bathroom of any kind, let alone the marble-clad, mirrored varieties of *Vogue Living*. Very reasonably, they decided their ablution arrangements may be a trifle deficient or infra-dig for an 80-year-old mum, so Roy had rigged a bath outside the shed. It sat on the red earth, unplumbed, screened by a couple of layers of green shade cloth. The only problem was, the shade cloth didn't actually shield it from view. Mum would, for all intents and purposes, be bathing in the open!

'Ooh,' she said, peering over the top of the shade cloth. Then she turned with a polite smile and a shrug of acceptance: 'It is very nice, *ja*?'

Meanwhile, Roy was ringmaster to a group of Aboriginal children in the cattleyards. 'Aboriginal people taught me so much; now I'll teach you,' he told them. And he began a gruff, rapid-fire patter about horsemanship: how to approach your mount, how to swing up into the saddle, how to turn in a confined space, how to have confidence in the presence of a horse, and why a horse is your greatest mate in the bush. 'You'd die for your mate,' he told them. 'If you've been galloping his guts out,

give *him* a drink first.' The young faces looked on — some anxious to try their hand; others apparently bored. Many of these kids, aged between 12 and 22, had never been bush before.

They came from the Kimberley's major centres — Kununurra, Halls Creek, Broome, Wyndham and the remote settlement of Kalumburu — under the auspices of various government health, education and family services agencies for a four-day conference aimed at promoting self-esteem, pride, respect and the Kimberley culture. They would hear speakers delivering anti-smoking, safe sex and nutritional messages, reminding them: 'You are the future — be proud.' The camp was called 'Young, Black and Deadly' — and yes, I needed confirmation that 'deadly' was slang for 'really good'!

At-risk young Aborigines learn horsemanship at Roy Walker's Kimberley camp.

After his lesson in the cattleyards, Roy began preparing to feed the masses. As he sliced dozens of onions to join the hamburgers on the griller, I chided him: 'You bark a lot, but you don't really bite, do you?'

'When I say "jump", they move,' he shot back. 'They must learn discipline. The one on the tail end is the one I want — he's going too slow.' Then he looked at me in momentary silence before the wide moustache broadened into a half smile and the mask of gruffness slipped.

'Yeah, I'm really a softie. My colonial oath I am.'

Kununurra — Aboriginal for 'Meeting of the Waters' — is the eastern gateway to the Kimberley; a new town founded 35 years ago as a construction centre for the mighty Ord River development. Like so many northern development schemes it was branded a white elephant in its early days, largely because of the failure of the first experimental crops on the vast, fertile river flats. The planting of rice seemed like a good idea at the time, but when a flock of magpie geese, reputed to number some 700,000, descended and stripped the irrigated paddocks bare, the thinking caps went back on. Cotton was tried, but it was ravaged by insect pests.

It is said today there is a crop for every letter of the alphabet grown on the rich Ord flatlands. Asparagus to zucchini; if it will grow anywhere, it will grow here. Ninety per cent of Australia's supply of melons — water, rock or honeydew — comes from the Ord's endless plains, but sugarcane is increasingly the staple. A new refinery, the first in Australia for a quarter of a century, was commissioned in 1996, and most of its output is destined for the Asian market.

The Ord irrigation area is a vast foodbowl with enormous potential. So far, the surface has just been scratched. The first stage of 14,000 hectares under irrigation represents a mere 11 per cent of the total available area, and is now fully taken up. The second stage of a further 50,000 hectares is under way, and cotton is set to make a comeback. The Australian research organisation, the CSIRO, has developed new, bug-resistant strains of cotton which are expected to be suitable for the tropics, as well as lowering the industry's dependence on chemicals in other areas such as the fragile black soil plains of New South Wales.

The Ord River dam, which creates Lake Argyle, was facilitated by a gift of nature. The Ord drains a huge area reaching into the Northern Territory to the east, the Durack Ranges to the west, and more than 200 kilometres inland from Wyndham, where it reaches the sea. At the site of the dam, the river flowed through a narrow gorge. It was a relatively simple matter to plug the gorge with about two million cubic metres of rock and clay, 300 metres wide at its crest, and suddenly a 2000-square-kilometre lake was created. This is nine times the surface area of Sydney Harbour, and the volume of water held is, incredibly, 254 times greater than Sydney Harbour. The locals measure the lake's holding in Sydharbs. And everyone living in Kununurra knows another statistic: if the dam were to burst, they would have 27 minutes to check their insurance before the tidal wave hit.

Kununurra has another industry — tourism. Its airport is the third busiest in Western Australia, and the 19th busiest in the nation, which is an eye-opening statistic for a town of just 5000 people. The volume of take-offs and landings is mainly due to a buoyant sightseeing industry, with the Bungle Bungle Range the prime destination. This

The Argyle Dam, Western Australia . . . 254 Sydharbs of water.

extraordinary 350 million-year-old massif of deeply weathered sandstone covered by striped layers of silica and lichen — looking like an endless succession of Taj Mahals — now rivals Uluru (Ayers Rock) as a must-see drawcard for tourists.

Most see the Bungles from the air, passengers in a nose-to-tail succession of fixed-wing aircraft which follow a strict figure-eight flight path over the range before breaking off to return to Kununurra via the giant Argyle diamond mine. It is a spectacular and awesome flight, especially if you can conspire to return as the sun sets over the mighty Lake Argyle. Other visitors buzz the rocks in little bubble-nose helicopters, doors off, cameras protruding as they pirouette over narrow chasms and deep gorges.

The experience from the ground is entirely different. To properly get the feel of the Bungles

it is worth doing both — either entering by road and taking a helicopter flight, or flying in and taking a 4WD day trip before flying out. Getting both perspectives allows the total picture of an extraordinarily fragile work of nature which, the experts predict, will erode to obliteration in the next 100 million years as wind and rain tear at the fine coating of silica to ravage the soft rock below.

At Echidna Gorge, the effect of water is starkly seen as the visitor enters a narrow chasm, 50 metres deep and only two metres wide, walking on a bed of rounded pebbles towards a vast circular amphitheatre, 50 metres across, carved out of the rock by swirling whirlpools of monsoonal rain. These whirlpool features appear frequently, the smallest being just planter-tub size, where pebbles become trapped in watercourses, relentlessly scouring into the soft rock.

The Ord River irrigation area . . . everything from asparagus to zucchini.

Mirriwung men, the giant Gangi Nganang, painted on the ceiling of a cave in the Keep River National Park, near Kununurra, Western Australia . . . visitors from space?

Creek beds look like pock-marked petrified waves, testimony to the erosive power of the seasons.

The largest of these features is Cathedral Gorge, a giant atrium of rock surrounding a deep waterhole carved by the torrents of thousands of Wets. As we gazed at this incredible structure we were startled by the sound of a didgeridoo, warbling and reverberating around us. So perfect were the acoustics that the sound enveloped us, and it took some time before I could locate the player — my son Kenton, a diminutive figure perched high on a rock ledge. As he played, tourists stood stock-still in awe, drifting into their own Dreamtimes. It was a magical moment in a magical place.

This is no picnic, this drive. We've come diagonally across the centre of the nation, Sydney to Kununurra, for a welcome breather with children and grandchildren. But we've kept up a cracking pace, visiting the Bungle Bungle Range, dropping in at El Questro, the Kimberley tourist mecca, and exploring the eerie rock art galleries of the Keep River National Park, where the Gangi Nganang figures have provoked speculation about visitors from space. And now we face a torrid 3200-kilometre west–east crossing across the Top End and the Gulf Country to Cairns.

Driving is a good way to explore; much better than travelling by air. By road you enter slowly, and absorb the power of the scenery; the solitude; the scale of it all. Oh, the scale. I have been struggling to find a word for it. Big? Too small. Huge? Not big enough. Immense, enormous, monumental, stupendous, infinite? Not quite right. Indescribable? Yes, demonstrably, but I must keep working on it. There must be a word for it.

Driving is also wearying. As the kilometres clicked by, the explorer inside me struggled to mount a convincing argument that another

The Bungle Bungle Range . . . deep chasms of ancient beauty.

Cooinda (Yellow Waters) in Kakadu National Park, Arnhem Land, Northern Territory . . . extraordinary displays.

stop to look and learn was more important than reaching our destination. It's not that I found the road from Kununurra to Katherine boring (far from it; it's spectacular and beautiful), but I did find it gruelling, and this made my interest in the tourist destinations along the way somewhat cursory. We took a helicopter ride over the Katherine Gorge, stopping for a couple of hours where a day or two was needed to do it justice. We camped overnight at Cooinda (Yellow Waters) in Kakadu National Park, and took a half-day boat ride among the extraordinary display of water birds, crocodiles and heavenly waterlilies, so that we could say we had been there, done that.

I was antipathetic about Kakadu. Perhaps we had been too far off the beaten track, where tourists don't go, where the real Australia glows, and you can walk around, drinking it all in, at your own pace, making your own path rather than being herded from boardwalk to boardwalk, following the hustling arrows which seem inevitably to end at a 'No entry' sign. Kakadu is the Top End's best-known national park, but its majesty is dimmed and its serenity shattered by the hundreds of thousands of tourists who clamber over and through it each year.

Or perhaps I am spoiled, because I have been to the other side. Kakadu is but a pipe-opener for the wondrous beauty of Arnhem Land.

This is where it began; this prying into the hidden nooks and crannies of Australia. Port Essington and the Victoria Settlement, where the Poms clung to the edges of a continent they couldn't understand; the King River, where we went to find fish and lost ourselves in a land time forgot; and the Goomadeer River, where we dropped out of the sky to share, for a week, a gritty shore with

crocodiles. Three times I had been drawn back to Arnhem Land; each time further into it; each time to new discoveries — about it, and about myself.

To me, Arnhem Land is the most beautiful, spiritual, powerful and inspiring part of Australia. It is also the part least likely to be seen by Australians. The entire area from Oenpelli in the west to Gove in the east, and from Croker Island in the north to the Limmen Bight in the south is Aboriginal land, and permits are required to enter. Facilities for travellers are all but non-existent, and roads are few and undeveloped. This is both bad and good: it means most Australians will never see or feel the power of this remarkable region, and that, in turn, means it is least likely to suffer under the impact of hordes of human feet. This land has a fragile beauty which is both breathtaking and bemusing. Allow yourself to be absorbed by it and its sense of timelessness, and it challenges your perceptions of reality: this is so untouched, so natural, so perfectly the way it was, and is, and will forever be, that it must be defined as *real* — as in, the way nature made it. Unspoiled by human hands. Yet, as you confront your departure date and a return to your life in the city, you realise it isn't *your* reality. Arnhem Land's reality is shaped by time, tides, winds, monsoons, and the seven distinct seasons of the year which come and go in solitude; *your* reality is shaped by cars, and smog, and traffic jams and fast foods, and the daily rituals of a society which overcomes, rather than heeds, the distractions and dictates of nature.

Our first contact with Arnhem Land was made in 1991 when we visited the site of what was soon to become the Seven Spirit Bay wilderness resort at the entrance to Port

Katherine Gorge, Northern Territory . . . helicopter ride.

Essington. This was one of Australia's first eco-resort projects, where well-heeled holiday-makers could experience the sublime serenity of the Cobourg Peninsula's coastal rainforests, white beaches and fecund fishing grounds. It was a brave enterprise, brought into being by a sensitive Darwin lawyer named Lex Silvester, but it proved to be overcapitalised and soon changed ownership. The resort won many tourism awards for its design and service, but it still struggles to attract clientele away from the more gaudy monstrosities of marble and concrete which litter the east coast from Surfers Paradise to Port Douglas.

Port Essington is an imposing stretch of protected water, 30 kilometres long and about ten kilometres wide, and was the chosen site for a British trading port established in 1837. The global strategists who pored over maps of the new world in Whitehall were worried about the influence of the Dutch in the East Indies, and had long felt the need to establish their presence in Australia's north. Two previous attempts had failed when they decided to set up the Victoria Settlement deep inside Port Essington. For 11 years a small garrison of marines clung tenuously to this harsh patch of land, and to walk through the ruins today is to marvel at both the stupidity of its sponsors and the tenacity of its settlers. All that is left are the crumbling stone stumps of rotund fireplaces and chimneys built in Cornish style from local rocks, a few foundations, the shell of a hospital building, an ammunition magazine dug deep into the dry red earth, and a haunting graveyard of men, women and children who lost the fight against climate and disease. The bush has all but taken over these remains, scattered over a couple of hundred hectares, but the relics fire the imagination and pose endless questions about those who decreed its existence. Imagine: here is a spot of virgin tropical bush, filled with straggling trees and mangrove-fringed shores; the temperature hovers around 32°C year-round; a monsoonal Wet dominates from December to March, an arid Dry from April to November. Spanish, Dutch, Portuguese and English explorers have dismissed this coast as pestilence-ridden for centuries, yet the British decide it is a vital spot to monitor and service the trade route from Java to Torres Strait and the western Pacific, so they dust off plans for a settlement. But, you ask, why build snug Cornish cottages of stone and wood? Each fireplace was an open cooking area, with room for the occupants to snuggle around the fire. No doubt that was good design for chilly Cornwall, but it was unthinking, architectural idiocy in the 32°C tropics. The sleeping areas attached to the chimneys were made of prefabricated wooden frames which termites gratefully ate out within a year. Crops regularly failed under the assault of birds and insects; starvation was the constant companion of those who clung wearily to the outpost, and morale ebbed away under the heavy weight of the kind of loneliness which comes from complete isolation at the edge of the world. When the Victoria Settlement was abandoned in 1848, it would be almost 30 years before another attempt was made to establish a northern port, this time at Port Darwin.

And yet . . . as we headed north aboard Lex Silvester's yacht *Touché*, and I looked back across the mirror-calm waters, searching to find where the water met the sky, squinting at the shimmering mirage of low hills on each side of the bay, I could see in this nothingness what might have been: towers of reflective glass punching into the sky, a sweeping bridge linking the eastern and western sides, high enough in the centre to allow supertankers to pass freely underneath, elevated concrete ribbons of expressways where the mangroves clutched the muddy shores, sprawling suburbia beyond, capped by a smudge of brown smog sealing a thriving city against the pure blue sky. For Victoria Settlement was meant to become a great trading city like Singapore. If its planners and founders had had half an inkling of what they were dealing with, and how to come to terms with the natural environment, it might have succeeded.

But back to reality. The untouched reality of gliding through waters so calm and clear that manta rays could be seen metres below, their wings creating lazy boils on the surface; shoals of hardyheads bubbling the water as they massed in defence against the silver flashes of an unknown predator; a crocodile, its presence betrayed by just a nostril above the water; mudcrabs presented as pastel-grey orbs on white sand washed with turquoise; a sawfish in the shallows, and a caved-in, disused freshwater well fed by a clear spring which replenished thirsty sailors a century ago at Record Point. This is a truly remarkable, beautiful place.

Lex Silvester grew up in the Western District of Victoria, a few kilometres from Ashford. He is a couple of years younger than me, and we never met, but we did fish for eels in the same creeks. When he graduated from Melbourne University he had a law degree and a passion for fishing, far more intense than my passing interest. The law, he decided, could provide his bread and butter, but the

sport of fishing would nourish his soul. So he vowed to practise where the fishing was best, and 28 years ago headed for Darwin.

Aboard *Touché* in the Arafura Sea, we hooked up great trevally, cobia, Spanish mackerel, coral trout and queenfish, and I was infected by the bug of tropical sportfishing. I was entranced by Lex's stories of barramundi fishing in the rivers and estuaries of the territory coast; places revered as the Holy Grails of sports fishing: the Daly, the Adelaide, the Mary, the Wildman, the South Alligator, the East Alligator. And the King. A fabulous river for barra, Lex said.

So we planned a camp beside the King: my son Scott, Jolly Jol Simpson, newspaper editor John Hartigan and myself; barramundi rookies with the best guides in the business

— Lex and his mate, Les Woodbridge. We left Darwin in convoy, out across the flood plains of the Adelaide and Mary rivers, through Kakadu National Park, Jabiru and Onepelli, across the East Alligator River lined with paperbarks and ghost gums, and into Arnhem Land proper. We sat slackjawed on the rock where Paul Hogan posed as Crocodile Dundee in the opening sequence of his worldwide hit movie, and gazed in awe across the flood plain, its lagoons crammed with red lilies, ducks and waterfowl. We sensed the spirituality of the place, and a kind of metamorphosis — urban to somewhere — came over us. We bumped slowly over the black soil plains, the surface rutted by the movement of buffalo in the Wet, with rock outcrops jutting from the plains; galleries of ancient art and repositories of uranium. As we settled into our camp beside the King, 400 kilometres east of Darwin, Les and Lex commandeered our watches. City time, territory time, any time, was forgone in favour of the timelessness of this place.

The weather refused to be friendly that week, and onshore winds confused the tides, meaning we had to graft for our fish. But we didn't care: fishing was fun, but a small part of the total experience. We saw crocodiles jumping out of the water for a breakfast of flying foxes hanging from the low branches of a giant riverside mangrove; we looked through invisible water in a cathedral-like creek and exchanged stares with hovering fish; we climbed a riverside outcrop called Old Woman Rock and saw our place within the entire river delta; we encouraged angelfish to shoot jets of water at our lures in the vain hope that they may knock an insect out of the sky; we spotted egrets, osprey, sea eagles, brahminy kites, sacred kingfishers, night herons, beach thick-knees and magpie geese; we explored a tiny pocket of rare melaleuca and mangrove rainforest fed by a freshwater spring beside the river, and we stepped ashore in the smouldering wake of a fire (sparked by lightning or local Aborigines perhaps 100 kilometres from here) to be startled by the broken remains of a champagne bottle. Further exploration unearthed bullet shells, mounds of broken glass, and evidence of wells, all entirely hidden until the fire stripped it of its protective undergrowth. Research by Les later revealed it to be the long-lost site of a 1910 prospectors' camp.

We had an incredibly good time, succumbing to the surreal thought that we could make this our new reality, then resisting it, reluctantly, as the time came to withdraw and return to our true reality of life in the cities. We collectively heaped praise on our guides, and when Les casually said: 'If you think this is something special, you ought to see the Goomadeer,' we pinned him to a promise that we would do it again — further out; further into the sacred and astonishing heart of Arnhem Land.

We upped the ante for the Goomadeer: six of us, three boats, three guides, a makeshift camp on a gritty deposit of shells at the river mouth, and no way in except by sea or air. We called ourselves Authors, Artists, Cooks and the Cove — Tom Keneally, internationally acclaimed author; John Hartigan, now a newspaper editor-in-chief, making a return visit; Adrian Read, former editor of *Gourmet* magazine and public relations expert with many wine industry clients; John Howley, a noted Melbourne artist who was my high school art teacher for a short period in the 1950s; and the Cove — financial services consultant Steve Beaumont who affects a bushman's air while living for rugby, rhyming slang, guitar strumming, and jokes, jokes and more jokes. Our guides were Lex Silvester and Les Woodbridge again, plus Russell Kenny, a professional contemporary of Les's, whose piscatorial knowledge was infinite, thus rendering as unnecessary his awareness of matters beyond fish. When he twigged, some days into the week, that Tom Keneally was an author of considerable note, he observed with great respect: 'You must be a walkin' fuckin' dictionary, then.'

Tom was, in fact, very much in the news at the time. He was chair of the Australian Republican Movement, and I a director, and we had taken the opportunity to call a

New pioneers of the Goomadeer, Arnhem Land (l to r): the author, Adrian Read, John Howley, John Hartigan, Stephen (the Cove) Beaumont and Tom Keneally.

press conference to help spread the message while in Darwin. Tom eloquently — as always — put the case for a republic, and along the way reminded the then Prime Minister, Paul Keating, that the quest for a republic was not his exclusive political preserve; that the people might just want a say in it, and there could be no party political ownership of a cause so deeply attached to our national identity. This perfectly logical proposition provoked headlines down south, and as we drove out of Darwin we had to stop beside the Stuart Highway while Tom used a mobile phone to do an ABC radio interview with the late Andrew Olle. This further stirred the pot, and at Jabiru we chuckled as we swiped a poster from *The Australian* saying:

KENEALLY DUMPS ON KEATING

Tom Keneally… a state of creative defencelessness.

and fiddlestick jabiru nests. Our pilot's instructions were to look for three boats, and set us down — quite easy, really, on this shore so desolate it had been ignored for eons.

Greeting us was the realisation that we must share the coming week with the true owner of this patch — *Crocodilus porosus*. Our guides explained the rules: don't get in their way, and they'll leave you alone. But the Cove, for all his bushie swagger, made a note in our diary: 'We were visited at lunch by two crocs surfacing 50 metres away; one quite large. I felt uneasy, but showed bravado by eating on. I can't seem to dismiss from the subconscious our camp's proximity to these beasts. It makes sleeping difficult — even with a pistol at the ready.' Tom, too, reflected on the crocs. An unseasonable storm on our first night drenched us, and Tom wrote: 'We huddled defenceless in the cookhouse and depended utterly on the storm's passing. We wake to dry our gear in a steaming sun. We hear that crocs can outrun us. We are therefore in a state of creative defence-lessness. We are children again. It is a release to be defenceless, as long as the elements and the fauna don't get you.'

After our first day our city instincts called us to the river to lather up with shampoo and rid ourselves of the day's clag — layers of sunscreen and insect repellent — on our bodies. We did so fleetingly, uneasily, with a minimum of fuss because while we washed Les sat on an upturned drum on the beach, a .357 magnum revolver stuck in his sock, keeping nit; a cockatoo on the lookout for crocodiles which may be attracted by our splashing about. Strangely, bathing was replaced with a quick wash beside the river for the rest of the trip.

We had come to fish, and we were rewarded early. Within minutes of putting a

Then we disappeared, for all intents and purposes, off the face of the earth, without phones, faxes, TV, radio, or any method of communicating at all! Find us if you can, fellas!

Our guides had travelled ahead of us, loading their boats with everything needed for seven self-contained days in the wilderness — generator, freezers, cooking equipment, tents, food, libations, fishing gear — at the King River camp. They then battled their heavily laden craft through heavy seas for more than 60 kilometres east, around Braithwaite Point, to the mouth of the Goomadeer in Junction Bay. We gathered at Jabiru airport to be choppered 130 kilometres across the plains, past the giant sacred sandstone pillar known as Nimbuwah, over scattering wild brumbies

Exploring the capillaries of the Goomadeer . . . meandering for miles.

The mouth of the Goomadeer River — a sand spit covered in shells.

rod in his hand, Tom, trolling, hooked up a 13-kilogram barra. 'I think for Tom it was an out-of-body experience,' Lex wrote in the diary. 'Such concentration, such amazement, bewilderment, compressed into the moment. The fish jumped, cartwheeling, great head shaking, so that the angler feels the wild gyrations at the rod tip. The fish was very attached to Tom via lure, line and rod, and didn't let go. For us, the guides, there is no finer moment.' Tom was delighted with his good fortune. It was the first, and biggest, fish of the trip, and he chortled as he warned: 'Just wait until I learn how to cast!' (When he did, he also caught the second-biggest barra of the week — a mere 4.5 kilograms.) In spite of the weather, which Lex recorded 'blew a thousand bastards all week', we all got fish, with all but a few returned to the river.

Adrian inspired a sublime sunset beach barbecue of barramundi and mangrove jacks wrapped in foil, and mudcrabs boiled in their own juices on the glowing coals. There can be no better gastronomic experience on this earth.

'Somehow,' Adrian wrote, 'fishing isn't the thing. It provides a framework for all kinds of other things that don't have a word like "fishing" to describe them.' Like: a sunset return from a nearby creek when our boat was paced by a silver razorfish, jumping out of the water, skimming alongside us, over and over again for hundreds of metres, as if it were stitching the sea to the sky. Like: a ride up a creek at high tide, out on to the salt pans of scalded red, ochre, yellow and white, following the capillaries of water-giving life to their extremities, meandering for miles; so flat, so vast; so stunted; like motoring on the moon. Like: cutting through what Tom called 'sea-borne acreages of brown coral spawn which reeked of life and reminded me we

were from the sea.' How incredibly fortunate we were to be there when, once a year, the coral sent its spawn into the unknown; endless strands of sperm, smelling of wet hay — or was it freshly baked biscuit? — covering hundreds of square kilometres with only chance to decide if a single cell would merge with another to give life to a new coral polyp. The lottery of life.

At nights we gathered around the trestle table, drank too much, ate too much, talked and lied too much, sang too many old songs, badly, and pondered our place. Lex summed it up by noting the 'conflict between human endeavour, fears and experience, and the landscape. The paradox is that continued existence involves merging with our landscape and finding, like all the other players in the great survival game, a place that sustains us.

Tom contributed a valedictory on our last night: 'This time next week we'll have been taken alive by the great urban crocodile, answering another more fretful master than the croc we saw tonight a few hundred yards downriver. He knows he's getting this place back in a day's time. Meantime he has proved himself an admirable beast — as Lex says, they live well with humans if the appropriate protocols are observed, and we hope they will be until we have returned the river utterly to him.' It was a prayerful wish, very nearly not fulfilled.

Our guides set out in their boats early the next morning, catching the tides back to the King River, while we waited for the helicopter to pluck us back to civilisation. I went out with John Howley and the Cove on a breathtaking ride over the Arnhem Land escarpment, leaving John Hartigan, Adrian and Tom to sit out the two-hour wait before the chopper returned for them. They reported that the leaden weight of isolation and fear (what if the chopper doesn't come back?) descended on them as the minutes ticked by. To keep themselves occupied, they went for a walk along the beach. Tom, striding out in front, was jolted rigid — gobsmacked — when the large croc he had noted the night before broke from a small stand of mangroves and bolted for the sea just arm's lengths in front of him. It moved with such terrifying power and speed that for some moments the trio could do no more than stand rooted to their spots, white-faced, jelly-legged and hearts pumping.

Years on, we still get blank looks and puzzled stares when the Goomadeer alumni get together. Our wives — and Tom's daughters — immediately accuse us of participating in a week of unrelenting boys' bonding, and have yet to be persuaded that this was not the case. People who have neither heard of the Goomadeer, nor can picture its place halfway between Darwin and Gove along the flat top of Australia, nod politely when we explain, but they cannot comprehend our babbling reminiscences. I still find it difficult to position the Goomadeer within the cache of life's experiences, save that I know it was the highlight of my enlightenment about Australia's most beautiful jewel — Arnhem Land — and a virulent stimulus to embrace more of the hidden treasures of this incredible land. Heads down, tails up in our cities, we are oblivious of so much around us.

We drew breath again in Darwin. It's a vibrant place with a feel of frontier finesse. Frontier normally means a dearth of services and a tatty look. But Darwin has been rebuilt since the 1975 Cyclone Tracy disaster to exacting standards — supported by large licks of Commonwealth money. Without this contribution from the nation's taxpayers, Darwin couldn't have funded its resurrection. I doubt there is any other city in the nation with a population of around 80,000 with six-lane arterial roads, overpasses, fully kerbed streets, multistorey buildings, a $125 million Parliament House for 25 MPs, and such well-coiffed public parks. In this respect it reminds me of a tropical Canberra; ironic given the propensity of its people to bite the hand that feeds them by speaking ill of Canberra and its politicians.

Darwin is — and always has been — the most racially mixed city in the nation. Chinese immigrants lured by the gold rushes of the 19th century have contributed to Darwin's affairs for decades. A growing Asian community continues this tradition, and Darwin has become Australia's first Free Trade Development Zone, with its focus to the north, rather than the south. Northern Territory politicians have made careers out of ignoring Canberra and dealing direct with Asian leaders. And why not? Darwin is closer to Jakarta, Singapore, Brunei and Manila than it is to Melbourne. A stroll through the crowded Parap or Mindil Beach markets, absorbing the smells of laksa, noodles, curries and satays, the colours of mangoes, custard apples, guava and melons, the exotic fashions of batik and tie-dyed sarongs, and the sounds of Thai, Laotian, Indonesian and Vietnamese chatter, gives the southern visitor a demonstration that here, at least, the melting pot is bubbling away well, creating a distinctive culture of its own.

But there is a dark side to Darwin which, by its nature, extends over the entire territory. There is a frontier attitude to politics and power. Since the Northern Territory achieved self-government more than 20 years ago it has been ruled by the

Country Liberal Party (CLP), conservatives who have neither felt the requirement, nor heeded any call, for the kinds of checks and balances that are inherent in older, and more sophisticated, political systems. This is in part due to the simple frontier philosophy of their constituents, who see a problem and roll over it; who see a mountain and move it. They don't see, and aren't encouraged by their representative government to see, any problem with taking short cuts to achieve an objective. They don't question the lack of account-ability in many government actions, and the concept of conflict of interest often bemuses them. Allegations of shady deals are frequently made, but fade away on a sea of disinterest. It's as if the populace sees

nothing wrong, hypothetically, with a land developer being in charge of zoning laws. He'd know a bit about it, wouldn't he?

The CLP has faithfully represented this streak of independence found among people who live in remote places largely free of rules, regulations and red tape. Up north, it's a way of life, along with a tough approach to law'n'order. There's no mucking about with miscreants in the territory: in a harking back to the 18th century, offences against property (not persons) are dealt with by the mandatory sentencing of those convicted to 14 days in gaol. This has led to the incarceration of men, women and children for crimes as heinous as the theft of a $2.50 can of beer. Those who complain about the harshness of this law are told: 'Don't do the

Corroboree at Milikapiti... vibrant and enchanting.

Waiting for sunrise at Milikapiti, Melville Island.

crime and you won't do the time.' This law is a Dark Age blot on the territory, and through the willingness of local politicians and their followers to put aside legal, moral and social niceties, one-quarter of the Northern Territory's people have suffered grievously: the Aboriginal population. Each election, the CLP shamelessly rattles the can labelled 'preserve our way of life'. That's code for white dominance and keeping the indigenous people subjugated, poor, unhealthy and in their place. It's a shamelessly racist attitude, and it resides deeply throughout the territory's power structures.

The lure of another joust with the elusive 15-kilogram barra of my dreams enticed us to Melville Island — to a new fishing camp established by Les Woodbridge at Milikapiti, on the shores of Snake Bay. This is the home of the Tiwi islanders, a gentle people whose distinct cultures reflect their centuries of interaction with the Macassans to the north and the mainland nations to the south. There, the old world met the new before the amazed eyes of Roger Fishman, a Los Angeles-based marketing executive for News Corporation, who had come to Milikapiti to pursue his eponymous hobby.

Les had negotiated his fishing rights with the local elders and established his camp on a high promontory of land adjacent to the community. Part of his agreement was that the locals would provide, on request and for a fee, a cultural experience for visiting fishos. The community relied heavily on its thriving

Mary Elizabeth Moreen ... 'a cultural thing.'

Milikapiti children... learning their dances.

art industry — works by local artists are displayed in museums and galleries as far afield as New York and Paris — and the local elders wanted to build this economic base through tourism.

We were the first to accept the offer. We were told that ten or a dozen men would take part in the ceremony, but when we returned from our day on the water, almost the entire town had turned out in gala mood — fully initiated men in bright red lap-laps with scarred chests and ceremonial paint, women in cotton dresses, their faces smeared with ochre, hordes of children, two local priests, plus white social workers and art centre managers. They staged their ritual dances in the smoke and dust, feet thumping the ground to the rhythms of sturdy sticks beaten

on upturned saucepans, chants and shouts filling the air. As master of ceremonies Pedro Wonaeamirri announced each segment — 'This is the crocodile dance'; 'This is the snake dance' — the adult males surged forward and back, forward and back, arms waving, hands twirling and clapping while the women stood in a semi-circle, chanting and clapping to the rhythms. And then the kids took over, repeating the movements of their teachers. It was vibrant and enchanting, and Roger was amazed and delighted.

As the dancers departed, clutching their fee, for the social club, I chatted with tribal elder Mary Elizabeth Moreen as she painstakingly painted an elaborate design of traditional armbands in red, yellow and white ochre on a background of black. 'I am doing this as a cultural thing . . . to teach my grandchildren about our culture,' she said. Then she asked: 'Where are you from?'

'Sydney . . . and that man in the white T-shirt is from America.'

'America, eh? What's he do?'

'He's from Hollywood. He's in the movies.'

'Ahh,' Mary Elizabeth said. 'My favourite movie is *Titanic*.'

Roger could scarcely believe his ears. His job is to oversee marketing for News Corporation, which includes Fox Studios, makers of *Titanic*. The aim is to get the message to the ends of the earth, and blow me down, here he was, for all intents and purposes at the end of the earth, hearing people as far removed from his culture as was imaginable, freely nominating his product as their favourite.

'Unbelievable!' Roger cried. 'It was released on video only two weeks ago.' He grabbed my video camera. 'I want to take a film of this back to my boss,' he said, laughing. 'He won't believe it!' So Roger began a personal market survey, quizzing Mary Elizabeth and her daughter Amy about their viewing habits. *The Simpsons*, *The X Files*, *Terminator II* — all Fox products — featured high on their lists, to Roger's delight.

I pondered the questions about cultural preservation which we had previously contemplated in the Tanami Desert. Here was a community carving out an economic future by drawing on its ancient cultures of dance and art. And yet it was switched on to, and knowledgeable about, the most modern extravaganzas Hollywood could dream up. At Milikapiti, there was no sense of cultural clash; just cultural coexistence.

Back in Darwin we spent a day with Lex Silvester, wrestling with the complexities of reconciliation. As a territorian for 28 years, a barrister involved in land rights claims, a strong supporter of reconciliation and as a humanist, he has taken a keen interest in these questions. As he talked, I listened.

'It is what the Aboriginal people were before European settlement that should define how they are seen today,' he said. 'In common with the world's other indigenes they had systems of belief, law and government that were, in the absence of any technological development in their societies, fully integrated into their physical environment. That integration was defined by climate, the seasons, their visual and spiritual view of the cosmos, and the fauna and flora they shared their earth with. That was their existence, which was expressed in dance, painting, oral literature and, above all, in ceremony and in caring for the country. It was an existence which, at any level of understanding, attained its own perfection.

'The imposition of European land title laws, the massacres, the forcible removals and the stolen generation of children was not acquisition without compensation, as we might see it, but a destruction of the foundations of their existence. Without the land, its sites, dreamings, ceremonies, history, stories, hunting, food gathering etc, their existence effectively ceased.

'It was that which land rights sought to restore. And these rights, creatures of the law of the Commonwealth, confer upon those whose existence was attached to the land — Aboriginal people who can demonstrate membership of local descent groups and spiritual affiliation through teaching, knowledge and involvement in ceremony — a right to claim unalienated Crown land in the Northern Territory, which resulted in exclusive possession.

'That, unfortunately, has been seen by many Aborigines and their advisers as a way to secure ownership of land within the European notion of ownership — some call it a land grab — which is at odds with the original concept of existence. Existence was never defined by the need for exclusive possession. Aborigines have no difficulty in sharing land and resources when it suits them, provided sacred sites remain protected and access for ceremonial and custodial duty is preserved. What has happened is that vast tracts of land have been granted for the exclusive use and possession of Aboriginal people, in perpetuity. That in itself is not undesirable, but the title is inalienable to the extent that it cannot be subdivided, leased, mortgaged or developed in the normal way. By shutting out commerce from this land, huge limits are placed on the rights of Aboriginal people to determine the use of their land. To me this is short-sighted. It might seem viable and relevant today, but who knows what future generations will want to do?

'It is a system of land title which mitigates against Aboriginal self-determination and self-reliance because the system all but shuts out normal commercial financing of development and ventures. Future generations of Aboriginal landowners will be held forever mendicant by a centralised and, arguably, unresponsive administrative structure. Much of the land held under Aboriginal freehold title is economically marginal by any standard. Land rights could have been structured to allow coexistence between old-style pastoral industry activities involving European capital and management, and the rights necessary for the coexistence with Aboriginal rights and values, and other ventures. In the long run, I think the

exclusive use and possession of Aboriginal land will be seen as bad for Aboriginal interests. It's been divisive and, ultimately, destructive to say, in effect, that what is needed for a continued existence coincides with the legal equivalent of a grant of freehold title.

'The lines are blurred, but the rights conferred by native title appear in many cases to be being used not for the preservation of the "existence", but as a lever to extract money and other benefits, as demonstrated by the Aboriginal association near Katherine which gave up its native title rights in exchange for a promise of a kidney dialysis machine at the local hospital. If freehold title in the European sense is said to be required for the existence, then it is wrong to use the existence to justify a land grab. There could be no better example than the Croker Islands sea claim, where exclusive ownership and possession was sought for the seabed surrounding the islands, and all the resources above and below it. The Federal Court has held that the rights exist, but not exclusively, and that finding is destined for review by the High Court. But even to make the claim got the politics, especially of reconciliation, badly wrong. Because their demands were exclusionary, they were seen as excessive and that has angered the non-Aboriginal population of the territory.

'European settlement rendered lost forever the exclusivity of the existence. It says a lot about our culture that we could not coexist, hence the genocide. But sadly, Aboriginal people, perhaps blinded by misery, don't now see that the genesis of the problem today is that the positions are reversed. While white Australia has, through *Wik* et al, adopted the principle of coexistence, Aboriginal Australia has judged it to be impossible.

A land rights court hearing in the open near the Roper River, Northern Territory.

'The reality today is that neither side can exist without the other. The future for Aboriginal people in Australia is defined by what remains — the remnants: art, dance, oral history and ceremonies; and the landscape in which it was formed. They are the basis of the future. They may be merely remnants, but they remain in a modern world, and they're strong and vibrant and powerful. There is no turning back; there is no escape from that. It's a world where the future of those remnants can only be defined by the place that Aborigines can carve for themselves in it. And I can't see the future best served by a mind-set that seeks to recreate or preserve by exclusive use and possession what is long gone; by a mind-set that is mired in bitterness and recrimination;

that depends for its validity on the pretence that European Australia, being responsible for the demise of this perfect existence, should now pay the debt with endless compensation.

'Aboriginal Australia should be judged by how, without letting go of their ancient existence and all it meant, they can survive and adapt in today's world, and in the future. It is when I look at how, in so many positive respects, Aboriginal people are doing that, that I am most in awe of that old existence. But sadly, it is when I look at that part of the present condition of this race of people which is bitter, introspective and, worst, dependent, that I see not the remnants of the existence, but the existence forgotten; forgotten by its very own owners.

'As Aboriginals have structured this, it is they who are and forever will remain as mendicants because, very simply, exclusive possession and occupation of homelands is not required for the continuation of the existence. They assume white Australia will fund the future of the existence on those terms. It's a bad call.

'What is required is a system of ownership which preserves the existence but otherwise facilitates normal commercial use and development of the land, regardless of cultural origin, based on principles of mutual obligation, universal respect for the remnants of the "existence", and the imperatives of land management and utilisation in a modern world.

'I don't think modern Australia will forever embrace an Aboriginal future that involves subsidies for living in the past. The adaptability of the remnants, as I have defined them, is what will determine the outcome. It is conceivable that the Aboriginal existence can then become one of the set pieces of everyone's future. I am afraid that, as Aboriginal Australia presently writes the plot, the existence has very little future, unless it is exemplified by fourth-world health, housing, education and living conditions.

'I see the future as being only in coexistence, where each has rights and attaching to those rights are obligations. We can mutually coexist. We don't need to apologise to each other; but we need reconciliation as an essential tool with which to educate present and future generations — and especially because reconciliation is required to underpin mutual obligation. Above all, we need respect. Mutual respect and mutual obligation.

'But really, I am a *balanda* [white man]. What would I know?'

The cruise down the Stuart Highway to Mataranka was a gentle run to calm us before we hit the bulldust and rough stuff beyond Roper Bar. Most places in the outback can claim a brush with fame, of sorts, and Mataranka has seized on its proximity to Elsey station, the location for Jeannie Gunn's 1908 book, *We of the Never Never*. A giant statue of Henry Peckham, the packhorse mailman known to generations of schoolchildren as The Fizzer, stands outside an art gallery at the old homestead, and in my let's-get-on-with-it-'coz-it's-a-long-way-to-Cairns mood, I felt it was all a bit like that: a fizzer.

The road to Roper Bar is lined by millions of termite mounds; some chocolate-brown, others red; some spires, some looking like grey, melting blobs. Sometimes there was only one type; at others two types were side by side. The termite mounds stood among flourishing kapok trees, their distinctive yellow flowers adding a surreal spatter of dots over the grey-green foliage, red earth and deep-blue sky. In places, infestations of spider webs hung from every tree, as if entire branches were swathed in bandages. I asked which spider produced these webs, but the local shook his head. He hadn't been anywhere else, so he didn't realise spiders don't make webs like this everywhere.

We bade farewell to the bitumen 40 kilometres west of Roper Bar and were welcomed on the outskirts of the town by a sign which read: 'Roper Bar. Population 14. 1 Rottweiler, 1 Jack Russell, 1 Guard Dog, 1 Cockatoo (still the same one). Have a Nice Day!' We mooched around the area, cast for barra below the rock bar on the river (to no avail) and pushed on along the Great Top Road, through open flatlands, narrow valleys

Termite mounds on the road to Roper Bar, Northern Territory… spires and melting blobs.

and the ancient hills of the Tarwallah Ranges, and on, relentlessly on, to Borroloola.

About 800 people live in Borroloola today. It was originally established when an enterprising trader called 'Black Jack' Reid sailed his ketch up the McArthur River in 1885 and built a slab-hut store to sell provisions — and booze — to the passing trade. It was a canny move, because he had gained seaborne access to the Gulf Track, over which thousands of hopeful prospectors were passing en route to the Kimberley goldfields. Black Jack didn't concern himself with the niceties of liquor licences, and Borroloola soon became the wildest, roughest, gunfighting, brawling town in the north — home to 'the scum of Northern Australia', according to government officials. But the rush ended as quickly as it began, and the white population fell to a mere six people.

Borroloola should have disappeared as quickly as it began. But the river access gave it a reason for continued existence, and today the establishment of the major McArthur River silver, lead and zinc mine, with its associated port facilities at the quaintly named Bing Bong, has provided the town with a relative boom. It is now a government administrative centre, as well as providing most services to travellers, although not always in the well-scrubbed way we come to expect on more travelled routes. We suffered a stone-fractured tyre on the way into Borroloola, but we were able to get a new one fitted by Terry Fisher at his Steptoe-style garage, where a pet black pig wandered with dogs and other assorted animals among the wrecks which lay ready for cannibalisation as spare parts for God knows what might break down next. That tyre lasted 44 kilometres; it, too, was fractured as we drove into Bing Bong. Terry, tut-tutting about our amazingly bad luck, reported there were no more tyres of our size in town, but he cleverly managed a repair

Borroloola mechanic Terry Fisher with pet pig.

using gussets and glue which enabled us to carry on, if nervously.

Borroloola is an open town; open in the sense that it is slap-bang in the centre of the Narwinbi Aboriginal Land. But the local owners have decided they don't object to visitors; they don't require permits to enter; they don't wish to claim the rights to exclusion which other communities have imposed; and they don't wish to ban liquor. They proudly talk of their colour-blindness in Borroloola. There is no black and white here; we can live together perfectly well, they say. And yet there are two main bars in the Borroloola Inn, separated by a wall with a rarely used door. On one side, the Aborigines drink; on the other side, the whites drink. There is no law which says there cannot be

crossovers between the bars, and it does happen. But, from our observations, rarely. There is a *self-imposed* apartheid in this colour-blind town.

'My name,' said the elderly gentleman, 'is William Shadforth.' We shook hands in the white bar of the Borroloola Inn. He wore a Persil-white shirt, neatly pressed, a $20 note peering from the top pocket, buff-coloured chinos and polished riding boots. His smile creased his eyes as he explained he had noticed me smoking a pipe. 'I haven't seen anyone smoke a pipe since the fifties,' he said. 'You must be a very intelligent gentleman.'

'We're a dying breed,' I joked. 'It's a dumb thing to do.'

'No — no; very distinguished.'

Debbie, behind the bar, whispered to Wendy. 'Look out, Willie wants to get you to go fishing. It'll cost you 100 bucks.'

And so began our adventure with King Willie, Scottish-Aboriginal-Australian, stockman, drover, scallywag, black pastoralist, father of ten, grandfather of 33, great-grandfather of 29. Willie is a genuine character with a cheeky, lived-in face, well-worn but knowing, a quick smile and a hearty chuckle. Wendy took an immediate shine to him — and he to her — and described his face as 'beautiful and caring'.

Bit by bit, in a scatter-shot kind of way, we learned his story. I can't vouch for its accuracy, because information from a variety of sources, including Willie himself, often varied from one telling to the next. He told us he was 80, but later amended that, saying he had dropped a couple of years in 1942 to join the army. There are discrepancies over cattle numbers and prices paid for property, and vague tales of land transactions where the only common thread was that Willie had pulled off a financial coup. But none of that seemed to me to diminish the central point of interest in Willie: here was a black pastoralist; the legal owner of the 1500-square-kilometre Seven Emu station, with a 50-kilometre frontage to the Gulf, west of Borroloola. The High Court's *Wik* decision had decreed that native title rights could coexist with pastoral leases, but in the event of a dispute over the use of land, pastoral interests would prevail. If the Aboriginal Willie found himself in dispute

King Willie Shadforth and his 'castle' . . . 'I like it here . . . '

with the pastoral Willie, which way would Willie decide?

Willie is a descendant of a prominent wool industry family from the well-to-do Sydney suburb of Mosman, where the quiet, leafy Shadforth Street today records the family's long association with the area. His white grandfather was Harry Shadforth who, in 1895, was manager of Wollogorang station which sprawled over the Queensland–Northern Territory border, west of the area known as Hell's Gate (so named because it marked the end of the policed area of Queensland: through the gate, travellers were on their own in an era of pitched battles between settlers and indigenous peoples).

One story tells of a confrontation between both of Willie's grandfathers, where Harry Shadforth was speared in the backside by Willie's maternal grandfather; others tell of tensions between the black and white Shadforth families. A white woman, researching her family tree and claiming Harry Shadforth as her grandfather (which would make her a half-cousin of Willie's), loudly protested against 'those dreadful Aboriginal people who adopted grandfather's name'. She refused to accept that a liaison between a white man and a black woman was an unremarkable part of life in this area at the turn of the century, and retreated from Wollogorang in a great huff.

Willie grew up on Wollogorang station, and received privileges not enjoyed by tribal Aborigines. He was an 'inside' person, meaning he was entitled to eat inside the homestead with the whites and other half-castes, while the tribal blacks 'ate out by the woodheap', according to current station owner Paul Zlotkowski. 'He was considered more of a white person than black,' he said. 'But he told me a few years ago it was better

now to be a blackfella. I assumed he meant you get more benefits.' Willie became a top-notch horseman and drover on Wollogorang, but in 1960 opportunity came his way. Seven Emu station came on the market, and Willie acquired the lease for — according to legend — 100 head of cattle. Willie says it was 400 head, each worth 'five quid', making his purchase price $4000. He doesn't deny it was the best deal he ever did.

He chuckles when asked about other deals — like twice selling half the property for cash down-payments then repossessing it when payments faltered, or spending a government grant of $50,000, then neglecting to sign the papers which would have obliged him to repay it — but he offers no denial, confirmation or explanation other than an impish grin. Whatever the details, Willie says he became Australia's first black pastoralist, and still is.

As we chatted in the bar, Willie established my interest in fishing and regaled us with tales of monster catches of barramundi and mudcrabs at the mouth of the Robinson River, the western boundary of Seven Emu. People came from all around Australia to fish there, he said, and we could drive to the edge of the Gulf. So we arranged to meet next morning: we would give Willie a lift back to his kingdom, and for this favour, he would waive his $100 fee.

'So what would you do if someone came and claimed a sacred site on Seven Emu?' I asked as we drove the 100 kilometres to the Robinson River.

'Tell 'em to get lost,' pastoral Willie snapped back. 'There are no sacred sites on my land. It's my land, I've paid for it, and I've worked for it. Anyone who comes looking for sacred sites can look somewhere else. There's none on my land.'

Willie was emphatic. But the Garawa

people have lived in this region for eons. The eastern portion of Seven Emu is made up of rocky, thickly wooded, undulating formations, with many rivers and creeks running through it; a rich food source. It is inconceivable that there are no sites of spiritual significance within that 1500 square kilometres. But not to pastoral Willie.

'My mob is a lost race,' Aboriginal Willie said. 'Lost. Definitely lost.'

'Why? I would have thought you had a wonderful culture. It's important to preserve the cultures, isn't it?'

'What culture?'

'In the land.'

'They're lost. They wouldn't know what to do with the land around here.'

'What about Arnhem Land? That's just up the road from here.'

'I don't know about Arnhem Land. I'm thinking about here. I don't care what the rest of them do. I'm myself. I look after what's mine.'

I was jolted by Willie's lack of concern for his people. I asked him about reconciliation.

'We're all human beings,' he said. 'I don't care who you are or what you are. We're all human beings; we've all got the same blood; white blood, Aboriginal blood, it's all the same. I've lived the white way and I've lived the tribal way. There is no difference.' And he said it again: 'We're all human beings.'

This became Willie's mantra. Whenever I raised the subject of black and white relations, he responded in the same way. It was as if he, merged in two cultures, rejected any definition of either; he was simply himself, of no colour and no culture, an individual who had shaped his own life, done it his way; and if he could do it, so could others — black, white or brindle.

'That's right,' he said. 'That's me. I don't care about government and this and that and all those things. I'm only interested in getting up in the morning, going here, going there, doing what I want to do. What else would I want?'

I decided that in any argument between pastoral Willie and Aboriginal Willie, Willie would win.

We drove across a rocky bar in the Robinson River and up a steep embankment. Perched on the edge of the river banks was a sprawling pair of open-sided huts, corrugated roofs held aloft by rough-hewn logs, a mosquito net hanging from the exposed rafters, deck chairs strewn about, iron beds with green hide springing, rusty 200-litre drums as rubbish bins, and a kerosene refrigerator against a single panel of wall. This was Willie's home.

'The station homestead is up that way,' he said, pointing. 'But what do I want to live there for? Why do I want a big house? I like it here, and I'm wealthy enough to do as I like.'

We sat at his table and chewed the fat. Willie brought out *National Geographic* and *Reader's Digest* magazines — at least ten years old — and expressed his amazement at pictures taken from a space probe on a long-forgotten fly-by of Mars. 'How could they do that?' he asked. 'It makes you wonder.' He repeated the phrase several times as I showed him the satphone, and he watched, shaking his head, as Wendy responded to a message from a client in Los Angeles. We talked of computing, and satellites, and converging communications, and the search for life in the universe, and we agreed: it makes you wonder.

As we drove along the Robinson River, Willie stopped us on a high cliff overlooking a bend in the river. 'This,' he announced, 'is where I'm going to have my next honeymoon!' It was a beautiful vista of shady paperbarks growing from the stony bottom of the river, overhung with enormous carbeen, Moreton Bay ash and cedar trees.

'But what about crocodiles?' Wendy asked.

'They won't eat you,' said Willie. 'Not if you keep a fire going.'

Wendy remained unconvinced as we made our way towards the Gulf, pounced on a couple who hadn't paid Willie's $100 entrance fee — 'stay a minute or stay a month; it's all the same price' — and fished (without luck) around the river mouth. We did a trade with the campers, a live mudcrab in return for some meat, and decided to set up camp for the night at Willie's honeymoon spot.

We made a fire and cooked the crab on its back in the coals, then prepared to settle into our tent. At Wendy's insistence, I stoked the fire high with wood to ward off the crocs. In the early hours of the morning I became aware she was no longer inside the tent. Stumbling around among the sand, pebbles and water-rounded rocks, I found her locked inside the Pajero, wrapped in her sleeping bag. When she woke she blurted out that she had woken in the night and seen that the fire had gone out, and could no longer sleep in the tent because, for sure and certain, the crocs would come and get her!

I didn't confess that I knew the only wood available — paperbark, which has no more body than a rolled-up newspaper — wouldn't burn all night. If I had told her, she wouldn't have slept at all! But I wondered why she left me there.

We backtracked from Seven Emu and turned east on to the Great Top Road again. The relentless drive would continue, with road conditions varying according to when they had last seen a grader. Most times they were pitted and corrugated so badly they 'would shake Christ off the cross', as one wag put it.

And if the corrugations didn't get you, the bulldust would. By now we were very weary travellers, but we had no choice but to plough on, through the thickly wooded areas of the eastern territory, into the more open forests of western Queensland, past the famous Hell's Gate roadhouse, skirting the permit-only Doomagee Aboriginal community, and on to the low-lying flats surrounding Burketown. The disappointing aspect of this drive is that you never once get to see the Gulf; even Burketown, which is said to be 'on the Gulf', is 30 kilometres inland, on the muddy banks of the Albert River. While it is an important shire administration centre, a provisioning point for the cattle stations dotted around it and a tourist stop, Burketown fails to excite or to live up to its old reputation of being one of the wildest frontier towns in the nation. The only clue to the hellraising that might have gone on here is gleaned from the messages — ranging from the obscene to the profane — scrawled on the walls of the pub.

A welcome break from the dusty monotony of this Gulf crossing comes at the Leichhardt River, where a causeway crosses the rocky riverbed just above the picturesque Leichhardt Falls. Corellas in their thousands perch in spreading eucalypts beside the river, occasionally taking to the air in a squawking, squealing mass. Halfway across the causeway was a sign made of welded bore casing in the shape of a cross, with wrought iron letters attached: 'GOD IS'. Yes, well: God is . . . what? Good question. This enigmatic message provoked more than theological thoughts: who put it there? And why? The answers were provided by Mrs Lenore Camp, widow of former Floraville station owner Walter Camp. Long after passing the sign in the river I phoned and explained I had been thinking about the sign for months, and with

Burke and Wills, Camp 119 at the Bynoe River near Normanton, Queensland… this is as far as they got.

a triumphant chuckle Mrs Camp explained: 'My husband felt the urge to prove his faith, so he put it up in the early seventies. It is a complete sentence, you realise — with a verb and a predicate — and it was meant to make people think about faith. You see, it worked on you.' But, she admitted, it is possible to misread the sign. She told of a traveller who negotiated the crossing when the river was high. Asked if he had struck any trouble in the swift-flowing waters, he said: 'Not really … it was a bit hairy at first, but OK after I got to God Island!'

An hour or so down the track we saw the spot where Burke and Wills ended their cross-country rush at Camp 119, beside the Bynoe River. Like the modern-day traveller, the explorers could taste the tidal salt in the creek water, but they couldn't make their way through the mudflats and mangroves to the true coast. So they blazed trees around their lonely camp and headed south to oblivion.

Today, some of the trees remain, and a cairn marks the spot.

Normanton is the largest of the Gulf towns and is the home of the railway to nowhere — the Gulflander, which now offers tourist runs to its destination at the old gold diggings of Croydon. We shadowed the track, finding — joy, oh joy — bitumen at last! Then we ploughed on to Gilbert River, Georgetown, Mt Surprise, and over the Great Dividing Range and the Atherton Tableland into Cairns, gratefully.

I left Wendy holidaying with a friend on a beach north of Cairns and flew to a business appointment in Melbourne. Driving past the World Congress Centre, where the Reconciliation Convention had been held two months previously, I cursed the lack of insight into ways to resolve the differences between black and white. But perhaps I was being unfair on myself: if I could solve it in two months, it would have been fixed years ago by greater minds. Nothing I had seen or done had changed my fundamental thinking: that this nation must come to terms with its past in a way which removes all impediments to a shared future. The only way this can happen is for non-indigenous Australians to pay proper respect to Aboriginal cultural beliefs and prior ownership, and in return, for Aboriginal Australians to accept that a shared future is possible. It is not morally or socially acceptable for us to say, 'You must accept our ways'; we must accept that their ways are equally valid, and worthy of preservation. In modern Australia, their ways — their existence — may be, as Lex Silvester observed, sadly remnants of a more complete past, but they are worthy of celebration in a nation which professes to embrace diversity. In the form of art, artifacts, dance and Dreamtime stories, they also have the capacity to financially underpin their own preservation.

It is dangerous to generalise about the state of Aboriginal Australia where differences between tribes, cultures, languages, needs, desires and politics are at least as — if not more — diverse than in the rest of multicultural Australia. No single template fits all situations. But some generalisations were firming in my mind.

Saying sorry isn't admitting guilt. Today's generations weren't responsible for the massacres, poisoned waterholes, the gunpoint pursuit of indigenous people to deprive them of their land, or the forced removal of children. These actions, unconscionable today, were a product of their times, and times change. We needn't feel responsible or guilty, but we can be sorry. A national apology would cost nothing; it would be a meaningful gesture, and would remove a reason for a backward-looking source of anger, thereby allowing a new focus on the future. If guilt comes into this equation anywhere, it is that we live today in a society which largely prefers ignorance over knowledge, with a leadership which recognises prior ownership but tries to suppress it. The shame of Australia today is embodied in the political pursuit of a plan to deny Aborigines the right to negotiate about the use of their land. What's wrong with negotiation? Isn't that what we have learned to do since childhood? Isn't that how we live and trade on this earth? Isn't that how we settle all differences, and reach all agreements, including the *Wik* legislation itself? Negotiation is the very process by which we come to terms, and arrive at viable, lasting, sharing, agreeable outcomes. What can possibly be wrong with that?

But not all fault lies at the feet of European Australians. Aboriginal leaders — notably the political players of the Aboriginal and Torres Strait Islander Commission (ATSIC) — haven't been without fault. They have made decisions which many non-indigenous Australians, eager for reconciliation, find hard to accept. They have put land ownership before living conditions. It is one thing to own, in modern legal terms, the land which created the existence, but it is another to continue that existence in Third World conditions. Surely the health and well-being of their people was of the highest priority, but vast sums have gone into land acquisition rather than water supplies, sewerage services, schools and health centres which are sadly lacking in many communities. The politics of land above all else does nothing to improve them. White Australia's frustration on this point led to the army being brought in as project engineers to build water and sewerage services. Aboriginal communities could, and should, have done this, with consequential benefits through jobs and skills development. Education should be approached in a cooperative way. Schools should teach indigenous languages and cultures, as well as preparing kids to live in today's society. In many communities the cry is to preserve the culture, while the evidence is that the kids, especially, don't want to live it. Education is an essential bridge to living in a modern world — a life to which many indigenous people aspire. Aboriginal leaders need to recognise that native title laws are an attempt to establish a framework of fairness — not a green light for a gigantic land grab. Some of their ambit claims, like claims over all land between high- and low-water marks and thousands of square kilometres of sea, are ill-advised examples of this. Their cause is ill-served by attempts to lock up their lands behind metaphorical electric fences; it's provocative and resented because, while it might make sense in terms of the way the world was before the arrival of Europeans, it doesn't reflect the realities of modern Australia where 18 million non-indigenous people share the land, and will continue to do so.

ATSIC also assumes its annual $1 billion budget is a bottomless pit, derived from the belief that white Australians were driven by guilt. The truth is that the giant well of support for Aboriginal Australia is the product of our belief in a fair go for all, and the greatest threat to its continued existence is a mendicant mind-set which sees the money as a right and an obligation (and therefore available to be ripped off, no strings attached), rather than as a means by

which the injustices of the past can be overcome. If Aboriginal Australia is to continue to expect Australians to dig deep to fund fairness in all parts of our society, their leaders need to adopt a policy of mutual obligation, recognising that many of their problems can only be overcome if they contribute to the solution. It's not good enough to dismiss the rubbish littering our communities as a product of Western culture, or to insist that violence against women, or child sex abuse, should be ignored with the mysterious suggestion that these are tribal matters, and therefore the business of no-one but themselves. If the rest of us are required to confront our social problems, like booze and drugs, the same needs and responses, with appropriate cultural deferences, should apply to Aboriginal communities.

These are well-intentioned criticisms, and need not divert us in any way from the goal of a mutual, shared future. Mistakes have been made by both sides (usually with the result of more distress and disempowerment of Aboriginal Australians) and they cannot be undone. The clock cannot be turned back. But the errors can be put behind us. The moral justice of the Aboriginal cause is overwhelming, and it can be achieved through all sides adopting the single principle behind the High Court's *Wik* decision: coexistence. If enough Australians were prepared to stand up and demand a future based on sharing and coexisting, our leaders would have no choice but to follow.

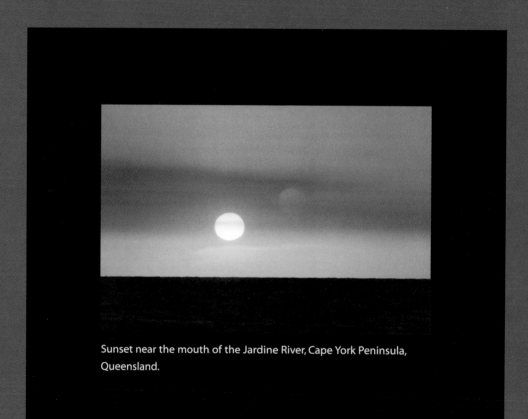

Sunset near the mouth of the Jardine River, Cape York Peninsula, Queensland.

eight

What do you call the top of Australia? The Tip, of course. And that was the focus of our attention as we paused in Cairns, serviced the Pajero and planned our assault on what has been termed the greatest adventure drive in the nation. We were headed north to Cape York, 1000 kilometres away, across rivers and roads so rough, remote and potentially hazardous that military-style planning was called for. We adopted the popular approach to the journey — two weeks up and two days back, savouring the many moods of this huge finger of land which is roughly the size of Victoria, but with a population of only 15,000. This strategy allowed time to explore the national parks and historical spots along the way, and to ease ourselves into Tip time, which would totally disconnect us from the world. Once at the Tip, we would stay as long as we could, then dash back along the east coast to home, almost 3500 kilometres away.

A rare clearing in the Daintree Wet Tropics area, Queensland.

We put Cairns, Port Douglas and Mossman behind us before crossing the Daintree River by ferry to enter one of Australia's World Heritage areas, the incredibly rich, diverse and precious Daintree rainforests. This area had been an environmental battleground in the 1970s, when the awakening green movement stood up against the commercial desecration of the area promoted by Queensland's Bjelke-Petersen government. The protesters failed to stop a road being bulldozed through the area, and they failed to stop small parcels of unserviced land being sold as housing subdivisions. But they won the war in 1988 when 900,000 hectares of tropical rainforest between Townsville and Cooktown was declared the Wet Tropics World Heritage area. Now the long process of repair is under way. A joint federal and state buy-back program encourages landowners to sell their blocks for permanent preservation, or, if they wish to continue living in the area, they are offered incentives to preserve the natural values of their land. The assault on the Daintree was a costly, pigheaded mistake by Sir Joh Bjelke-Petersen, the former Queensland strong-man Premier, but, we observed with a twinge of guilt, we were the beneficiaries, because the road gave us access to absorb the sights, sounds and incredibly fresh smells of the rainforests.

The Daintree area is classified as one of the most important wet areas in the world because it is seen by scientists as an evolutionary link to our past. Millions of years ago marsupial moles snuffled through the soft ground; at night, gliding possums and bats swooped through the rainforest, and pygmy possums scampered through the branches. On the forest floor, carnivorous kangaroos and marsupial lions hunted the forebears of today's skinks, geckos and scrub fowls. Unlike the rest of Australia the Daintree rainforest survived the cold, arid climates of passing ice ages and today, 13 out of the world's 19 families of primitive flowering plants are still found here; green dinosaurs.

The Wet Tropics is the most biologically diverse place on the Australian continent, with more than 1000 different rainforest trees, 900 varieties of shrubs, 450 different types of vines, about 400 herbs, 150 epiphytes (plants which require host plants), 40 palms and 333 different ferns, including a giant King fern identical to its ancestors which lived 250 million years ago. Many of the species surviving here are found nowhere else in the world, and some animals are also unique. Fossils show that tree-dwelling possums came down to ground level to live on fallen fruit, fungi and insects and evolved into today's kangaroos. But some, like the unique Bennett's tree kangaroo, were tempted back to the trees in search of food when the continent began to dry out, returning to the lifestyle their ancestors had abandoned.

We didn't see any of these rare creatures, but we figured it was nice to know they were there and wouldn't be hurried to extinction by Joh's invading hordes of semi-suburban bush dwellers. As we poked along the narrow track, we marvelled at the dappled light, the clarity of the gently flowing creeks, the vines hanging from the trees — waiting for Tarzan? — the incredible variety of palms filtering light through every imaginable shade of green. Mountains towered above us inland,

and we caught occasional glimpses of the sea down precipitous slopes to the east. The beauty, and the fizzy, highly oxygenated air thrilled us as we made our way through Cape Tribulation, laboured in low ratio up challenging mountain ridges, crossed the dramatic Bloomfield River, detoured to the Bloomfield Falls, still running strongly even in the dry, passed through the Cedar Bay National Park, and marvelled at the enormity of the shattered granite blocks which make up Black Mountain, before reaching Cooktown.

Outback pubs are marvellous places. I recall the thrill of my first visit to the Bark Hut Inn at Annaburroo, halfway between Darwin and Jabiru. Signs on the walls reflect a raw bush humour — such as a feral pig's rear quarters, stuffed and mounted on a wooden plaque, with the words 'WE GIVE CREDIT' above the trophy, and 'WE DO' below. Most Australians, even slyly grinning teenagers, make the translation — 'We give credit — pig's arse we do' — but it frequently needs explaining to foreign visitors who may be more comfortable with the more prissy, 'Please do not ask for credit as refusal may cause offence.'

Pubs of all sizes and descriptions dot the outback landscape. Scrawled messages on walls, bumper stickers, banknotes and drinks coasters from around the world can be interesting reading over a cool ale, and conversations with publicans — usually the font of all local knowledge — can be highly rewarding. But after a while, these pubs take on a certain sameness. There is a limit to the number of times you can laugh at the same jokes: 'A camel can go without a drink for eight days, but who wants to be a camel?', or 'I don't have a drinking problem. I drink, I get drunk, I fall down. No problem',

"CARLTON"

"I ALLUS HAS WAN AT ELEVEN"

or 'Cows may come and cows may go, but bull in this place goes on forever.'

At Rossville, just south of Cooktown, we came across the Lion's Den Hotel, a hole-in-the-wall which is little changed since it was built in 1875 to service the tin miners scrabbling for a living in these hills. The place reeked of character, its walls lined with old tools and implements, its rafters holding the memorabilia of more than a century. And on a wall, out the back, towards the gents, I found a gem: the Legend of Sam Knott.

Sam Knott was born in Devonshire, England, in 1841 and died choking on a bone from oxtail stew in Paddy McVeigh's Upper Yarra Hotel on 23 May 1907. His death was premature, not because Sam didn't live to a great age (he was

66) but because he didn't live to see how famous he would become.

Sam was the man on the poster printed by Carlton and United Breweries Ltd standing at the bar, clutching his beer and saying: 'I allus has wan at eleven.' His portrait adorns hotels and bars all over Australia. Yet Sam never saw it. He died just a few days before it was released.

Sam Knott, alias Griffith, came to Australia in 1888 to make his fortune fossicking for gold. He wandered off to the Upper Yarra Valley and around the hills searching for the precious metal which always eluded him. He later became a timber getter, hotel yardman and rouseabout. His favourite waterhole was the Upper Yarra Hotel. A confirmed bachelor, Sam could regale visitors with stories for hours. The story has it that when he worked for Paddy McVeigh as a hotel yardman, Paddy paid him his one pound a week with the same banknote. When that pound note left Paddy's till to pay Sam, it always finished up back in its special place in the till before the day was out. Sam took his place at the bar every day at 11 am. One morning in 1906 a young artist entered the bar at the same time, saw Sam about to down his first for the day, and said to him: 'You look as though you're enjoying that.' 'Aye', said Sam, 'I allus has wan at eleven.' The young artist sketched Sam on the spot — beer, beard, bowyangs and boots — and took the drawing back to Melbourne with the idea of selling it to a brewery. Carlton Brewery bought the portrait and decided to have it printed and distributed. But these things take time. The six biggest breweries in Melbourne, including Carlton, were going through the long drawn-out merging process to become Carlton and United Breweries, so it was well into 1907 before the poster was ready for distribution. Just days before it arrived in the Upper Yarra

Valley, Sam Knott choked on an oxtail bone in the hotel and died.

But if Sam's death was somewhat bizarre, his burial was even more so. Paddy had to build a coffin, but there was one major problem — there was no suitable timber. So he scrounged bits and pieces of packing cases, butter boxes, etc, nailed them all together and placed Sam inside. The next problem was getting Sam to the old Warburton cemetery, 40 kilometres away over a rough and slippery road accessed only by horse and dray, and even then at some risk. Two locals, George Stacpoole and John Maginn, were given the job of driving Sam to Warburton where they were to meet the minister. But on the way Sam's patchwork coffin slipped off the back of the dray and smashed. Stacpoole and Maginn loaded him back on the dray, but his feet were sticking out the broken end of the coffin. When they arrived in Warburton in pouring rain the minister was late and, the story goes, they decided on a noggin or two to keep warm until the minister arrived. They propped Sam up at the bar to see whether their drinking companions would notice if they were drinking with a dead man. Later Sam and what was left of the coffin were placed before the hotel fireplace. When the minister still didn't arrive, they decided to bury Sam anyway and headed for the graveside, accompanied by a local identity, Tom Crowley, to make up the funeral entourage. But the coffin was beyond it, and Sam was propped up between the driver and passengers for his last journey. Even so, they still had trouble. The grave was full of water and Sam kept floating to the surface. Tom Crowley reported later they had to weigh him down with rocks so they could fill the grave in. It was then that the Reverend William

The Bloomfield Falls, south of Cooktown, Queensland.

Williams arrived. 'Have you said a prayer over Sam?' he asked. 'No,' they said, 'just "poor old Sam".' So the reverend said a prayer for Sam and earned his burial fee of ten shillings.

Sam's grave is unmarked, but his influence was felt years later. The brewery poster became so popular and well known it was used to swing the argument away from the temperance movement when Victoria held a referendum on prohibition in 1930. The pro-drinking lobby released a cartoon of a miserable Sam weeping into his cup of tea, saying: 'I allus used to have wan at eleven.' It was enough to swing the vote against prohibition.

Cooktown calls itself the Queen of the North, and it's not an idle boast. It is a pretty place, and its beauty is equalled by its position in Australia's history. For it was here, in the mouth of the Endeavour River, that Lieutenant James Cook careened the *Endeavour* for seven weeks in 1770 to repair the damage caused when he struck part of the Great Barrier Reef, 50 kilometres south. For a week, in imminent danger of sinking, all hands manned the pumps, and heavy items were jettisoned, as Cook struggled to find a suitable landfall. One can imagine his relief as the mouth of the river came into view.

We booked into the delightful Seaview Motel, overlooking Cook's landing place, and in the evenings, as the sun brought tints of gold, orange and pink to the mangroves across the river, we sat on the lawn, imagining the scene 227 years earlier: the ship high on the sand, a makeshift blacksmith's forge, storage tents, carpenter's workshop, a butchery, pens for pigs and sheep, fishing nets drying in the sun. It would have looked like a tiny village, and that is why Cooktown today claims to be the site of Australia's first European settlement.

Cook no doubt cursed his bad luck, and

The Endeavour River, Cooktown, from Grassy Hill . . . Lieutenant Cook careened the *Endeavour* here in 1770.

worried about how he was to escape the reef which hemmed him in from the open sea, but the unscheduled stopover did have its benefits. For it was here that the kangaroo was first seen and described, and the botanists Banks and Solander discovered 180 plant species new to science. It was to be more than 100 years after Cook departed — and threaded his ship through the Reef near Lizard Island — before Europeans arrived back in Cooktown, this time rushing through it in their thousands on their way to the Palmer River goldfields.

Today Cooktown reeks of history, with several monuments to Cook, museums and points of historical interest. A climb to the Grassy Hill Lookout, on a 260 million-year-old knob of granite, presents the same vista Cook took in — towering mountains inland, and treacherous shoals and sandbars out to sea. The population is about 1600 today, and Cooktown exudes a sophisticated, confident air. Compared to some towns of a similar size, it has class — mainly because of the number of southern folk who have turned their backs on the cities and headed north to new frontiers. It has been a procession pushing ever northwards for decades — beyond the Gold Coast, beyond the Sunshine Coast, beyond the tropical cities of Townsville and Cairns — and, now, safely beyond the booming tourist Mecca of Port Douglas. Cooktown has the feeling of being 'the next big thing', and it is to be hoped that, as it grows, it doesn't succumb to the same sort of overdevelopment which has ruined the sleepy charms of places like Port Douglas.

A striking example of the southerners who migrate north for a new life is Joy Earles, who turned her back on Melbourne soon after her father died in 1994, and joined a partnership to run a restaurant on a historic old Sydney

MV *Burragi* … Sydney Harbour tender, now a restaurant at Cooktown.

Harbour ferry now moored in the Endeavour River. Somehow it seems a fitting resting place for the old MV *Burragi* — Aboriginal for 'Black Bird of the Water'. Once a familiar sight on the harbour, puttering around the birthplace of the nation, she now floats near the exact spot where Cook and his crew established 'the first European settlement'.

The *Burragi* was built and named SS *Isis* in 1910. Her role was as a small tug and water tender, used mainly around the Goat Island shipyard until 1957 when she was converted to a diesel-powered passenger ferry and re-named. The closure of the shipyard in 1991 made her redundant and her owners, the Maritime Services Board, moved to scrap her. But there was an outcry, with the Seamen's Union and the Sydney Maritime Museum mounting a campaign to save the *Burragi*, and the vessel was given a maritime heritage listing. She was then sold and refurbished as a floating restaurant with French tapestries, glass portholes, and Sir Robert Menzies' old bedroom rug on the saloon floor.

She was again offered for sale, and Cooktown chef (and former Melburnian)

Warren Edsell saw the advertisement. He teamed up with Margaret Vohland, whose husband runs a local earthmoving business, and the consortium was then joined by Joy. The *Burragi* was prepared for the long journey north, but everything that could go wrong, did. She slammed into a reef off Coffs Harbour, nearly sank, and spent three costly weeks on a slip while a three-metre section of her keel was replaced. But with a new skipper, the *Burragi* completed the remaining 1200 nautical-mile journey to Cooktown in less than 13 days, and now rests calmly as a charming addition to one of the more sophisticated, enterprising and pleasant places of the Far North.

We were surprised, in a Cooktown restaurant, to find King Island beef on the menu. Why, in the far, far north where beef cattle graze all around, import beef from the lush pastures of the far, far south? 'Because the local stuff isn't good enough,' came the reply. You can say that again. We had long ago given up on good food in the boondocks, and the mere recognition that travellers might like more than a greasy hamburger made us grateful to the restaurateurs of Cooktown.

Australian food has come a long way since the meat-and-three-veg days of the 1950s. Chefs have become celebrities, and the pursuit of new flavours, new ingredients and new sensations has spawned a growing East-meets-West industry. For the first time, it can be legitimately claimed in the 1990s that Australia has a unique cuisine, pioneered by the likes of Sydney's Neil Perry, Tetsuya Wakuda and Serge Dansereau, Adelaide's Cheong Liew and Maggie Beer, and Melbourne's Stephanie Alexander. All have received world recognition for their talent, and a growing number of Australian wine and food lovers have enthusiastically embraced their creations.

Region of origin produce is increasingly acclaimed: Queensland mudcrabs, Streaky Bay scallops, Western Australian marrons, rock lobster and yabbies, Pacific oysters, Illabo milk-fed lamb, Riverina rice, Gippsland and Tasmanian farmhouse cheeses, Kervella goat's cheese from Western Australia and tropical fruits from Far North Queensland.

But none of this means a hill of beans outside the major cities. Put simply, food in the outback is appallingly bad. This applies at every level — ingredients, cooking, presentation and service. Score two out of ten for each; and the two is there only because, in the end, it's food to keep the body's engines firing. A necessary evil.

Nobody expects to find Neil Perry or Stephanie Alexander slaving away in a hot kitchen in Borroloola, Burketown or Birdsville. Nobody expects silver service and fine dining in Coen, Karratha or Katherine. It's only fair that you accept lower standards in areas where the population can't support the investment needed to establish a ritzy restaurant. But it's not unreasonable to expect that, wherever you are, ingredients might be fresh, cooking might be more thoughtful than cindering both sides of a slab of beef, and presentation and service might be something less than slovenly.

Bush motels and pubs around the country offer the same repetitious selection — schnitzels, chicken kiev, T-bone steaks, seafood baskets, hamburgers with the lot, and chips. Universally, they come pre-packaged from the freezer; universally, they taste like cardboard; and invariably they are trimmed with limp salads with a slice of orange on the

The Elim coloured sands, north of Cooktown.

top. The worst area for sustained bad food was across the top. In Georgetown, our last stopover before Cairns, we were presented with a huge slab of local beef — so large it hung over the sides of our plates — encased by a rind of yellow fat, held together by glutinous sinews and lumps of lard. By the time we had removed this excess, the edible content had fortunately been reduced by half, but that looked like grey shoe leather and tasted the same. Nevertheless, we ate it.

We developed a defence against the culinary equation that outback equals outrage. During our Cairns stopover I flew to Melbourne for a week's business. I acquired there some fine cuts of beef, lamb and pork at an up-market butchery, had them put through the cryovac process which vacuum-seals the cuts in individual airtight plastic bags, carried them on board on the return flight, and popped them into our Engel car fridge, where they could stay perfectly fresh for a month or more. In our camps up and down Cape York we ate triumphantly well, with reasonably fresh vegetables acquired every few days and fine meats cooked on a heavy iron skillet resting on the coals of open campfires. A delicious way to beat the system!

There are two ways to tackle the Cape: straight up the middle, or by meandering through the national parks and reserves which dot the map. We chose the latter, making for Hopevale, and on to the extraordinarily pretty Elim coloured sands north of Cooktown.

When the tides are right, it's possible to drive on to the beach and travel almost 15 kilometres along the coast towards Cape Flattery. The key attraction is the deeply weathered chasms of sand — ochre, yellow,

black, white, cream, brown and red — which have been exposed in the massive sandhills which dominate on the seaward side of the Battle Camp Range. At various points, water, filtered and fresh, streams from the base of the sandhills, cutting rivulets through the sand as it makes its way to the sea.

After Elim we turned back west and battled our way over atrocious roads into the Lakefield National Park, fording creeks, cursing the potholes, bulldust and corrugations, but noting pretty spots on the map with exotic names — Battle Camp, Mick Finn Waterholes, Red Lily Lagoon, Suicide Waterhole, Mosquito Waterhole. The Lakefield detour links up with the main road again at Musgrave where an original wooden pole from the old telegraph line to the Cape still stands. Immediately below it is a Telstra phone box, powered by a solar cell fitted to its roof. Times change.

The traveller's centre at Musgrave is just off a crossroads. Cows browse on the airstrip adjacent to the old telegraph station. After fuel and a sandwich, I swung on to the main road and settled down for the 100-kilometre run to Coen. After 15 kilometres, Wendy said: 'I think we're going the wrong way.'

'I've got a dollar to say you're wrong,' I said. Who's the driver here? Who's the navigator? Who's the map reader, the planner, the one who can tell almost to the minute what time we'll arrive at our next town? But I looked for the sun. It was cloudy. Could she be right?

Wendy was looking for the sun, too, holding her wrist high, so she could point 12 o'clock at the sun and calculate north by dividing the space between 12 and the hour hand. This was the girl who couldn't read a compass before we left. Now she was a bloody bush woman!

I drove on. She nagged on. I had nagging doubts. So I stopped, got out the compass — and did a red-faced U-turn. She got the dollar.

The little town of Coen, known as the capital of the Cape because it is a service centre approximately at the halfway mark, is a rough-and-tumble place with most of the action happening at the Exchange Hotel in the main drag. Someone with a sense of humour has added an S to the sign on the roof. It would be a hit in Kings Cross, Sydney, but somehow this whole country seemed too masculine, too butch, for the sex change joke to be credible. But we weren't put off. We booked a room for the night. We enjoyed camping, but given the choice between a bed in a hotel room, no matter how sparse, and the hard yakka of putting up the tent and establishing a camp, I would go for the easy option. This was particularly so when we faced the task of making and breaking camp on consecutive days. Dragging all the bits and pieces down from the roof rack at the end of a hard day's drive, then cleaning them all, and putting them back in the right order and right place the next morning, wasn't always my idea of fun. The night before Coen we had camped at Kalpower Crossing in the Lakefield National Park, and we planned the next day to head into the Iron Range National Park, where there were no facilities other than camping spots. We veered east off the main road north of the Archer River roadhouse and immediately had our pace reduced to about 25 kilometres an hour by the narrow, rutted track conditions. The river crossings here were the deepest and roughest we had experienced, but the scenery made it all worthwhile. From the tops of the ridges of the Sir William Thompson Range we could see the majestic Mt Tozer, which we skirted to the north. The foliage was changing, too, with masses of blackboy plants, their soft green flouncing spikes wafting in the breeze. And we were struck by changes in the ever-present termite mounds: a few kilometres back they were angular and slender; now they looked like statues with flowing robes of white marble. And fringing every creek was rainforest, bigger, darker than the Daintree, although in smaller patches. It was extraordinary to drive out of thin scrub into these amazing cathedrals of foliage reaching for the sky; huge trees encased in creepers falling 50 metres across our paths, broadleafed bamboos, a variety of palms, and masses of delicate maidenhair ferns. And, just as abruptly as we entered, we would drive back into the bright sunlight to find ourselves on the open plains of a verdant grassland.

Our destination was Portland Roads, a tiny community on the sea where the fishing, it is said, was excellent. But there were no facilities here, and no welcoming smiles from the locals, either. Indeed, we felt our presence was resented, so we headed for the camping ground at Chilli Beach. This involved a six-kilometre drive along a soggy track, where axle-deep black mud gave the Pajero a proper work-out while a twitching, over-anxious Wendy gave me the same. But we made it through, the Pajero covered in mud and looking decidedly battle-weary, only to be puzzled by the arrival of another vehicle a short while later, as clean as a whistle.

'That mud was pretty rough going,' I said.

'What mud?' they asked.

'That section a couple of kilometres back. We very nearly got bogged.'

'Didn't you see the detour?'

Well, no.

Chilli Beach is exposed to the ever-blowing south-easterly trade winds, and the palms

Rainforest in the Iron Range National Park... cathedrals of foliage.

which fringe the beach and the creek behind it take on the shape of boomerangs, bent backwards by the wind. We took a drive down the beach to pick up driftwood for our campfire nestled behind a wind barrier, and were disgusted by the filth of the place. Flotsam and jetsam in the form of plastics and garbage from the thousands of ships which are piloted through the narrow channels between the reefs is blown up on beaches along this coast. We found one container with a ship's name attached to its neck on a still-legible tag. I felt like handing it in to the authorities and calling for the owner to be charged with littering.

Overnight rain turned the detour around the bog into another touch-and-go encounter on the way out, and our plan to make our way back to the main road just south of the Moreton telegraph station was blocked by the Pascoe River. A vehicle in front of us had just made it through the 80 centimetres of water flowing quickly over the causeway, but it — and its occupants — had been drenched. We decided that discretion was the better part of valour, and opted to retrace our steps. This, in turn, meant doubling back to the Archer River roadhouse for fuel, because the extra distance and slow going put a big question mark over our ability to make it to the next fuel supplies at Bamaga. This wasn't country to take chances in.

The 120 kilometres between the Archer and Wenlock rivers is corrugated — three to a metre — and the landscape is corrugated on a larger scale, too. Undulations take us up, over a crest, then down into a watercourse; up and down, up and down, kilometre after kilometre. The driver is forever on the brakes, slowing for a dip, then powering up again to reach cruising speed, only to be quickly on the brakes again for another infernal dip.

But it's kind of fun, because some wag has enhanced the ubiquitous yellow-and-black roadside DIP warning signs with some witty additions: DIPpity-doo-dah, DIP toe through the tulips, Dear Dorothy DIP, serenDIPity, skinny DIPping, DIP ya wick, DIPsomania, cheese DIP, DIP in my heart, DIP stick, lucky DIP, slippery DIP, big DIPper, and the inevitable DIP shit. I suspect the author, with a quick wit, precise hand and willingness to stop every kilometre or so, is named Gary. One of the signs proclaimed Gary DIPped Sarah.

The real adventure begins at the Wenlock. From here to the Jardine, 155 kilometres north, the track follows the old telegraph line, its surviving steel poles invariably twisted and bent by cyclones, falling branches or encounters with vehicles. To call it a track is to dignify it. Skeins of interwoven tyre marks push relentlessly north, barred frequently by fallen trees, washaways, the torn-up surface of impassable bogs, and sometimes three-metre-high termite mounds. This is slow-go country — it's rare to get above 25 kilometres an hour — and while the track redefines the word 'roughness', Wendy was strangely accepting of it. At slow speeds, she reasoned, nothing much would happen even if we did get stuck.

Drivers coming into this region have to know what they're about, and what to do in

The Telegraph Track to The Tip… tracks woven among washaways.

case of trouble. Spare wheels, winch, snatch straps, high-lift jack, and supplies of fuel, water and food are essentials. Depending on the season, the innumerable river and creek crossings will involve driving through water up to a metre deep, and it's necessary to prepare vehicles — particularly those with petrol engines — for these encounters.

At the Wenlock River we crossed to the northern bank to find several campers enjoying a mirthful watch on the ford. They were laughing about the owner of a new Landcruiser who stopped at the water's edge, removed his fan belts to stop water being thrown up within the engine compartment and perhaps putting the electrical system out of action, and tied a tarpaulin over the front of the vehicle to act as the bow on a boat, minimising the possibility of a surge of water over the motor. All wise precautions. Then he drove through 30 centimetres of water — barely enough to get his axles wet!

At each of the crossings we stopped to survey the route. Most involved a steep and usually rough descent down the banks of the creek to the water's edge, and occasionally a drive of perhaps 100 metres along the creek to the crossing point. Most fords have solid rock or gravel bottoms which can be seen through the clear water, so it's not difficult to identify holes or other pitfalls. Often it's necessary to zigzag across the river to avoid holes, and on some crossings this meant precision was essential. But the apprehension we felt at the first of these crossings soon evaporated into confidence. Stop, walk-through, pick your line, low ratio, low gear, constant revs, then gun it up the bank. Easy. Good fun. We felt a growing sense of adventure. And then we came to Gunshot Creek.

This is the daddy of them all! Most drivers take a 27-kilometre detour via the Heathlands

Ranger Station which avoids Gunshot, but I wanted to see what this fabled crossing was all about. As we approached, we met a convoy of film crew vehicles, and the driver of the lead car told us: 'You can't get through up there.' Hmm, maybe. We kept going, rounded a bend and stopped in our tracks. The road disappeared in front of us. A deep, clay-based slippery dip led at 45 degrees into a muddy boghole adjacent to the creek. At the moment I arrived, an old Landcruiser was face-down in the mud, its engine stalled. Two other vehicles were parked, dripping mud, on the other side. The Landcruiser engine fired up again and it lurched through the river amid whoops of delight from four triumphant men savouring their victory. Wendy stood aghast at the top of the drop-off into the mudhole and said: 'You've got to be kidding. You can't get through that!'

'C'mon,' they shouted from the other side. 'Don't be a chicken!'

'You're mad,' Wendy cried.

I weighed it up. It was very steep, for sure. Once the back wheels were over the top lip of the drop-off, there was nowhere to go but down into the bog. But, they had just driven out of it, and they were on the other side with snatch straps at the ready. And this is Gunshot, I reasoned, the ultimate challenge on the Telegraph Track. So I said we'd give it a go, knowing it was at the extremity of capabilities for myself and the vehicle, and that I wouldn't have the guts to try it without the guys on the other side of the creek.

Wendy protested loudly, so I gave her the video camera and sent her paddling across the creek. One of the other guys took my still camera, and I inched towards the lip of the drop-off. From the driver's position I could see nothing but fresh air. My front wheels went over and the nose of the car pointed

Gunshot Creek... the ultimate challenge on the track to The Tip.

down, down, and finally the back wheels cleared the lip. Then, under full brakes, I slid gently down the last metre until the nose plunged into the mud and we rested for a moment, my windscreen view entirely filled with a close-up of mud. I gunned it and the Pajero leapt forward, like a startled animal, out of the bog, into the creek, and — swoosh — with water sweeping over the bonnet, up on to the dry bank. We had made it! Wendy, shaking, joined us as we cracked a beer with the blokes, and we dubbed ourselves the Road Warriors of Gunshot Creek.

The landscape was different now. The straggly ironbarks and bloodwoods had given way to gently sloping heathlands, giving a softer appearance to the ever-narrowing finger of land, now just 80 kilo-metres wide from the Gulf of Carpentaria to the east and the Great Barrier Reef to the west. We pressed on to the pretty Fruit Bat Falls at Eliot Creek, encountering the deepest of all river crossings. The Telegraph Track was getting rougher by now — hardly

possible, we thought — but there were a number of escape routes linking us to the new developmental road which skirts the rivers and swamps to the east. Before that road was built the final hurdle on the run to the top was at the Jardine River, where the ford was 150 metres wide and usually about 1.2 metres deep. But travellers today are encouraged to use the ferry, ten kilometres downriver from the old crossing, and local chat had it that the indigenous owners of the ferry operation had turned encouragement into necessity by blasting a deep hole in the ford!

There is considerable resentment about the ferry. It costs $80 to make a return trip — a little more than a minute on the water each way — and this is seen by many travellers as legalised theft. Chatter among travellers says a crossing can be negotiated for a slab of beer, and the local owners don't pay any fee at all. Yet the ferry operation is heavily subsidised, and a fuel station on the southern bank of the Jardine has closed, allegedly

The Jardine River, Far North Queensland . . . serenely blissful.

because funds weren't available to pay for supplies.

But the ferry ticket also provides a permit for any number of camping sites north of the Jardine, all of which is either Injinoo Aboriginal land or national park. It's a high price for a ferry ride — but not a high price for a permit to visit The Tip for as long as you wish. (Similar permits for the desert parks of South Australia cost $60 — without a ferry ride!)

The ferry operates from 8 am to 5 pm and we arrived too late to make it across, so we pitched our tent beside the Jardine and fished from its banks. It was a glorious, moon-filled night; serene and beautiful, followed by a blissfully still sunrise. Wendy was concerned about crocodiles — doubly so, because a man

had been taken in these waters a few years ago — but we were well up the bank, and if the crocs were there, they observed the appropriate protocols and stayed away.

From the Jardine it was a bone-shaking, corrugated 50-kilometre run to Bamaga, and a further 38 kilometres to The Tip. After almost 15,000 kilometres and two months on the road, we could almost taste it.

The Dutch were the first Europeans here. In 1606 William Janz (sometimes Jansz) was blown to the western side of Cape York and named several prominent landmarks — including Duyfken Point on the high red cliffs which were to be identified in the 1950s as the world's richest bauxite mine at Weipa. Cook passed by in 1770, and Edmund Kennedy was speared to death in retaliation for shooting Aborigines on the first trek to the Cape in 1848. The Queensland government established a permanent settlement at Somerset in 1864, and appointed John Jardine as magistrate. The Jardine dynasty — sons Frank and Alick — pushed a mob of cattle north from Rockhampton in an epic journey in 1865 to take advantage of their father's fiefdom, and John took over as magistrate, ruling the northern Cape for almost 70 years with uncompromising fierceness and brutality. The native population was reduced over 40 years from about 3000 to 300 through disease, shootings and kidnappings.

Another kind of invasion took place during the Second World War, when thousands of American and Australian soldiers poured in to make the Cape a staging base for the war effort in New Guinea. Sixty known aircraft wrecks dot the area around the Bamaga airstrip — the wartime Higginsfield air base — and some are today designated as war graves. The quiet isolation surrounding these wrecks is a silent reminder of how close war came to our shores. The Injinoo people contributed greatly to the war effort, acting as guides and couriers, but were hardly rewarded: immediately after the war their lands, livestock and gardens were confiscated, their movements restricted and their children removed — many to Hopevale, 1000 kilometres south. Even in the 1960s, the Mapoon community was removed at gunpoint, their houses, store and church torched, to make way for the Comalco bauxite mine at Weipa (even though their land has never been mined) and resettled at Mandingu, or New Mapoon, south-west of The Tip. This tight government control wasn't relaxed until 1985, when the indigenous people were given the right to re-

establish a form of self-administration. One can only wonder about the motives of government when we learn that, even then, it was illegal for Aboriginal people to own or operate any business other than the sale of alcohol.

A low-powered FM radio service at the Jardine crossing provides warning of yet another threatened invasion. An announcer gravely intones: 'Today the area is still in danger — not from the marauding foreign armies that Frank Jardine or the WWII generals were worried about — but from invaders with even more potential to devastate Australia. The region is geographically very close to Papua New Guinea and South-east Asian countries where we know serious pests and diseases occur. One, of most concern, is the dreaded screw worm fly. It looks like an ordinary blowfly, but its feeding habits are much more horrid. The female screw worm fly lays her eggs in the flesh of any warm-blooded animal, and soon, the eggs hatch and the emerging maggots feed on the living flesh. Native and domestic animals, as well as livestock and humans, are at risk. This hideous pest's proximity to northern Australia is of great concern.' We saw screw worm fly traps, and passed through a 35-kilometre livestock buffer fence which stretches from coast to coast north of the Jardine, but fortunately, we saw no screw worm flies.

There were 25 4WD vehicles in the car park at the Pajinka Wilderness Lodge when we arrived for our walk to The Tip. They displayed number plates from every state of the nation. No matter the starting point of our odysseys, the time it had taken us to get here, or the adventures we had had along the way — we had but one destination. With the exception of Byron Bay in the east, the extremities of our mainland are in relatively remote places: Wilsons Promontory to the south, Shark Bay to the west and Cape York in the north, but none required the effort, planning and commitment needed to make it to The Tip. We would savour this.

The first part of the walk traverses a patch of rainforest which gives way abruptly to mangrove-lined Frangipani Beach, curving wide, white and shallow to the east. The rainforest boardwalk becomes a steep climb over red rocks up a bluff which runs all the way to The Tip. It is deceptive: as you climb, a ridge appears ahead, topped by a cairn of stones orginally placed by the indigenous people but now enhanced by others. As the ridge falls away steeply towards the eastern sea, the winds blast from the south, and the stone cairn beckons as your destination. But when you get there, a bronze plaque on the highest point indicates distances — 3020 kilometres to Melbourne, 3000 kilometres to Denpasar in Bali, 3610 to Hobart — and a vista unfolds below. It is a further 500-metre walk over boulders and steep rock faces to the point where the Australian continent disappears into the sea. As we made our way down, skirting rock pools, we noticed with disgust a graffitist had daubed the name 'Callisto' in white paint on a prominent rock. We muttered about idiocy and bastardry before posing in front of the stainless steel sign: *You are standing at the northernmost point of the Australian continent: 10 deg 41.41 minutes south latitude; 142 deg 31.82 minutes east longitude.*

We had made it! We felt such a sense of achievement — is triumph too grand a word? — as we dabbled our feet in the fast-flowing water ripping through the narrow channel between The Tip and York and Eborac islands. We set up the satphone and called

friends at home. 'We're on top of the world,' we said, before scaling down our boast to: 'Well, on top of Australia, anyway.'

The camping areas at The Tip are unserviced, so we made for Punsand Bay Private Reserve, which bills itself as 'the best camp site in Australia'. It's no idle boast. Blessed with 500 metres of beachfront, within sight of The Tip and Thursday Island across the water, it offered stunning sunsets, beach fishing, tranquillity and congeniality. Our tent was 20 metres from the water's edge. Bliss!

Further along the beach we found our Road Warriors from Gunshot Creek — Alan Briggs, Warwick DeRose, Warren Ackerly and Peter Mill — four dedicated off-roaders from Melbourne who gave Wendy top marks for her adventurous spirit. They had left their wives or partners at home.

We spent some days exploring the region: walking through the northernmost rainforest in Australia, the Lockerbie Scrub, named by John Jardine after his ancestral roots in Scotland, and now recognised as an important habitat for migratory birds flying south from Papua New Guinea; picking our way through the ruins of a wartime communications centre from which coast watchers flashed news of Japanese air activity; and tracing the prewar undersea telephone cable where it entered the sea at, appropriately, Cable Beach. This cable was cut when the Japanese took over Singapore and was never repaired.

We felt relaxed and at home at Punsand Bay. We marvelled at how far we had come — not in the physical sense, but in our acceptance of bush ways and bush life. When we left Sydney on the first trip, Wendy was tartly critical of the standard of accommodation in our first motel. But bit by bit she came to accept that the lack of city

A sense of triumph… we made it to The Tip.

conveniences was more than offset by the impact of discovery; of seeing things she never knew existed; of experiencing the beauty of unspoiled nature; of finding new ways to do things — even going to the toilet armed with a shovel. Conventional standards were meaningless in the bush. She wasn't even fazed when advised to take a sturdy stick into the campground shower block at Kalpowar Crossing in Lakefield National Park because it was shared with a three-metre python!

Compared to this, we felt Punsand Bay was the very centre of civilisation at The Tip. Friendly staff led by manager Geoff Hintz gave advice, provided meals if we wished,

and freely gave guests the run of the place. But we were as disconnected from the realities of life in Australia as we could possibly be. No-one knew what was happening down south, and no-one seemed to care.

But we had an appointment to keep. We flew to Cairns, then on to Hayman Island for Rupert Murdoch's retirement dinner for Ken Cowley, the executive chairman of News Limited in Australia. I had known Ken for 25 years, and while it had been a long time since I had worked with him, I was chuffed to be invited to this event and to mingle with more than 200 guests including politicians, captains of industry and News executives —

Punsand Bay… the centre of civilisation at The Tip.

arguably the most connected people in the nation. For most of them this was a relaxing weekend away from the pressures of their jobs; a welcome escape from the winter winds of Sydney or Melbourne. For us it was an eye-opening reminder of how remote from this rarefied life we had become. Where Punsand was an open wooden building made of local logs nestling among palms and natural scrub, Hayman was a sprawling complex of concrete, marble and glass, a $350 million monument to the last word in luxury, decorated with statues of glass sea goddesses lying over languid waterfalls, bronze brolgas stalking in tinkling fountains, soapstone Chinese lions guarding sweeping ponds of koi carp, surrounded by manicured lawns, hedges of hibiscus and vibrantly coloured Hobie cats, drifting, waiting for a

puff of wind off well-coiffed beaches. Purposeful staff clop-clopped over marble floors between the deep pile carpets and delivered well-trained smiles and salutations. A shop window displayed a tiny T-shirt bearing the words 'Trainee Millionaire', and the prices for the designer apparel on display reinforced the need to be one, well-trained indeed, before entering.

The Hayman weekend — a brief brush with the lifestyles of the rich and famous — was, we figured, as remote from the reality of most Australians' lives as our camp on the beach at Punsand Bay. We had travelled in a weekend from one extreme to the other; from a relaxed, egalitarian resting place, utterly free of airs and graces, to the golden peak of aspirational luxury, available only to the well-heeled chosen few. We flew back to The

The Road Warriors from Gunshot Creek *(l to r)* – Warwick DeRose, Peter Mill, Warren Ackerly and Alan Briggs.

Tip, reflecting on the stark contrasts, and when we got back to our tent on the sand, we were greeted with a genuine and cheery, 'Welcome home.'

West of The Tip is one of the 137 islands which dot the sea from Cape York to Papua New Guinea. The most immediate is named Possession Island, where it all began, in a legal sense. For it was here that Lieutenant James Cook, having rounded the Cape and observed the coast disappearing southward, calculated that he had arrived at the pre-discovered shores of William Janz. Beating against the south-east trade winds, he was unable to make it safely back to the mainland, so he went ashore on the island, through jagged coral and rocks, with a handful of marines. There he formally took possession of the whole of the eastern coast of Australia 'from

Making friends at Punsand Bay with a green tree frog.

the latitude of 38 deg south to this place' in the name of King George III, and fired a musket volley which was answered from the ship. Canons would have been used to formally salute this addition to the British possessions, but they had been jettisoned south of Cooktown, to lighten the *Endeavour* as it struggled to stay afloat after its encounter with the Great Barrier Reef.

Standing on a rocky knob on the western side of the island, Cook may have doubted the long-term value of the coast he had surveyed. While he had been impressed by the meadows he had seen first at Botany Bay, he was much less enthusiastic about the coast to the north, and especially doubtful about the ferocity of the natives he had seen at Cooktown. But he could not have guessed that more than a century after his declaration on 22 August 1770, a goldmine would be sunk just 30 metres from the spot on which he stood, and more than 3000 ounces of precious metal extracted before the vein ran out. The entrance to the shaft is still open — dark, dangerous and forbidding — but the mine is now just a home for bats. Nevertheless, its presence is a metaphor for the unknown riches Cook claimed in the name of Mad King George, simply because he judged the land to be empty of any form of civilisation he understood.

A plaque — gold lettering on polished granite — is fixed to a white cairn marking the spot. It was put there for the 1988 Australian Bicentenary, replacing an original bronze plaque which had been stolen some years before and used — according to local legend — as a barbecue plate in a suburban Brisbane garden. We guffawed at this quintessentially Ocker tale: where else in the world would a significant piece of national history do duty burning chops and snags on

a backyard barbie? The plate was recovered from a 1990 garage sale, and is now in a Brisbane museum, safe from the further indignity of fatty snags.

Our visit to Possession Island was a detour on a 40-kilometre run south to the mouth of the Jardine, where fishing guide Scott Oldfield had promised we would catch barramundi. We left in the mid-afternoon to take advantage of the early evening tides, with Scott confident he could safely navigate home by the light of the night's full moon.

We made our way through liquid gold seas as the sun set massively over the Gulf, and Scott expertly threaded his way through the sandbars which make the mouth of the Jardine accessible to experts only. We caught several barra, and Scott poked his way through seemingly unbreachable barriers of overhanging mangroves to take us to his favourite barra hole where he had triumphed in a recent fishing competition. It was a delightful night, but the moon was sinking low on the horizon as we left the Jardine and headed north, our wake shimmering silver in the moonlight behind, and the lights of the Seisia community port blinking green ahead of us. A few minutes into the trip the moon disappeared behind clouds, and we faced almost 40 kilometres of reef-strewn water in the blackness of night. I couldn't escape the feeling that this was one of the greatest follies of my life as Scott occasionally swept the sea ahead with his torch. Three times we ran aground on sand before we made it back to Punsand at 2 am, greatly relieved. Only then did Scott admit he chose to risk running aground on the sandbars near the shore, because 100 metres across the channel he couldn't see were the jagged fangs of treacherous coral reefs!

Possession Island . . . the original plaque became a barbecue plate.

Two weeks up, two days back. After nine weeks on the road, we didn't spare the horses on the run down the coast. Somewhere on the endless corrugations north of Laura we split our rear differential, and puzzled over a build-up of oil spattering on the rear window until Rockhampton, where we had the choice of a three-day wait for a new one or a quick $50 weld. The weld still holds today.

We spent half a day watching the whales in Hervey Bay. Six days after leaving the Cape we arrived, weary, in Sydney to prepare for our next departure.

Cable Beach, Broome, Western Australia . . . camel rides at sunset.

chapter nine

We often have trouble defining our national identity. Perhaps it's because the processes involved are, after more than 200 years, still incomplete. Perhaps it's because we have changed our self-perceptions so often. At the beginning, we knew we were little more than a conveniently distant prison camp where the dregs of another society could be consigned and forgotten. Slowly, we came to recognise our worth as a colonial outpost growing rich on the twin pillars of golden nuggets and the golden fleece, and we demanded our right to govern our own affairs. After federation, we didn't hesitate to prove we were a nation of sturdy, self-sacrificing youths, ready to answer the call to defend the Motherland and, by so doing, snatch our manhood from the glorious failure of Anzac. We came to see ourselves as a fortress island of white in a sea of perilous yellow; rejecting those from the outside but ready to look after our mates in tough times. In my lifetime we have begun to take pride from the more modern definition of ourselves as a tolerant, inclusive, multicultural people, maintaining at least one constant legacy from our bastard beginnings: our egalitarian willingness to give a fair go to all. When we have made peace among ourselves over our capacity to extend that same fair go to our indigenous people, thrown off the final constitutional ties to Britain, and stand at the dawn of the new millennium as a fully independent Australian republic, waving our new flag, perhaps we will find it easier to define ourselves.

These processes aren't easy; nor are they sudden. But from time to time they are given a fillip from unexpected sources as *expressions* of Australianness which are more easily absorbed into our consciousness than definitions. When artists Tom Roberts and Arthur Streeton limned their idealist bushland scenes they not only portrayed distinctive Australian, rather than European, light for the first time, but built into their works Australian emotions. Lost in the bush, inside a shearing shed, dusty drovers on horses at full stretch; these were the emotional hooks for Australian life at the turn of the century. Sidney Nolan and Albert Tucker made further leaps with their realist works: Nolan, in his larrikin Ned Kelly series, grasping the deep-seated Australian emotional link between underdogs and oppressors, and Tucker reflecting the harshness of war with his portrayal of women.

In the early 1980s a young designer, art director and painter named Ken Done burst into our consciousness. His sunny, simple, exuberant art seemed to radiate the essence of modern Australia, encapsulating the boldness, the vibrance and the insouciance of our good-natured bays'n'beaches lifestyle in statements of resounding colour, big and bright, which often rendered form incidental.

Today Ken, and his designer wife Judy, are an extraordinarily successful team, and their brand is so well known and respected around the world that in Japan, for instance, 'Done' is seen as shorthand for Australia.

The passion of Ken's work extends to (or perhaps leaps from) the man himself. He is an enthusiastic, emotional Australian, instinctively confident about his work and our place in the world. He doesn't subscribe to the self-doubt which niggles at many of us who, paradoxically, say Australia is the best country on earth, yet worry about our many troubles. For Ken, Australia *is* the best place in the world.

In recent years, Ken and Judy have swept aside their global assault on feel-good design and fashion, withdrawing from partnership agreements where final approval for products was in the hands of others. They found no joy in seeing their designs adapted for what they felt were inappropriate uses, or created by others in their signature style. They found irritation at the gleeful chant of their opponents and detractors: Over-Done. They shrugged as their name, their brand, withdrew from American and Japanese chainstores: so what? For Ken and Judy, less became more — fewer hassles, fewer disappointments that their partners didn't quite *get* it; fewer employees; more time for themselves; more time for golf; more time for discovery; and more time for Ken to paint.

It is not unusual for artists who leap outside the conventional to be dismissed by their contemporaries. Ken Done has been pilloried at home, while being lavishly praised in Paris, London and Tokyo. He has been a victim of his own success — the tall poppy syndrome which afflicts many of those who rise above the norm in Australia. In time, when the memory of his Sydney

Ken Done paints in his cave above Chinamans Beach, Sydney Harbour.

Harbour T-shirts is replaced by an unbiased assessment of his later works — and those yet to come in the most creative period of his life — he may be belatedly granted a place at the forefront in the evolution of Australian art.

We lived near each other on Sydney's Chinaman's Beach, and as Judy walked their old dog, Spot, we'd chat over our fence. As this project grew in my mind, I wondered how Ken would meet the challenge of painting Lake Eyre: it's all white out there, with the sun on the lake, and he's Australia's foremost colourist. How would he paint white? But the gods conspired, and by spring 1997, autumn and winter rains across the centre had turned the desert into a mass of wildflowers and sturdy, determined stockfeed which would keep the cattle in good condition for at least two seasons. So we set

out for the blooming desert to see if we could *feel* the essence of Australia.

We linked up in Adelaide, Ken and Judy checking out of their splendid marble suite at the Hyatt hotel and observing with (I couldn't tell which) suspicion or anticipation the neat trailer which would unfold as their tent home for the next week.

We set sail for the north, through Port Augusta, Quorn and Hawker, shadowing the pale purple Flinders Ranges, to the old railway town of Beltana. A little further north — just south of the coal-mining town of Leigh Creek — was our first objective, the towering buttresses of Yalkarinha Gorge in Trebilcock Creek, at dusk. This was Opera in the Outback, a splendid but contradictory notion if ever there were one: take the soaring crescendos of high opera out of the rococo

After the Opera . . . party time with the rollicking Bushwhackers.

splendour of La Scala et al, and place it in the rocky majesty of a dry creek bed in the outback; discard bow ties and tails in favour of Akubra hats and R. M. Williams boots; and merge the crystal clarity of soprano Dame Kiri Te Kanawa's voice with the haunting bass rhythms of Dreamtime songs performed by the local Adnyamathanha women's choir — all beneath the ghostly branches of river gums and the canopy of the Milky Way. Only in Australia!

This was the second Opera in the Outback concert, and people had come to it from across the nation and, indeed, from around the world. Deluging rain had made the first two days of the festivities a nightmare for organisers and concert-goers alike, but it cleared for the main event. This was a massive logistic operation, involving 70 semi-trailer loads of equipment, including more than 1100 lights, 37 switchboards, 42 power generators, 300 mobile toilets and showers, 13 hectares of camp sites, and almost 100,000 meals to be supplied over the four-day event, washed down with 1500 dozen bottles of wine and 100,000 cans of beer. Seven satellite dishes provided communications, including temporary Telstra payphones in the gorge.

The program began at dusk. As the sun disappeared, leaving blushing pink in the sky, the undersides of the white-boughed sprawling gums were lit with orange, white, pink and blue lights. Cockatoos screeched and crickets chirped as an Adnyamathanha elder welcomed us to his people's land; moths fluttered towards the bright stage lights, buzzing the orchestra, and the Southern Cross peered through the branches of the trees. Then Dame Kiri began a program of high opera classics and lighter musical fare. She was at her most impressive with pure opera: somehow Irving Berlin, Richard Rodgers and Andrew Lloyd Webber seemed out of place — both from her, and in this setting. But then, so did the chardonnay set from the cities, and the bemused look on some of the faces of the bush folk reflected this.

But not the Bushwhackers. This internationally-known Australian bush band from Sydney, lagerphone, fiddle, squeezebox and all, performed for the audience after the main concert and as the food and wine flowed; the night of grand opera turned into a swinging, rollicking bush party. The young danced with the old, Japanese girls rocked along to *Waltzing Matilda*, and black stockmen and white station owners' wives kicked up the dust, together, colourblind and enthusiastically.

I lived up here when I was three. Leigh Creek, Copley, Telford; they were all familiar names from my early years, yet I have virtually no memory of the places. I do recall two incidents: picking my way through saltbush, prickles hurting my feet, crying out to my brother: 'Wait for me! Wait for me!' It's tough being the youngest kid in dry saltbush country. I also remember hiding in fear under the tankstand while my father searched for me: we kids had been playing house in the foundation trenches of a building he was working on, and we had defecated in a trench. Was he annoyed at this behaviour? Does a kid shit in a trench?

My family has other Leigh Creek stories: how my brother and I, with some other kids, climbed on to the scaffolding of the new school building and threw to the ground all the bricks which had been stacked up there, ready for laying; how my mother kept weather records at Leigh Creek, and never saw the thermometer go below 96°F (35°C) for the entire month of February; how we used a Coolgardie safe — a wooden box draped with a wet hessian bag — to try to keep food cool, but the temperature inside was 90 degrees so we became the first folk in Leigh Creek to get a kerosene refrigerator.

My mother also tells the story of how, aged three, I threw my boot out the open window of *The Ghan* — a huffing, puffing, smelly and sooty old steam train in those days — somewhere around Pitchie Ritchie Pass. (Who are the wags who persistently paint out the first letters of each word on the sign which marks this route through the southern Flinders Ranges?) She reported the loss to the driver when we reached Port Augusta and, believe it or not, he spotted it beside the track on his return journey, stopped, picked it up and returned it to her. I guess train drivers did things like that in the 1940s.

The Ghan is the subject of another story. Back in the old days, before the new line was built from Tarcoola to The Alice, the track went via Leigh Creek to Marree, and along the Oodnadatta Track, through rivers and creeks which were mostly dry. But when the rains came, washaways and protracted delays were common. The story goes that a

The Beltana races . . . camels, donkeys, ferrets and waddling ducks.

pregnant woman was becoming increasingly agitated by flood delays, and repeatedly asked the driver: 'When are we going to get there?' After hearing the same question many times over some days, the driver snapped and demanded to know: 'What's the hurry?'

'I think I'm about to have my baby.'

'Well, you shouldn't have got on the train in that condition.'

'I wasn't in this condition when I got on the train!'

Boom boom.

After the opera, we went to the Beltana races, where the city and the bush came together for a day of bizarre fun and games. If horse races were on the program, I missed them, being far too preoccupied with the ferret races, the camel races, the donkey races and the Indian waddling duck races. Wendy sat in the dust, under a broad umbrella, for a wellness massage. Ken and Judy mingled with the crowd, marvelling at the assortment of hats, and Ken did a drawing of the scene which he called Race Meeting. It showed black and white, together.

At Marree we fuelled up to the brim and took on our last supplies. This is where the roads divide — left to Oodnadatta and Alice Springs; right to Birdsville. Travellers leaving Marree are warned by a large roadside sign: 'You are entering remote territory', followed by a checklist: 'Do you have water? Spare tyres? Fuel supplies? Food?' I glanced at it and said 'yes' to each. Ken and Judy later said it had a profound impact on them, because never before had

Camels ready to race at Beltana.

they been to a place where remoteness itself could be life-threatening.

Our destination was Muloorina station, 55 kilometres north of Marree, across naked gibber plains, a horizon-to-horizon vista of nothingness which left Ken and Judy awed. 'There's got to be a word to describe this,' I said to Ken, again rejecting *big, huge, vast, massive* or even *gargantuan*. 'Let's think about it,' he said, as we drove out of the desert, into Muloorina, an oasis of trees, homesteads, wool and machinery sheds, shearer's quarters, an aircraft hangar, and the thing which made it all possible — a shady billabong of permanent water, overhung by branches, lined by reeds, and rippled by fish and swooping birds.

Muloorina is here because water is here. It surges up from the Great Artesian Basin, through a bore pipe sunk 540 metres into the desert, 20 litres of it every second under 120 pounds per square inch pressure, too hot, at 56°C, to hold your hand in. And as it flows, steaming, into the billabong, it drives an electric turbine which provides the entire homestead complex with its power.

What genius! A sustainable source of energy drawn from a sustainable source of life. This is the legacy of Stephen Elliot Lovell Price, who completed school to grade 1; who never learned to read or write anything other than his own name, yet designed and built machines which tamed the desert. Elliot Price was the grandfather of the station's current owner, Malcolm Mitchell, who speaks reverently of the achievements of the man he calls 'Gran'ad'.

'He came here in 1935–36, with Grandma and three kids, plus all their worldly goods, on the back of an old truck with a stationary engine bolted on the tray,' said Malcolm. 'The engine drove the rear wheels via a pulley

Malcolm Mitchell . . . the outflow from Gran'ad's bore-water turbine.

with three gears. It took him three weeks to get up from Peterborough in the mid-north.

'He had been up this way in the twenties, putting down a bore out towards Anna Creek for Sidney Kidman. Muloorina had been a government camel-breeding station, raising camels to carry goods up and down the Birdsville Track, but the government abandoned it in 1920. By the time Gran'ad got here the camels were feral and had eaten all the bush. It took years to grow back after he shot a lot of them. He had only two wells then, and employed Aborigines to shepherd his sheep and lock 'em away from the dingoes at night.

'He died here in 1969, aged 71, and is buried up on the rise there.' A plaque by the grave notes: 'Largely by his own character

Malcolm Mitchell . . . Gran'ad's junk heap at Muloorina station, South Australia.

and enterprise he pioneered and developed this property for more than 30 years. It now stands as a shining example of what can be achieved in the face of hardship and adversity.'

An incredible example from one of the great Australian bush pioneers. With no education except that from the university of hard knocks, he designed and built an amazing range of contraptions. Apart from the bore water turbine to deliver power, Elliot Price made two gyrocopters, cobbled together, Heath-Robinson style, from bits of wood, steel and corrugated iron, and powered by Volkswagen engines. One of them crashed; the shell of the other, grounded by the Department of Civil Aviation because it didn't have dual magnetos and other safety

systems, lies in the Muloornia tip, its corrugated iron stabilisers still intact. Alongside is the skeleton of a gee-whiz fun machine made for the kids. It consisted of an old car seat bolted to a wooden base, complete with safety rails, and four plough discs fitted underneath. The name of the game was to take it on to the firm salt crust of Lake Eyre, tow it behind a Landrover, drive in an arc until it was at the end of a whip, like a waterskier, and release it. It would spin madly across the lake surface accompanied by the howls of delight of kids who clearly worshipped Gran'ad.

There was also a sheep rattling device. Necessity being the mother of invention, when drought filled the fleeces with dust and made shearing a near-impossibility, Elliot

The Coorong, South Australia . . . saved from pollution.

Price designed a contraption which, driven by a vehicle power take-off, shook and rattled the sand from their wool.

All these items, together with the original Second World War Blitz and trailer which carried *Bluebird* on to the lake for Donald Campbell's 1964 world speed record of 401.3 miles (650 kilometres) per hour (still the fastest speed attained by a vehicle driven through its wheels), lie in the Muloorina tip. Nothing is thrown out here. It's an incredible junkyard; a museum of 20th century mechanical development and one man's tinkering genius.

Ken, strolling about the Muloorina environs soon after dawn, picked up a piece of rusted flat steel, a piece of bent No 8 fencing wire and the broken remains of a

Ken Done finds art in junk at Muloorina station.

steel comb. Only an artist could have seen in these pieces of scrap a form which, when stuck together with Araldite, made a miniature sculpture evoking the sun, the sparse trees, the cattle and the land. Finding bent, broken, rusted and forged shapes of steel in the tip, he made a sculpture in the style of Robert Klippel in the sand and prostrated himself to photograph it. Malcolm looked on with bemused interest. For him, a tip is a tip; a place to store things which might one day come in handy; a place to put things out of sight when they are worn out or broken. Ken saw it as a treasure trove of shapes; an archeological Aladdin's Cave of the way we were, and will never be again.

We pored over large-scale maps with Malcolm and his wife, Colleen, as he briefed us before we set off to the lake. There is just one approved road leading to the shore from the station, and casual visitors aren't entitled to move off it. But Malcolm and Colleen offered us the status of guests, and sketched on the map the approximate position of station tracks which would take us further afield. He suggested we camp at a spot called Prescott Point, where the *Bluebird* base was established for Campbell's runs across Madigan Gulf. To get there we had to pick up a shotline which intersected the track leading to a place called Scalloped Bay. These shotlines were bulldozed, straight as a die, many years ago as part of oil search activities. New technology makes them unnecessary these days, which is fortunate, because their scars are a disfiguring blight on the landscape. But the line we wanted must have been very faint because, try as we might, we couldn't find it. Instead, we found ourselves bogged in soft mud on a claypan a couple of kilometres from our destination.

Getting bogged is embarrassing. Travelling to Adelaide to pick up Ken and Judy, I had taken my mother, Alfreda, on a nostalgic visit to our old stamping grounds in Western Victoria, then up the South Australian coast towards Robe, where she had spent her honeymoon with my father at the end of 1938.

We had time on our side so I turned off Highway 1 south of Robe to look at the lake system encompassing Lakes George, St Clair and Eliza. The south-east of South Australia was naturally a low-lying wetland, but it has been extensively drained to create rich grazing land, and has been environmentally abused by the large cellulose industry feeding off massive pine forests in the area. Years ago, as editor of the Adelaide *Sunday Mail*, I had campaigned against this damage and achieved tighter controls over the industry's effluent discharges which no longer colour the lakes pollution-pink as a by-product of our love affair with designer-coloured toilet paper.

We found ourselves on a well-graded dirt road called Bog Lane, running alongside the Little Dip Conservation Park. I saw a narrow track leading, I thought, to the beach, and turned into it. I wanted to see the sea, enjoy the majesty of the sandhills I knew to be out there, and maybe, just maybe, drive up the beach into Robe. That would be a bit of adventuring the old dear, at 85, could brag to her friends about.

We passed a sign which warned of soft sand and turned into a side track up a sandhill. The wheels dug in, and as I reversed out Alfreda suggested we return to the road.

'Mother,' I said sternly, 'I know what I'm doing. I've done all this before. This is like a highway compared to some of the tracks we've been on.'

'Yes, dear,' she said.

I found another track and we powered up

it, good as gold, and down the sweeping side of the sandhill towards the beach. The sand was soft, but presented no trouble. Deep tracks led on to the beach and continued along its high side as far as I could see.

No problems: just follow the wheel ruts; 4WD, high ratio.

We got 50 metres on to the beach before the Pajero stopped. I muttered a curse under my breath (mothers are good at moderating language, even in difficulties) and walked towards the water. It would firm up where it was wet. No. It got softer. I figured the best way forward was back. I put it in low ratio, locked the diffs and tried to reverse. No way. No back. No forward. Stuck.

Now, it's one thing to be stuck. It's quite another thing to admit it to your old mum who you've just shut up with an emphatic

'Mother, I know what I'm doing.' My silent question was: 'How am I going to get out of this?' The embarrassment, I meant. Oh, and the sand bog, too. Within seconds of telling her she was safe and protected from calamity with me, who knew it all, had done it all, I had put her in a jam.

'We're stuck,' I said, and she nodded. Bless her. Just a nod. Not a gloating, cutting 'I told you so,' or even an 'I know' through gritted teeth — code for 'You stupid bloody idiot.' Just a simple, accepting, trusting nod. I got the shovel down from the roof rack and cleared the sand behind the tyres. I dropped the tyre pressure to about 25 pounds. No luck. I dug out more sand, front and back, and lowered the tyres to 20 pounds. I gave it another go, rocking back and forth. No

Bogged on the beach with Alfreda . . . 'Mother, I know what I'm doing!'

way. The car was digging itself deeper and deeper into the sand, until ultimately it sat with its chassis, gearbox and diffs *in* the sand. I looked around for posts or timber I could use to anchor my winch. There was nothing except for small bushes which I put under the wheels for grip. Still no good. I sweated, dug under wheels again but watched as they turned freely, with no grip at all, spewing sand into the air. Four-wheel drive? No-wheel drive!

Mother sat in the car some of the time, saying little. She got out to pick up driftwood and shells to help the tyres grip. She needed to go to the loo, and struggled to the end of the beach, her walking stick giving no support in the soft sand. How long, I wondered, since this urbane and sophisticated woman had squat-peed in the bush? Would her indignity corrode our relationship? What could I do to demonstrate I was in command; that I had a plan; that I had a way of getting out?

It was she who first mentioned the satphone. At first I refused to entertain the idea. I must get out myself; I must use my knowledge; I must use my common sense; I must use my bush craft. I must.

'Please use the phone, dear,' she said. 'It would be sensible. We could get help.'

Then: 'Please. Please do it for me.'

What do you say? 'Mother, I know what I'm doing' seemed inadequate, because clearly I didn't anymore. But to do it for her meant I had to admit my failure; face my embarrassment; capitulate in the face of a crisis, and submit to the greater forces of others.

'Do it for me,' she said again. I reached for the phone, called the Telstra operator, and got the number for the South Australian Royal Automobile Association. I heard the RAA contractor at Robe call across his

workshop: 'Hey, Robbie, there's a guy stuck on the beach. Want to earn some money?' Robbie obviously gave the thumbs up to that, because the contractor told me: 'We'll be there in 30 minutes.' And they were.

I introduced myself to Robbie and his mate Steve with the old line: 'Hi, I'm Mark and I haven't been so embarrassed since my helicopter was repossessed.' They laughed as they assessed the situation, estimated the length of ropes, chains and snatch straps we could put together to give them firm ground and traction. Their first try was to pull on the rope and snatch straps. No go. They pulled with the snatch straps only, hoping the elasticity in the straps would hoick me out like a stone leaving a catapult. I didn't feel a thing.

And so it went. Collective heads at work. Alfreda stood high on the beach, in the sun,

Bogged near Lake Eyre . . . a complicated recovery.

Wendy's hat on her high hair, watching as we pulled it this way and pulled it that way. We got out the winch, but it just pulled their anchoring ute towards the beach. Nothing was working. They talked of going back to Robe for a tractor. They told me not to feel bad about it; plenty of people had got stuck here. I looked at the tide, now closer to the car. We decided to dig it out. They put in four-fifths of the effort as we cleared the underside of the car. As the sand was removed, the weight of the vehicle returned to the wheels. I dropped the tyre pressures even further, and we tied on the snatch straps again for one more, heroic effort.

I put it into reverse; 4WD, low ratio, diffs locked. Gave it heaps. And it sprang out of its hole, furiously revving backwards across the beach. On firm ground at last, Robbie commented that the snatch straps never got tight. A muted triumph: I had driven out on my own!

We laughed the laughs of relieved men as we cracked a beer and pumped up the tyres. Alfreda made her way along the beach to ceremoniously note the names of our saviours: Robert Scott and Steven Kennett. Thanks, fellas, and how much do I owe you? They wouldn't take more than a slab of beer each. Don't let anyone tell you the great Australian tradition of helping a bloke in trouble is dead.

At Lake Eyre, our bog in the clay was complicated by the trailer we were towing. Ken toiled in the sun to dig a hole for the spare wheel to anchor our winch so that we could pull the trailer free of the car, but then we couldn't get the winch to work. Helpful advice from Wendy and Judy — 'Are you sure it's not back to front?' — didn't help,

Out of the bog . . . a storm develops over Lake Eyre.

either. So we manhandled the trailer free and eventually got out.

Sharp-eyed Judy spotted a track to the west, and we followed it to a bluff on the lake shore. The sun was setting, so we found a spot in the lee of the hill and pitched our tents, a trifle skew-whiff in the rising wind. We sat at the edge of a ten-metre drop, blown away by the infinity of the lake before us, and Ken proffered the solution to my long search for an appropriate word.

'Vaaaaaaaaaaaaaaaaaaaaaaaaaast,' he screamed into the wind, before adding: 'With 24 As.' Why didn't I think of that? 'But even that trivialises it,' said ken, 'because it's a vision you see from the front of your eyes, the side of your eyes and the back of your head. When you focus on the horizon, if you can discern it in the shimmering heat, you realise

you can see absolutely forever.' Or at least, we figured from the map, 25 kilometres to the eastern shore of the lake, where hillocks or sandhills appeared suspended on the horizon.

'I can't paint this,' said Ken. 'No-one in the world can, because there isn't a big enough canvas.' But the artist, undaunted, began to sketch, fountain pen lines scribbling across the blank pages of a hardback sketchbook. 'The only way to approach this is to paint something of your feeling about it, an idea about it, or something that triggers within the viewer the absolute majesty, the amazingness, the phantasmagorical-ness — I don't have enough words to describe how old it is or how big it is. And then you have to try to make some references to the people who were here before, the things that have happened here, to try to put it all together.'

The vast expanses of Lake Eyre... no canvas big enough.

The pen sketched ideas, and then added colour: colour by word rather than crayon. Starting at the top of the page, Ken wrote: Dove grey, lilac/mauve, eggshell grey/blue, pale peach, yellow, pink and yellow . . . Then came the horizon, and the colour notes continued to the bottom of the page, sensing the reflections: pale blue, mauve, warm fur, grey/khaki, mouse brown, and then the blobs of sage green dotting the shoreline below us. So much for the theory that it's all white out here! The lake, when dry and salt crusted, is harshly, powerfully, squintingly white in the sun; but when rain dissolves the salt it turns to a dun and disappointing brown, streaked by different hues reflecting the sky in its wettest parts.

The light constantly changed as Ken sketched, and if his colour chart was right for one instant, it had changed the next, and the next. Shafts of light broke through the cloud cover and lit up the lake; the warm fur and khaki colours took on pink hues, and crisscrossing, crystalline slashes of light formed the letter 'W' falling from the sky on to the lake amid the clouds and rainstorms to our west. We were in for a buffeting storm that night.

The next day, as we walked on the lake, our camp on the cliff a mere dot behind us, our tracks etched into the ever-softer mud, Ken said softly: 'It's like walking on a sea of khaki.' Back at the base he immediately made a painting with that title, adding at the last moment, marks evoking Aboriginal carvings and a *Bluebird* speed record car . . . 'some references to the people who were here before and the things that have happened here.'

The people who were here before. The things that have happened here. It was a prescient remark. In a satphone call to Malcolm and Colleen to confirm our safety I told them we hadn't found the shotline, but were camped on a bluff west of our intended destination. Malcolm knew the spot, and said it was of great interest to scientists because fragments of the eggs of giant emus had been found here. Giant emus! We immediately renamed our home Dinosaur Bluff.

By a pure fluke we had plonked ourselves beside one of the most interesting and little-known scientific research sites in the nation. Here, on chaotic ridges of gypcrete which looked like the skin of a lizard with a reptilian resistance to the ravages of time, was the evidence of life going back 100 millennia — evidence to support the belief that the first human invasion of this land had an impact on

Lake Eyre from 'Dinosaur Bluff'… a buffeting strom.

the natural environment every bit as profound as the recent invasion of Europeans.

The giant emu, or *Genyornis newtoni*, wasn't a dinosaur but a ponderous, lumbering bird which roamed towards the end of the Pleistocene period about 50–60,000 years ago. These birds were of a quite different lineage to today's emu, being three metres high and weighing up to 400 kilograms. They were part of the mega fauna — giant kangaroos, wombats and the cow-like diprotodons — which roamed Australia and feasted on lush tropical plants, leaving their bones to be found in fossil abundance at Riversleigh, Queensland, and at Lake Callabonna, 200 kilometres east of our camp.

The mega fauna, including *Genyornis newtoni*, disappeared suddenly about 45,000 years ago. Why? Scientists speculate it was because human migration over the land bridge from Asia occurred about 50,000 years ago, and the first migrants to this land

hunted the plentiful fauna to extinction. A critical site for evidence of this was here, where we sat. Scientists at the Australian National University, led by climatologist John McGee, have made frequent trips to this site to hunt for scraps of *Genyornis* eggs which, after isotope and DNA testing, have given clues to their diet and, therefore, the vegetation of the area at the time.

It is part of a remarkable scientific jigsaw, and the only tragedy is that John McGee is having to fight government budget cuts to be able to continue his research.

We talked into the night. About art: 'The drawings I did today were essentially caveman stuff,' said Ken. 'Man making his mark on something is a very caveman act, but what might happen to these drawings, how they might be used, where they might be exposed, where they might lead to, is extremely modern, so that's why I would like to be thought of as a modern artist.'

Ken Done creates on the shores of Lake Eyre… 'Like walking on a sea of khaki.'

After the storm… shafts of light reflect on the wet salt of Lake Eyre.

About Australia: We are approaching *our* millennium, and we want to have our house in order when it comes. As a nation, we seem to have lost our confidence. We love our country and wouldn't dream of living anywhere else, but we are shaken and unsettled by the problems facing us — coping with change, junkies, crooked cops, pernicious politicians and the economy. Out here, in our remoteness and the lake's vaaaaaaaaaaaaaaaaaaaaaaaaaastness, time merges the pastpresentfuture in a way which makes that world irrelevant. 2001 is just another tick in time out here. The lake has seen many millennia before.

On Malcolm: That chiselled, quintessential Australian face, itself a landscape with a hat on it, which showed so much pride as he took us through Gran'ad's junk heap — relics of an uneducated but remarkably smart mind which created this classical, romantic outback station beside a billabong amid the gibber.

Cavemen; pastpresentfuture; relics. Somehow, *Genyornis newtoni* joined us for our time at Dinosaur Bluff.

When we set up our camp, Ken unfurled his design for a new Australian flag. It is simple — a designer's solution; a representation of the Southern Cross — with the four main stars in golden yellow boldly placed on a rectangle of azure blue. The fifth star, the five-pointed ellipse, slips neatly into the lower right quadrant.

We flew it atop my beach fishing rod, anchored against the stiff wind by a single star picket pole on the bluff. It had a nice feel about it. We knew there was no-one here to share it with us, but it was our statement: here we were, remote from civilisation, adventurers under the Southern Cross, able to define our own Australian identity, and

salute it silently with a warm, embracing smile. Here, there would be no fights picked; nor would we be pilloried by those offended by the emphatic expunging of the British Union Jack, rampant top left.

I was particularly aware of the sensitivity over the Australian flag. In our earliest meetings, the committee of the Australian Republican Movement (ARM) made the decision to be a single-issue body, and not to take on board the republican cart all and sundry issues which would so weigh it down that the wheels could fall off. So, although the leading lights in the ARM supported a change in the flag, we bit our lips on this question, saying it was a matter for another time.

During my last stint on radio — on Sydney's 2GB in 1996 — I knew I could generate a passionate half-hour of talkback by saying we should get rid of the Union Jack. The great majority of callers were older people, mostly savagely opposed to my point of view. There was no surprise in that, because most of my listeners were in what the radio industry calls the 55+ demographic, and if the session had been conducted on a station with a younger audience profile, the response, I am sure, would have been the reverse. So I never regarded these outpourings as representative samples of the entire public, but they did represent a sincerely held point of view. Time and again, the arguments were put: our flag represents our history and we must not relinquish the Union Jack because it is part of our history; Australians have fought and died under this flag, and it would be an insult to our Diggers to change it; we have worn this flag proudly as a sporting nation for almost a century, and our athletes' achievements would be diminished if we tinkered with it. And so on...

They are spurious arguments. The flag was

the result of a design competition launched in 1903 with the proviso that the Union Jack must appear top right; it was modified in 1907, but its use was restricted to the role of various ensigns for the armed services. It wasn't our national flag during the First or Second World Wars; nor in Korea where we fought under the United Nations flag, nor even, technically, in Vietnam, which was never a declared war, and where we fought under the U.S. military command. The blue ensign became our official national flag by an Act of Parliament in 1953. But, it's true, most of us have grown up with the current Australian flag, and we have all felt pride as it has been raised to honour Australians of achievement: the men and women who died in past wars, our Olympic heroes, sporting teams and our representatives on a myriad of world stages. I mean no disrespect to that flag, but we have now outgrown it.

When Australia becomes a republic, it is unthinkable we should not have a new flag. As we update our constitutional arrangements, so too should we update our national logo in a way which clearly expresses something about all of us. That is the appeal of the Southern Cross; we all live under it. Always have; always will. And the dominant feature of the current flag, other than the Union Jack, is the Southern Cross. Only an incremental change is required to modernise this existing symbol of Australia. (Another possible candidate for an instantly recognisable Australian symbol is the kangaroo, but how do we explain that we shoot it, eat it and can it for pet food?)

There is no logic whatsoever in retaining the British flag in the corner of our flag when we break the ties that bind us to the British monarchy. To those who say it would be sacrilege to remove a part of our history, I say history remains with that flag which was our

Ready to roll . . . Judy and Ken Done after breaking camp at Dinosaur Bluff.

Jackboot Bore, on Muloorina station . . . warm and welcome artesian water for Ken Done.

national logo for almost the entire second half of the 20th century. Our new design should make new history.

When we broke camp at Dinosaur Bluff, I fixed the fishing pole to the Pajero, and we drove into the desert with the flag fluttering above us. This was, in part, a statement about us and who we were. But it was also a safety measure: unlikely as it was that we would meet anyone else out here, sandhills can swallow a vehicle from another's line of sight, and flying a flag in places like the Simpson Desert is standard procedure to warn others of your presence.

We drove to a spot on the map called Jackboot Bore, catching glimpses of the southern part of Lake Eyre as we went. There we rendezvoused with Malcolm and Colleen Mitchell, and their daughter Lee Anne. We gratefully ducked behind a piece of corrugated iron and into an old bathtub for a

welcome shower, the water sprinkling warm from the artesian well behind a welded sign saying 'JAC BOOT'. Malcolm had made it as a school project many years before, but the 'K' had been knocked out.

Malcolm and Colleen had offered to guide us to some spectacular viewing points on the lake shore, and to our next camp site. This was to become an extraordinary drive: 107 kilometres through the wilderness. No roads; not even tyre tracks to follow. Just Malcolm's dead reckoning to take us from place to place across saltbush-studded sandhills and plains, through creeks and washaways, across claypans and scalds, over sharp gibber ridges and along cliffs reminiscent of the Grand Canyon.

I would never have attempted this journey on my own. It would be absolute folly. But this is Malcolm's life and his property. He may not have been to these places for five years, but he had grown up here, where the land is so flat and the landmarks so few, and he instinctively knew precisely where he was.

Ken asked: 'Do you ever get lost?'

'Not out here,' Malcolm said. 'I just know my way around. But I'm not too sure of myself in the cities. I'm getting more relaxed in Adelaide these days, but I don't like places like Sydney. It's much too big.'

There was a short silence. Then he added: 'I did get lost once. Lego Land on the Gold Coast. I came out through the wrong gate and I didn't know where I was for almost half an hour.'

He said it so laconically, so unselfconsciously, it seemed a reasonable proposition. And it was. Those who have grown up in the cities instinctively develop the same appreciation for landmarks: turn left at the GPO; first exit after the bridge; go right at the Ampol station; first bus stop after the park; whatever: landmarks help define our existences. Malcolm's landmarks were his secrets; we would have ours. Yet his comment seemed to define the gulf between the cities and the bush and the essential living experiences for people who were poles apart, yet all the same: Australians.

We stopped for lunch on the eastern side of Babbage Peninsula, where the maps are so imprecise they show the shoreline as a dotted approximate. Overlooking Jackboot Bay, curiosity got the better of Malcolm.

'What does the flag mean?'

I sensed he may disapprove. It can be a touchy subject. What if he objected to this radical heresy on his land? But if Ken felt any similar doubts, he showed no sign of it. He explained that of all the symbols which could be used to represent Australia — kangaroos, koalas, Uluru, wattle; whatever — only one transcended time and place: the Southern

Across the wilderness . . . Ken Done's flag flies over Muloorina station.

Camel Canyon on the edge of Lake Eyre . . . crazy patterns of ochre.

Cross. Astronomers came to the south seas to observe it; the first humans here lived under it; no matter what our colour, creed or origins, no matter how young or old we are, where we've come from, or when we came, we all live under it today.

'So it just has to be the Southern Cross,' he said. 'And that has the great benefit of being evolutionary from our current flag. So the challenge as a designer was to fit the elements of the Southern Cross into the rectangle demanded of a flag.'

He sketched in the dust with a stick. 'In this design the four main stars are placed to represent the continent itself — at the north, south, east and west of the nation, with the fifth smaller star falling where Canberra is.' He smiled. 'We may not always like what

happens in Canberra, but it's our seat of government, and it's a happy and proper accident that the right place for the fifth star is where our government is situated. And the colours are important, too. The blue is taken from the sky — it's not the deep Royal blue of the current flag — and the gold is a deep and lustrous yellow to represent the optimism of the people; gold for the wealth of the nation and the future of this country.'

We drank our billy tea in our splendid isolation, and each of us reflected on our place — and the flag.

We drove on, Ken and Judy with Malcolm in the lead Landcruiser, Colleen and Lee Anne with Wendy and me — and the flag — in the Pajero. Every time Malcolm looked in his rear-view mirror to check that we were safely following, he saw the flag. Once, the bottom of it came adrift and we stopped to re-tie it. Ken said he would like me to have the flag as a memento, but I had another idea.

We drove north to a line of crumbling cliffs on Jackboot Bay. Water covered the lake surface, giving it a pink shade mixed with blue reflections from the sky. Across the bay we could see the Elliot Price Conservation Park, a section of the Hunt Peninsula which was never grazed, and will therefore be preserved in its pristine state forever.

We struck west through a series of washaways and creek beds which tested our vehicles to a huge dry gulf called Camel Canyon. Here, wind and rain have eaten into the chalky cliffs, 30 metres high, a kilometre or more from the lake's edge. Huge water courses have scoured the soil, leaving crazy patterns of ochre, browns, greys and whites between small rises encrusted with saltbush and sage. Words aren't sufficient to describe it, and even the camera lies: the high cliff edges merge with the colours of the valleys below as if they were on a single plane.

Awed, Ken asked: 'How many people come here?' Malcolm replied: 'You could count on the fingers of your hands the number of white people who have ever seen this.'

We crossed the Bonython Headland and made for Prominent Hill, 20 kilometres through profuse and brilliant wildflowers, to our south-west. Below it, we made camp at dusk on Dingo Soakage, and shared a wine with our hosts. We were immensely privileged to have been guided to parts of the lake which would otherwise have been utterly inaccessible to us, and we thanked

We made it to Dingo Soak (l to r): Ken Done, Lee Anne Mitchell, Colleen Mitchell, the author, Malcolm Mitchell and Judy Done.

A baby wedge-tailed eagle on the shores of Lake Eyre . . . fluffy and defenceless.

Malcolm and Colleen with deep conviction. We then ceremoniously lowered the flag from its fishing pole, folded it, and presented it to them as they prepared to return to Muloorina station. Within two days Malcolm had renovated and repainted the station flagpole, and run Ken's flag to the top. Tourists ask the same question Malcolm had posed: 'What does the flag mean?' and Malcolm and Colleen give them Ken's answers. Some say they like it; others grumble: 'You should fly the *Australian* flag.'

By the campfire that night Ken reflected: 'I was touched by today's incredible drive, and all it meant. A 100-kilometre journey through space and saltbush, never leaving Muloorina, all the time seeing you behind us with the flag flying. Malcolm could see it too, and after I explained why it was designed the

way it was, I could see it started to mean something to him.

'He was moved to receive it tonight; he wanted to have it; he understood, as did Colleen and Lee Anne, that this is a symbol about love of Australia, and not about disrespect for anything which went before. This is one symbol of our nation which represents absolutely everything that has happened on this continent from the first moment in time, and therefore that's the thing we should have — must have — on our flag.

'I hope we can get a wider group of people to feel the things he felt, and to understand this is a flag for *all* Australians — it's not *my* flag, a designer's flag, an artist's flag. And if you said to people, "It's up to you to decide which one you fly — the old one or the new one", I bet it wouldn't be long before we

Walking on water… Ken Done surveys the vastness of Lake Eyre at Belt Bay.

adopted the new one because everyone would come to see it — as Malcolm and Colleen did — as a symbol into which they could fit themselves.'

Our map marked our new camping spot with the words 'Dingo Soakage — position doubtful.' We knew where we were — on cracked and crusted clay, dotted with saltbush, behind the soft sand of a large lakeside lunette held firm by the roots of an extensive stand of trees which gave us ample firewood. Our only company was a baby wedge-tailed eagle, white and fluffy and defenceless, which nestled in a large nest of higgledy-piggledy sticks in a dead tree about 100 metres away. We approached cautiously, meaning no harm, but it greeted us with an instinctive fearsome look, beak open and eyes agog. Its mother circled on thermals high above, while dozens of green–grey finches zipped and zoomed into their tiny nests crafted elegantly and efficiently among the host eagle's sticks.

We walked out into Belt Bay. The lake had been wet at Dinosaur Bluff; but here it was covered in water, stretching north for 150 kilometres, a couple of centimetres deep at the edge; perhaps a metre deep in the Warburton Groove, a shallow ditch which marks the original course of the Warburton River right through the lake.

The sunlight sparkled on the salt and water; thousands of dead fish lined the edge, no more than five centimetres long, testimony to the ravaging harshness of nature which had spilled teeming life into the lake with the rains, only to take it just as suddenly as the heat sucked away the means to sustain that life.

The camp site at Dingo Soak . . . 'Will we get out of here?'

Walking into its vastness made Ken and Wendy, quite independently, do something which must have been instinctive. As each posed for a photograph, they threw out their arms, imitating Christ on the cross. Was it simply an attempt to embrace the unembraceable scale of the place — or to make it appear they were walking on water?

Squinting at the lake, Ken murmured: 'I've been to some amazing places on this planet, but I've never been to a place which is so remote and so far from other people. To look out at this lake, and the plains around us, is to somehow understand the scale of the place, and our consequent vulnerability.'

Ken hurried back to the camp and reached for his crayons. He sat at the table, marking a blob in black. 'I'm not sure where this is going,' he said. Then: 'Ah, yes . . .' and the blob took on a torso, a head and a hat; then legs and feet below, followed by, in descending order, feet, legs, buttocks, torso, head and hat. Four times he repeated the shapes, side by side, us and our reflections, colour coded according to our attire. Then, with three different coloured crayons between his curled fingers, he drew parallel lines above and below an indistinct horizon, before adding bold brushstrokes of hot yellow in the sky and white and magenta in the water and mud. To me, this was the quintessential Ken Done representation of our visit to the lake: four lonely figures in a sea of vulnerability.

The difficulties involved in capturing an infinite scale on a small piece of art board were challenging Ken. Having previously declared our world was too big to capture, he rose early the next morning to paint the universe. On a piece of white board he slapped black paint, leaving only a crescent moon and a touch of orange–red colour for our campfire. He moved his painting table into the lee of the Pajero to escape a stiff breeze, mixed white paint with a smidgin of blue on a brush, and held it above his head. 'This is the tricky bit,' he said. 'Anything could happen,' and with that he repeatedly tapped the brush. Spatters of paint fell in blobs, splashes and tiny sprays.

Ken stopped to look. Amazingly, a Southern Cross had fallen just above the horizon. He smiled the smile of an artist touched by serendipity. 'That's nice,' he said.

We drove up Prominent Hill, rested under a tree in the hot afternoon sun, snoozed in our tents, and made another excursion on to the lake at sunset. We breathed a sigh of relief when the sun went down and the flies mercifully disappeared, and talked into the night. Our isolation was splendid, but we all felt an underlying tension about it. Not that we were in any way threatened here (who could threaten us?), but there was one more unknown to confront: will we get out of here?

Campfire at Dingo Soak . . . Ken Done touched by serendipity.

Sunset over Lake Eyre at Dingo Soak.

Judy Done in the glorious soft hues of the Flinders Ranges, South Australia.

We were about 100 kilometres west of Muloorina, and the Oodnadatta Track was 60 kilometres to the south-west. Malcolm had shown me how to find the gate between Muloorina and the adjoining Anna Creek station, and given instructions on how to find our way out. We had maps, a compass, plenty of water and fuel, but now, only one spare tyre because one had fractured on a stone on Prominent Hill. In some places, Malcolm said, the track out was a bit indistinct. Remembering our inability to find the shotline to our proposed first camp site, we wondered *how* indistinct. Through a tossing-and-turning night, the notion of leaving Lake Eyre took on the elements of *escape*.

But the condemned men ate a hearty breakfast. We put the last of our bacon into a frypan with the rest of our eggs, slapped the last butter on burnt toast, and wolfed it down. Amazingly, a flight of seagulls arrived to scavenge our scraps. Where on earth did they come from? Doyles at Watson's Bay?

Packed, we said a fond farewell to Dingo Soak. From Prominent Hill we snatched our last glimpses of the lake. And then we headed into the unknown.

We found the gate, and followed a fence, as instructed, for 13 kilometres before turning south. The track was easy to follow, but in the vicinity of the bore thousands of cattle hooves had obliterated it. We drove in an arc on the

Wilpena Pound, South Australia . . . 600 million-year-old rocks.

southern side of the bore and eventually picked it up again and headed for an uncertain rendezvous with the Oodnadatta Track.

It wasn't to be easy. The rains that had fallen on us at Dinosaur Bluff had been much heavier here, and in places water covered the track for up to 100 metres. Fortunately, while the surface was muddy, the base was firm. I kept up my speed through these slippery patches, believing momentum was my best asset. I didn't relish the thought of becoming bogged here, but neither did my passengers relish the repeated slides and showers of mud and water.

The last few kilometres through the swampy branches of Warriner Creek were the hairiest. The track was seriously de-graded, and momentum wasn't an option.

But we made it, and triumphantly turned on to the Oodnadatta Track, having *escaped* from the lake.

Judy Done with a gnarled eucalypt in the Flinders Ranges.

We stopped at Coward Springs for a blissful bask in a warm natural spring and a satphone call to the Mitchells to confirm we were safely out. And then we drove on to Marree, passing again the remote area warning sign. We agreed a sign should be made in reverse: *Warning: You are now entering a reality zone; beware of power poles, traffic lights, shopping centres, phones, faxes, television, Big Macs, lunatic drivers, politicians and people on the make.* We chortled our way to Hawker for afternoon tea at the Quandong Cafe, where the woman serving our piping-hot scones, cream and quandong jam politely enquired where we had come from that day.

Ken said: 'Dingo Soak,' and Judy said: 'Belt Bay,' and the woman nodded, as if she knew. But she didn't.

This harsh brown land . . . the mid-north of South Australia, waiting for rain.

chapter ten

I took to the air for my next sweep around the nation. Ten kilometres into the sky, travelling at 850 kilometres an hour, looking down on the rippling red sand dunes and pointillist khakis of the outback scrub, the perspective is vastly different. By road, there is an osmotic interaction between the individual and the place, as the detailed complexity and constant changing of the environment is slowly absorbed. By air the big picture is dramatically displayed, but intimacy and texture are lost, and the haunting vastness is fleetingly framed and held in check by the smooth plastic mouldings of an aircraft cabin.

But I was on a schedule. Where my meandering up to this point had taken many months on the road, I now had allotted myself 15 days to dig into Australia's mining industry. It was a journey which would take me to Karratha in the west to marvel at space-age superstructures of stainless steel nestling among 2500 million-year-old rocks; to Roxby Downs in South Australia's north-west where men and women toil like termites half a kilometre underground; to Moomba in the desert, where a flaming infrastructure had materialised so suddenly as Jolly and I drove towards Innamincka months earlier; to Weipa in the far north, where in 1606 the Dutch sailor Janz had spotted the high red cliffs that contain the world's largest deposit of bauxite; and on to a nameless spot on the Gulf of Carpentaria, where an environmental crisis on the other side of the globe became the stimulus for a $1.3 billion investment in the Century zinc mine.

I was propelled along this path by a desire to understand, and perhaps reconcile, yet another Australian paradox: our love of big projects, the cult of national development which is deeply embedded in the psyche of my generation, against the growing realisation that the future lies in the small; in chips, in information technology, in financial services, in cyber-technology, and in the preservation rather than wholesale reshaping of our fragile environment.

To my father, the postwar Snowy Mountains Scheme was a grand and enticing adventure. He would tell us of his life in the mountains; how he and his companions would eat possums and barter their skins, and how it would be a miracle if the snows of the Australian alpine winters could be turned away from their short and wasteful runs to the sea and be diverted into the thirsty flatlands of the Murray and Murrumbidgee river basins. The first scoops of earth and rock were being drawn from the banks of the Eucumbene River when I toddled off to school; today the completed Snowy Mountains project — the largest engineering challenge ever undertaken in this country — feeds water to a vast inland irrigation industry and channels hydroelectric power into the homes of millions of people.

Strange, but even today when I fly over the mountains and spot the neat rows of pipes feeding water through massive tunnels to hydroelectric power stations, I feel my earliest connection to this land, gifted to me, unseen, by my father's entrancing tales.

Its legacy is deeply embedded into the minds of my generation. Many of us instinctively subscribe to the notion of national development through big projects and the belief that we can achieve anything if we put our minds to it. The Snowy scheme proved to us we were a nation of people who, if we dared to dream, could literally move mountains. In 1949, when Prime Minister Ben Chifley earned a salary of £4000 a year, the project was costed at £225 million. In today's terms that's about $12 billion. To build it today would cost more than $25 billion, but the scheme generates an aggregate of about $4 billion a year in power, agriculture and associated benefits.

Why don't we pipe the waters of Lake Argyle to Adelaide and Perth, and open up vast tracts of land between which needs little more than the magic potion of water?

We could turn back the Burdekin River and connect it to the Diamantina and irrigate the central and western Queensland savannah, providing secure water resources to an inland area the size of many Victorias. We could connect Alice Springs to Darwin by rail (as promised in 1911) and run fast trains fuelled by natural gas from the Mereenie oil and gas field, west of Alice Springs. We could establish a Very Fast Train service between Sydney, Melbourne and Canberra (for starters) to move people and freight by magnetic levitation at 500 kilometres an hour. We could spend $10 billion laying rail through the productive hinterlands west of the Great Dividing Range, from Melbourne to Darwin.

All these ideas have been regularly promoted, debated and pigeonholed in the past 30 years. They have foundered on economic uncertainty and environmental doubt — the latter propelled by a growing realisation that the triumphant Snowy Mountains Scheme may be having unintended consequences — killing the very areas it brought to life, and destroying the remnants of the Snowy River itself. The incessant use of water for irrigated crops in the Murrumbidgee Irrigation Area around Leeton and Griffith is causing the natural water table to rise, bringing salt to the surface and scalding it into flat wasteland. Just 1 per cent of the previous flow of water is now allowed to trickle down the once-mighty Snowy, sparking calls for a dramatic increase to return the system to its natural state. The yearning for big projects is being tempered by a fear of their consequences. It is doubtful that the Snowy scheme would have gone ahead today, because of environmental objections.

Yet we cannot exist without mining. To build and sustain the high-technology clever-country future of service industries and information technology, we must mine. Life would be impossible without it. As the Mining Industry Council puts it in a brochure aimed at school children, our bodies lack shells and tough hides, claws or sharp teeth. We can't run particularly fast, climb trees with exceptional skill, or fly without mechanical aid. In other words, we need clothes, we need knives and forks, we need homes, and we have come to rely on trains, planes and automobiles to get around. The council says we will each require 50 tonnes of iron ore, 55 tonnes of limestone, four tonnes of lead-zinc ore, 200 tonnes of black coal, 175 cubic metres of crude oil and 12 tonnes of phosphate rock — just for starters — to get through an average lifetime.

Plus aluminium for our drinks cans, cooking foil and cars; coal for plastics, electricity and bitumen roads; copper for radios, TV sets and electrical appliances; diamonds for drill bits; gold for computers; magnesium for rayon, glass, paints, paper and antacid tablets; manganese for personal deodorants; mineral sands for fibre optics, computer chips and ceramics; silver for films; tin for batteries; and zinc for our cricketers' lips and noses as they toil under a hot Gabba sun.

Mining benefits us all, at a variety of levels. Jobs, investment, profits; the money-go-round wouldn't be the same without the $30 billion generated by mining each year.

But lurking behind the acceptance of the need for mining are the wider arguments about sustainability. Mining activities contribute to greenhouse gases; global warming is looming as a major threat to life on this fragile planet. We say we need our cars, but they burn hydrocarbons; we need our electricity, but it is generated by coal, or gas or uranium. How much carbon dioxide can we spew into the atmosphere before we choke? How many Three Mile Islands or Chernobyls are waiting for us in the 21st century? How much hotter can Earth become before melting polar icecaps sink us beneath rising seas? What balances can we devise to give us a sustainable future?

Driving through the country is a scenic experience which can obscure the fact that Australia is more than a landscape. It is also an economy, where the land and its uses are inextricably entwined with economic outcomes. We used to think Australia rode metaphorically on the sheep's back; since the 1960s, miners have increasingly touted their economic importance. Also, mining is a very visible part of outback travel. Although it scratches a mere 0.02 per cent of the land surface — less than the space allocated to

Woodside's North West Shelf gas processing plant near Karratha, Western Australia . . . where space age meets stone age.

hotels, I was repeatedly told — mining is often the only reason for people to live in remote areas, and the single reason for infrastructure spending in regions which would be otherwise desolate. Yet, as passers-by, we were more often than not excluded from entry to mine sites. If, for instance, Jolly and I had knocked on the door at Moomba, we wouldn't have been granted permission to enter until faxes had been sent to headquarters in Adelaide, enquiries made, decisions taken, and permission or otherwise sent back to the gatekeeper. All that could take days.

Mining in Australia is worth more than $30 billion a year, 80 per cent of it being export income. It directly employs 82,000 people, plus a further 200,000 in related service industries and 425,000 in manufacturing jobs providing inputs to mining and energy projects. The industry pays almost $5 billion a year in taxes, charges, royalties and fees. Whichever way you look at it, mining is big business for the nation.

Yet the mining industry has a dubious name and a tarnished record. It has copped much flak over the years for what is

Dampier, Western Australia, foreshore . . . incredible riches under the sea.

perceived as its disregard for environmental issues, and its dismissal of the rights and interests of indigenous peoples. Much of this criticism is undoubtedly deserved and is recognised by mining organisations now strenuously trying to change their ways. The impact of this isn't yet being recognised throughout the nation, where a strange dichotomy exists in attitudes to mining.

Wherever we had travelled, we found that the local environment rated high on the list of concerns among the people with whom we yarned. In cities and towns, one-pub waystations and isolated camping grounds, among pastoralists and labourers, families and drifters, there was a unifying train of thought: that they lived in a beautiful part of the country which must be respected and protected. Even in communities which existed solely because of mineral operations, there

Burrup Peninsula near Karratha . . . red rock and oil rigs.

Woodside's North-west Shelf gas processing plant.

was an ambivalence about mining: concern was expressed that 'Australia has become just a giant quarry'. Yet those operations which supported their local communities were deemed to be all right. It was the others they were worried about. Perhaps this simply reflected an unwillingness among people to make judgments or come to conclusions over issues where their knowledge was limited; perhaps it was because they knew which side of their economic bread was buttered.

When William Dampier poked around the rocky coast of Western Australia at the Tropic of Capricorn in 1688 he described the natives who inhabited the barren, waterless land as 'the miserablest people in the world'. His descriptions of desolation and worthlessness stimulated no interest among the spice traders of Europe who continued doing business through the Dutch in Java, and the Great South Land slept on, more unwanted than undiscovered.

Ironic, then, to see it now. Nestled among the ancient rocks of the Burrup Peninsula, so red, so hot, and so hard they ping, is a petrified forest of steel, a spaghetti bowl of carefully crafted pipes, catalytic converters and heat exchangers which represent a $6 billion investment. A further $6 billion has been spent offshore developing the North West Shelf oil and gas fields, which have at least $40 billion worth of proved reserves — and probably enough to continue production for 100 years. Worthless indeed!

As with so many things Australian, it is the scale of the North West Shelf gas plant which first takes the breath away. And the audacity. Here, under a searing sun which bakes the rocks and sends thermometers past 50°C, causing heatwaves to dance on an uncertain horizon, the equivalent of *four and a half million* household refrigerators turn natural gas into liquid at −161°C. And the equivalent of a further three million refrigerators are being built. The mind boggles. Eight specially designed Liquified Natural Gas (LNG) ships, each named after a different migratory bird, shuttle back and forth between the Pilbara and Japanese ports, each containing 75 million cubic metres of natural gas, which in its compressed and liquefied form is reduced by a factor of 600 into 125,000 cubic metres of LNG. The ship engines are powered by their cargo — natural gas, with enough left aboard at the Japanese terminals to allow the return trip to the Burrup Peninsula.

Debate about sustainability may be a long time coming. The North West Shelf is likely to be still producing at the end of the 21st century. But when work started on the onshore facility, negotiations took place with local Aborigines over the necessary disturbance to the great piles of rocks which create the Burrup Peninsula, many of which carried ancient carvings. These were carefully shifted to a site away from the works. Some were placed face-down so that casual visitors couldn't see the sacred carvings on them, and they remain there today, awaiting the day when the gas fields are dry and the processing facilities are removed. They will then be returned to their original positions.

Bill MacRae, Woodside's Karratha spokesman, told a story about the Burrup's flint-hard red rocks, among the oldest in the world, which jut jaggedly from the ridges and valleys throughout the peninsula. A small area on a hill overlooking the Woodside processing area was levelled to allow the building of a visitors centre. 'We try to disturb as little as possible,' Bill said. 'But you can't keep everybody happy. We were once berated by a woman who complained of our environmental vandalism — for dumping all those rocks around the site!'

What we see on land is just part of the North West Shelf operation. A 135-kilometre pipeline runs under the sea to the North Rankin A platform, higher than Perth's tallest building, which sits on the seabed and collects gas from nearby wells. It is also connected to the Goodwyn platform, 23 kilometres south-west, and the Cossack Pioneer floating oil storage and loading vessel, 34 kilometres to the north-west. While the platforms are designed to withstand cyclonic winds of up to 215 kilometres an hour and waves of 23 metres, the Cossack Pioneer has to be disconnected from its subsea production wells when cyclones threaten. Loaded with more than a million barrels of stored oil, it rides out the cyclones at sea. Solar-powered buoys are deployed far out to sea during the cyclone season as an early warning system, sending a constant flow of data on wind strengths and wave heights, allowing up to 24 hours' notice of approaching storms. Where the space age meets the stone age, they've got everything covered.

The Roxby Downs mine in South Australia, up the road from Woomera, near Andamooka, very nearly didn't get off the ground. Or under it. A geological lottery 1600 million years ago very nearly put paid to the largest private investment currently being undertaken in Australia. The molten metals spewed out of that volcano left a two billion-tonne ore body which, when pulverised into a fine talcum-like powder, will yield 60 million tonnes of pure copper, one million tonnes of uranium, 24 tonnes of silver and about five tonnes of gold.

It was the uranium which nearly blew it. Approval for the mine had to run the gauntlet of federal and state parliaments, and intense opposition to uranium mining among the environmental lobby. But Western Mining Corporation (WMC), which has developed the

Roxby mine, didn't choose the mineral mix, which is unique in the world. The uranium — as well as the gold and silver — is simply a by-product of the main attraction: copper.

In revenue terms, 75 per cent of Roxby's value lies in copper, 20 per cent in uranium, and 5 per cent in gold and silver.

Like the North West Shelf, the visitor reels at the magnitude of the operation. But approaching from the air, there is relatively little to see: the Olympic Dam village appears as a green oasis of rooftops and trees; a crushing and smelting plant on several hectares north of the village looks insignificant on the red earth desert, and a couple of mine heads jut into the sky. And that's about it. But the surface evidence belies the extraordinary activity below. Already, 130 kilometres of tunnels — known

Underground at Roxby Downs, South Australia . . . like termites in overdrive.

Smelting at Roxby Downs . . . 99.99 per cent pure copper.

as drives — honeycomb the rock as teams of workers systematically work the multistoreyed stopes, chewing away at the rock, hauling it in 50-tonne trucks to the crushers, and whipping it to the surface in ten or twenty tonne skips, one to the minute. This amazing complex of catacombs is being extended by 28 kilometres a year, and the pace is quickening. Like termites in overdrive, men and women work drilling machines around the clock, putting them on autopilot during meal breaks at the underground canteen (known as the Hard Rock Cafe, of course); mechanics repair and service heavy equipment in giant caverns, their welding flashes flickering in the blackest of blackness; at every blind intersection horns blare and combine with the persistent beeps of reversing vehicles, a

Underground at Roxby Downs . . . running repairs.

symphony overwhelmed by the roar of rushing wind, like a jumbo jet in takeoff, at the base of the intake shafts which suck air, 15 tonnes of it for every tonne of ore taken out, from the surface. A decade into the operation, they've barely begun.

Construction under a sweltering sun at Roxby Downs
. . . Australia's largest private development.

Terry Quinn, who drove me down the tunnel to the mining operations centre almost half a kilometre below the surface, said WMC was spending $1.5 billion on a new smelter, a new refinery, the largest grinding mill in the world, another 140 houses in the village, a water pipeline from Muloorina and a new power line from Port Augusta. 'This is Australia's largest private development,' he said. 'But the profit years are yet to come.' You can excuse them for hoping that commodity prices stay up. Especially copper.

Malcolm Mitchell at Muloorina is concerned about the water. His bore, which Gran'ad first put down, delivers 2.3 mega-litres of water a day. The Roxby Downs bore,

recently sunk, will take almost 20 times as much each day, and channel it through 14,000 lengths of concrete-lined steel pipe — 110 kilometres in all — through the desert to the mine site. Further supplies come from closer borefields. It's the sustainability of this that worries Malcolm. Sure, artesian water has leaked from the desert at the mound springs south of Lake Eyre for eons, but when you have 150 bores sunk in South Australia since the coming of the pastoralists, 150 in the same artesian basin in New South Wales, and a greedy 3000 in Queensland, you can be excused for wondering when it might dry up. The experts say there isn't a problem. Malcolm's not an expert; he just lives there, worrying. And when the federal government promised to spend $280 million capping wasteful bores in Queensland, he figured he had good reason to be concerned.

The first thing I noticed in the admin-istration building at Roxby Downs was a framed statement of WMC's environmental policy, signed by the chairman, Hugh Morgan. It was the kind of mission statement which businesses indulged in during the late 1980s and into the 1990s. Motherhood stuff:

The company is committed to establishing compatibility between economic development and the main-tenance of the environment and therefore seeks to ensure that throughout all phases of its activity WMC personnel and contractors give proper consideration to the care of flora, fauna, air, land and water and to the community health and heritage which may be affected by these activities.

To fulfil this commitment the company will observe all environmental

Laying water pipes from Muloorina station to Roxby Downs . . . environmental concerns.

laws; progressively establish and maintain company-wide environmental standards; integrate environmental factors into planning and operational decisions; assess the potential environmental effects of our activities; regularly monitor and audit our environmental performance; continually improve our environmental performance including reducing the effects of emissions, developing opportunities for recycling and more efficiently using energy, water and other resources; rehabilitate the environment affected by our activities; conserve important populations of flora and fauna that may be affected; and promote environmental awareness.

The man whose job it is to put WMC's money where its mouth is is John Read, an ecologist who runs the Ecosystem Restoration and Research project within sight of the mine heads at Roxby Downs. Here, a 13-square-kilometre patch of lightly grazed desert has been fenced off in a joint experiment with the Adelaide University environmental department and the South Australian Department of Environment and Natural Resources, to see how quickly the desert returns to its natural state, and whether rare native fauna can be successfully reintroduced.

The fence is a determined-looking structure. Wire netting is buried to stop burrowing animals, like rabbits, getting through. The netting is then joined with a second band which rises above the top of the fence posts,

Western Mining Corporation ecologist John Read . . . protecting native fauna near Roxby Downs.

flopping outwards so that animals such as feral cats will fall backwards if they try to climb over it. Old rubber conveyor belts are laid beside the fence to prevent erosion and burrowing, and future plans include electrification. It will be a brave intruder indeed who tries to get through.

The location was chosen because the lack of water sources meant it had been very lightly grazed, and it included a variety of habitats — low stony rises, a swamp area, and various mixes of scrub trees. Mining may take place below in the future, requiring air shafts on the surface, but the impact of these will be minimal. In the meantime, vegetation and fauna are being closely monitored, and soon it is planned to introduce burrowing bettongs, bush-tailed bettongs, stick nest rats

and bilbies to the area. All previously lived here; all disappeared around the turn of the 20th century.

'You can blame a number of factors,' said John. 'Rabbits, feral cats, foxes have all contributed. We shot a feral cat a while back which had 29 lizards in its stomach, plus a mouse and a zebra finch. All were undigested, so they had been eaten that day. Work it out — one feed for one cat in one day — it wouldn't be long before the impact was felt.'

What if this ecological experiment is a wild success? What if the bilbies and bettongs return to their homeland and breed into flourishing colonies? How realistic is it to fence off not 13 square kilometres, but 1300, or 130,000 square kilometres, eradicate rabbits, foxes, cats, and other predators, such as humans? Who will fund it? Who will manage it? WMC gets brownie points for this experiment, and they'll get more if it is extended. But, worthwhile as it is, the likelihood is that this patch of bush can be no more than a model control centre to clearly demonstrate what we have lost.

In the mid-1960s I was a reporter on the Adelaide *News* when I flew north with Charles T. Easley, the head of South Australia and Northern Territory Oil Search (Santos) to report, with great excitement, the discovery of hydrocarbons in the Cooper Basin. It was New Year's Eve 1963 when the gas and condensate flowed, and we wrote rapturously of a great new economic future for the driest state in the driest continent on earth. Enough gas to supply all of Adelaide. And maybe Melbourne, and Sydney and Brisbane, too! Riches for all!

We slept in the desert, sand scooped away to accommodate our hips, marvelling at the canopy of stars blinking through the cold night air, dreaming of a Texan future for a state which had always had to graft for its growth. But during the same period, gas was discovered over the border in Queensland and offshore in Bass Strait, and the thought of South Australia becoming the supplier to the nation slipped away. Nevertheless, gas, ethane and oil pipelines radiate today from the Cooper Basin to Sydney, Canberra, Brisbane and Mt Isa.

On that first visit there were two wells: Gidgealpa 1 was dry, and Gidgealpa 2 hit paydirt. It is exhausted today, but Santos executive John Hudson took me there. It looks like any other well head, except for a sign which marks its significance among the 550 producing wells in the Moomba region. These are connected by hundreds of kilometres of underground pipelines, linking 20 satellite stations, and collecting billions of dollars worth of oil and gas for processing at the Moomba plant. Out in the desert, beam pumps — or nodding donkeys — work relentlessly around the clock, sucking millions of barrels of oil from formations up to 3000 metres below.

When Moomba got under way almost three decades ago, there were known gas reserves for 20 years of uninterrupted supply; today there are known reserves of 22 years. Indeed, there is a surfeit of gas, much of which is pumped back down dry holes and stored. But six rigs constantly traverse the desert, drilling wells in pursuit of more oil.

The men and women who work this outpost fly in from Adelaide for two weeks of

Drilling for oil near Moomba, South Australia . . . 550 producing wells.

ten- or 12-hour days, then fly home for two weeks off. Their desert life is one of regimented mealtimes, but they are fed well in a large canteen and can enjoy an evening beer — for a while. The bar shuts early: hangovers aren't required on the job.

When we returned to the Moomba village after a day touring the facilities in the sweltering desert, I was surprised to see a 4WD utility hooning around in a giant mud patch. Slipping, sliding, spinning and sending up showers of mud, it looked like great fun, but it had a serious intent: in rain periods the clay roads become as slippery as ice rinks, and in the past Santos lost an average of 15 vehicles a year in the hands of inexperienced wet weather drivers. So they set up a driver training program and haven't lost a vehicle since.

From the air, the footprint of the Moomba facility is nothing more than a postage stamp on a sheet of beige claypans, ochre sandhills and speckled grey saltbush. But the oil explorers have left an indelible mark on the landscape; a grid pattern of seismic shotlines bulldozed over decades. These have been necessary so that search teams could drive in perfectly straight lines, oblivious of obstructions, setting off explosive charges at regular intervals to map by shockwaves the subterranean structures. But regeneration on these cuts in the sand has been tortuously slow. Oilmen may dismiss them as mere collateral damage, but they are ugly scars. Technology has provided new answers, and now soft-tyred vehicles carry out the same work, with the evidence of their presence disappearing in a couple of years. Over the protests of environmentalists, search teams are moving into the highly sensitive Coongie Lakes region — wetlands which flood when Cooper Creek gets a big surge of water from

Queensland. The lakes are a crucial habitat for birdlife, and will be threatened if oil or gas wells expand into them. But the oil drillers say they can avoid this by setting up on the edges of the system and drilling diagonally into the hydrocarbon structures. Environmentalists remain sceptical.

The Comalco bauxite mine at Weipa has been operating longer than any other I visited on my sweep around Australia, and, if there is still a demand for aluminium in the world's cyberfuture, it could still be going in 2400. There are 3.6 billion tonnes of known bauxite deposits along Cape York's western coast, and Comalco is strip mining it at an average rate of ten million tonnes a year. Hulking yellow scraper machines, mated in tandem push–pull coupling, slice off 100 tonnes of topsoil on every pass; front-end loaders gulp 16 tonnes of ore at a time and flip 150 tonnes of it into bottom-dumping trucks which zoom along tabletop-smooth roads to rail dump stations. This is big. This is the biggest in the world.

Out of these flat coastal plains, noted by Janz in 1606, mapped by Tasman in 1802, and recognised for their significance by geologists in 1955, strip mining equals total environmental destruction. There is no other way. The rich band of bauxite lies under a metre of topsoil. First the trees which cover the virgin territory must be cut down and their roots ripped out; then the scrapers move in, nose to tail, like godzillas on heat, until the front one lowers its underbelly and strains against the weight of the soil it scoops into its giant hopper. The second monster nudges its rear and, roaring and snarling, they link up, on the move, the following vehicle pushing until the front hopper is full and raised clear of the ground; then the lead

Drilling for oil near Moomba . . . hard, dirty work.

Gas from the desert . . . a satellite gas plant near Moomba.

Loading bauxite at Weipa, Queensland . . . 300-tonne monsters.

vehicle pulls as the second scraper takes its fill, and they unhook and separately dump their guts on giant hillocks of rich dark topsoil, never stopping as they do the circle again, and again, 100 tonnes at a time.

Cleared of top soil, the loaders move in, chewing away at the pisolites of ore until the ironstone beneath the bauxite is exposed. The strippers move back in, dumping topsoil on the ironstone, and the bare earth is handed over to the regeneration teams. Each hectare of land is then planted with a pre-determined mix of about 2500 indigenous trees and shrubs which, ten years later, are virtually indistinguishable from the original low forests which cover the entire lease area. Native fauna returns to each rehabilitated area — through wildlife corridors deliberately left during mining operations — about three years after its original destruction. Experiments with revegetation to create a secondary forestry industry, using exotic trees like teak and mahogany, were abandoned because the trees didn't do well and the fauna failed to return.

The townsfolk of Weipa are a tight-knit community; a natural outcome among 2000 people in the middle of nowhere, most of whom are employed by Comalco or its service companies. By Cape York standards, they have all the facilities in the world, and they are proud of their schools, library, hospital, shopping complex, pub and recreation facilities. Michael Lobascher of Comalco talked me into joining the Weipa Hash House Harriers' weekly run around the township, destroying any benefit it might have delivered with several ice-cold stubbies at the red-faced end. The mums, dads and kids who gathered for the run gave a new definition to Australian bush friendliness. But they are a trifle bizarre: each year after the first rains of the Wet they stage the Running of the Bulls. At 3 am they gather to run a 1.5-kilometre course — in the nude! Along the way, contestants collect money for the Royal Flying Doctor Service, raising about $1000 in seven minutes. It started out as a run for blokes only, but in recent years some bullettes have joined in. I guess they pray for a moonless night.

Seventy kilometres north of Weipa is the Aboriginal settlement of Mapoon. The original Comalco mining lease, enshrined in a 1957 Queensland Act of Parliament, encompassed the Mapoon area, and gave Comalco virtual carte blanche to do as it pleased with any of its leasehold areas. The indigenous people weren't consulted before the Act was drafted; nor were they compensated in any way for the loss of their land. In what is now recognised as a shameful act of political and corporate power, the people of Mapoon were removed at gunpoint from their homes, with police burning houses, a store and a church to prevent their return. They were taken up the Cape to a settlement called New Mapoon, between Bamaga and Seisia.

The company attitude at the time was one of extreme arrogance. The Act gave it the

Front-end loader driver Jane Stevenson at Weipa . . . ten million tonnes a year.

right to steamroll away any impediment — real or imagined — to its mining interests, and these rights were executed with an attitude of: 'We've got the law on our side and we don't give a bugger what you think.' But mining never took place at Mapoon, and in 1977 the land was returned to the people. The gunpoint removal of the people served no purpose.

The Act conferring vast powers on Comalco hasn't been changed. But attitudes have. The fundamental catalyst for change was the *Mabo* native title decision of the High Court in 1992, followed by the *Wik* decision of 1996 which declared that native title rights could coexist alongside other rights under the Crown. The Wik people of Weipa took Comalco, the state of Queensland, other mining companies and

Strip-mining scrapers at Weipa . . . tandem godzillas on heat.

some other indigenous groups to the High Court in that landmark case. By then, according to Jamie Cullens, Comalco's manager of community relations at Weipa, 'We acknowledged that we had got it very wrong.'

He said: 'We said to ourselves, "This is a sea change, guys." We took into account changes in society, changes in attitudes, and changes in our management processes — plus other factors — and they all culminated in a new determination among the Rio Tinto group of companies (of which Comalco forms a part) that we wanted to lead the industry in how we dealt with indigenous issues. Up here on the West Cape we now have a very positive process under way which goes ahead independent of anything anyone says down south. Reconciliation is happening. It's a rocky road, but there is a determination to sit down and work through the issues.'

Rio Tinto's chief executive, Leon Davis, has signed and circulated a new policy towards Aboriginal and Torres Strait Islander people. Considering past actions, it is a breathtaking backflip, but a breakthrough for the locals:

This policy is based upon recognition and respect. Rio Tinto recognises that Aboriginal and Torres Strait Islands people in Australia have been disadvantaged and dispossessed, have a special connection to land and waters, and have native title rights recognised by law. Rio Tinto respects Aboriginal and Torres Strait Islands people's cultural diversity, aspirations for self sufficiency, and interest in land management. In all exploration and development in Australia, Rio Tinto will always consider Aboriginal and Torres Strait Islands people's issues; where there are traditional or historical connections to particular lands and waters, Rio Tinto will engage with Aboriginal and Torres Straits Islands stakeholders and their representatives to find mutually advantageous outcomes; outcomes for Aboriginal and Torres Strait Islands people will result from listening to them. Economic independence through direct employment, business development and training are among advantages that Rio Tinto will offer [with] strong support given to activities that are sustainable after Rio Tinto has left the area.

In the case of the Weipa mining operations, that could be a long time coming. But at the Aboriginal community of Napranum, just south of Weipa, the foundations of economic independence are being laid. Comalco handed over the assets of the Napranum community to the Napranum Aboriginal Corporation in 1996, and now offers support for the development of various business enterprises — a concrete block-making plant, a sawmill, carpentry and engineering workshops, a washed sand operation and a business development consultancy. Chief executive Sandy Callope concedes these businesses are small, but says they offer employment, and expresses hope for future expansion.

It is a small beginning, but it's a beginning, nevertheless. Perhaps it's also fitting that this process is taking place so close to the spot where the dispossession began — on Possession Island, 230 kilometres to the north.

Fairy lights festoon the banyan trees in downtown Cairns. Christmas is coming, and on a torpid night languid figures slump in doorways, on benches, in shadows, draped out, waiting for a breath of air. A man strums a guitar, eyes closed; youths shout at each other under flickering neon lights up a laneway; and the smells of Asian food hang over the beachfront park where Yothu Yindi performed on our last visit some months before. Across the way, its back to the city, is the forbidding, windowless, casino complex; a most appalling piece of architecture. Cairns is the favoured destination of tourists making for the Great Barrier Reef. It has grown enormously over the past two decades — in size, in facilities, and in importance as the de facto capital of Far North Queensland. But it has a fast-food, frontier culture, about as stimulating as its indolent night air.

Across the base of the cape to Normanton; oppressive heat, blue haze from horizon to horizon, the muddy flood plains at high tide, sun glinting off the sluggish capillaries of the Normanton River's salt-scalded flood plains; mud islands rising in the dirty water, a mangrove here, another there, beginning to populate them. The aircraft is a sweltering hotbox on the ground; blessed relief for a few minutes as we hop to Karumba and come into land over a new pub on a promontory with a huge and welcome sign on its roof: ICE COLD BEER.

Mining is one of the oldest industries in the world. It was only a matter of time before it became space-age. At Pasminco's new Century Zinc mine in north-west Queensland, the buckets of huge excavators are fitted with global positioning system (GPS) beacons. Information relayed via satellites will tell operators if the next gulp of dirt is rich ore, or worthless overburden.

To achieve this technological marvel, 500 drill holes were sunk in and around the zinc, lead and silver ore body, the first signs of which were identified in 1990, to build up a three-dimensional computer diagram of the mineralised zone. By plan, or by cross-section, the computer can tell exactly where the ore begins and ends; how deep it is in any given spot, and where the barren zones are between the two main floating segments of

A welcome sight at Karumba, Queensland.

ore. In some sections, it is virtually on the surface; in others, it will require 1.1 billion tonnes of overburden to be removed, creating a hole 300 metres deep. The computer also tells us there are almost 100 million tonnes of ore to be recovered: five million tonnes a year to be gouged out, crushed at the mine to the fineness of face powder, mixed with water and sent by a 300-kilometre pipeline to Karumba, dried into briquettes, shipped to the other side of the world, and turned into 450,000 tonnes a year of zinc concentrate. It's a $1.2 billion project, yet it very nearly didn't get off the ground.

The Century site was a discovery of CRA Exploration (part of Rio Tinto), but while it was clearly significant, it wasn't considered to be a bonanza. CRA entered into protracted negotiations with local owners in a confused native title environment during the mid-1990s, and Century became an on-again–off-again political battleground. But the project had the green light switched on when it was purchased by the Australian zinc and lead producer Pasminco Ltd for $345 million. The attraction for Pasminco was a problem it faced on the other side of the world, in The Netherlands, where it owns the Budel Zink smelter. During smelting, zinc produces a

Lawn Hill National Park, north-west Queensland, near the Century Zinc mine site . . . natural coexistence.

hazardous by-product called jarosite from iron and magnesium in the concentrate. Dutch authorities put Budel on notice that from 1998 (since extended by two years) it must cease producing and storing jarosite, or close. As luck would have it, the Century deposit is the only known location in the world where the concentrate is iron-free. So Pasminco, by buying the Century mine, could supply its own raw materials to Budel. Without this link, the Century project may have lapsed.

When I visited the site of the mine, earthworks were under way preparing for the crushing plant. The route for the underground pipeline carrying the slurry produced from the crushed ore has been defined, with local Aborigines advising on any potential disturbance to sacred sites between the mine and Karumba. It crosses five rivers, where engineers are boring directional tunnels under the riverbeds to drag the pipeline through. A massive storage shed has been built at Karumba, where the

slurry will be dried and loaded on to a barge for shipment to ore carriers anchored offshore in deeper waters in the Gulf. In spite of environmental concerns, this process has been approved by government because the alternative — a pipeline and rail transfer to Townsville — would have added $30 million a year to costs and made the project uneconomical. The Queensland government had its eye on the 4000 jobs Century will provide during its 20-odd-year life.

Doug Fishburn is a four-decade old timer in the mining industry. A consultant to the Century Zinc project, he is a former geologist whose main claim to fame is his discovery of the huge Ok Tedi copper and gold deposit in Papua New Guinea. 'You only get one in a lifetime,' he said with a chortle. 'There was nothing to it, really. In the mid-1960s geologists had cottoned to the idea of continental drift and the realisation that at certain places at the edges of geological plates you found copper and gold deposits. The

Bougainville mine was the first big one. I was working for an American company then, and we outfitted a ship with a helicopter deck and an atomic absorption device — very new in those days. We sailed along the PNG coast, the choppers putting us ashore in the morning; we'd walk up the creeks and collect samples, and be picked up in the evenings and flown back to the ship. Overnight the samples were assayed, and if there was any trace of copper or gold we'd go back for another look. We started at the eastern end of PNG and gradually worked westward — and I was the one who went furthest west.

'There were sniffs of copper in the Fly River, and from there it was just a matter of tracing it back up the river. Walking up the creeks we could see almost solid copper sulphides. Finding the mother lode was really a function of being the first person in the area who knew a bit about geology.'

Not surprisingly, given the environmental catastrophe of Ok Tedi, Doug has firm views about mining and the environment — including its impact on local communities. 'From a mining perspective, there wasn't much appreciation of environmental matters even 15 or 20 years ago,' he said. 'Today an environmentalist is the first person hired for any mine. Then someone to look after community issues. There have been lots of well-meaning people having a crack at these things, but we're not very good at it yet because we haven't done much of it. But in a decade or less there will be professional community people who do know what they're doing in the same way as we now have environmental people. It's a continual learning process.'

But to make the point that mining and national parks can coexist side by side, Doug took me to Lawn Hill National Park, 11 kilometres from the Century site. Here,

Myall Lakes, New South Wales . . . harnessing the power of the sun.

permanent springs feed deep rivers running through perpendicular gorges, red rocks soaring into the azure sky, waterlilies and remnants of ancient rainforests fringing a delightful desert oasis. At the Century site, there is no sign of Lawn Hill's proximity. At Lawn Hill, there is no sign of Century. Mining cannot occur in the national park, and the rocky hills of the mine area aren't worthy of national park status. So they coexist.

On the Myall Lakes, north of Newcastle, in New South Wales, we zigzag across a mirrored millpond on a houseboat, slowly absorbing the splendid beauty around us, feeling gratified that it is protected by National Parks legislation. Lynette Thorstensen embraces her children, Irena and Max, as black swans cruise by with barely a ripple; a squadron of pelicans approaches, ten o'clock high; shags dry their wings under a weak winter sun, and sea eagles nuzzle together high in the trees. 'These wonderful works of nature,' Lynette says, nodding at squirming Irena, almost two, and Max, 11 weeks, 'are why we must rethink our relationship with our environment because if we don't, their future is very unsure.'

Lynette is the former chief executive of Greenpeace Australia, a position she relinquished in 1995 to become the director of Greenpeace International's climate change program, based in Amsterdam. But she resigned from that extraordinarily influential post to return to Australia in 1996 to become a mother. 'It was amazing,' she said. 'Overnight I went from the absolutely macro — the future of all the world's climate — to the totally micro — a tiny premature baby in a little cottage in Rozelle. But, to me, both are equally important.'

Lynette's husband, Michael Ward, is a director of the Australian Republican Movement and a former head of the Health Promotions Unit of the New South Wales Health Department. In that role he planned and executed the 'Me No Fry' campaign to change the way we think about the dangers of exposure to the sun. The success of this campaign can be judged by observing little tykes on the beach in brightly coloured sunscreen suits, their noses and cheeks painted pink with zinc, wearing floppy Foreign Legion-style caps for neck protection. Sun protection is now a cool fashion statement for kids, and perhaps, in a generation or two, Australia will no longer be the melanoma capital of the world.

But it's to the sun that Lynette looks when she thinks about sustainability. 'Solar is the way to go,' she said. 'Its power can be harnessed, and it's free. No-one can own it. And that's why we are being held back in our national willingness to devote more and more to research and development of solar power: because powerful vested interests, particularly from the coal lobby, have too much to lose.'

Lynette is no banner-waving, rabid, tree-hugging, extreme greenie. She acknowledges the need for balance; accepts that mining is a necessity; concedes there are regions of lesser conservation value which wouldn't unduly suffer from invasive development; and endorses case-by-case negotiations to resolve environmental questions as more reasonable than don't-touch-a-thing sloganeering. 'But,' she adds, 'We must also concede that due care hasn't been taken in the past; that Australia has been battered around over the years; that there's been too much rape and pillage; and that there are some special areas of high conservation and biodiversity which deserve protection and which must be left alone.' The trick is to find the line that meets the objectives of all stakeholders, and that means

Lynette Thorstensen and Michael Ward with baby Max and Irena . . . 'these wonderful works of nature.'

vigorous debate over environmental issues will be with us for generations to come.

'It is a scandal that there isn't more effort put into solar research in Australia,' she said. 'We have the world's leading researchers, but they have been left to manage as best they can with very little government support. The key players in solar development are Japan, the U.S. and Germany. We even lag behind Greece in the amount of solar energy hooked up to the power grid. Why are we so myopic? Why, with our abundance of sun, can't we see the benefits of becoming a world leader in solar industries? This question frustrates the bright young things in the Green movement, and it's depressing to say it, but it's hard to find any reason for this myopia except that it's driven by the vested interests of the coal industry, in particular. They are a very powerful lobby. They dominate decision-making forums, certainly

within the Commonwealth Department of Primary Industry and Energy.

'But I'm an optimist. Eventually, good will work its way through. Everybody is an environmentalist — although some just aren't yet. There is an emerging generation which understands the nature of environmental problems. The environment movement actually represents more members than all the political parties combined. When you count the little land-care groups, all the small regional organisations, the coast-care groups, and the participation of the people from all walks of life on Clean Up Australia Day, it's quite extraordinary. We must overcome vested interests and "she'll be right" apathy and use some of our ingenuity to develop alternative energy resources. Solar, wind, waves — there is tremendous potential. And, after infrastructure costs, it's all free.'

Farmlands and the arteries of industry merge near
Portland, in Victoria's Western District.

chapter eleven

By now I was all bigged out. I felt the need to see the other side; to seek smallness and compactness, so we packed the Pajero again and headed for Tasmania. And the first thing we did was drive aboard the huge Bass Strait ferry, *Devil Cat*!

Tasmania is the smallest of the Australian states, representing 1 per cent of the total landmass, with a population of 475,000, or about 2.5 per cent of the nation. Because of its size and relative insignificance, it is often forgotten, or left off maps, much to the chagrin of its people. Yet the story of Tasmania today has many lessons for all of Australia as we — with our small, relatively insignificant population — seek to find our place in an increasingly global economy. In many respects, Tasmania is Australia writ small.

Tasmanians are busy today making a future from their past. This applies at three levels: the timeless wilderness beauty of the island's south-west is the springboard for a fast-growing eco-tourism industry; its European history as a convict settlement is a further drawcard for visitors; and its unique environmental advantages, combined with its small population, are driving its push to excel in niche food products which have gained a top-notch reputation in markets around the world.

If only the locals would realise it. The bitter fights behind efforts to switch Tasmanians' thinking from giving away their heritage in low-value exports such as wood chips, to exploiting high value-added products such as cheeses, fish and ferries, have occupied a generation. And the battles are not yet over.

The *Devil Cat* is a perfect example of a successful niche product, albeit not one derived from its past. Incat Australia of Hobart have specialised in making high-speed, wave-piercing car and passenger ferries for ten years — and they have snared 40 per cent of the world market. They have become market leaders, pioneering designs and manufacturing processes, and they have made shipbuilders around the world sit up and take notice. The American Marines are evaluating the cats as a means of transporting soldiers and their equipment to world trouble spots in the shortest time possible.

It's an unlikely business to find in little old Tasmania. Yet it happened, literally, by accident. Incat evolved from other boat-building companies, including the Sullivans Cove Ferry Company, which was formed in 1972 to operate a fleet of 'bushranger' ferries — named after famous Tasmanian bushrangers — on Hobart's Derwent River. When the bulk ore carrier *Illawarra* crashed into the Tasman Bridge in 1975, cutting the link between Hobart's western and eastern shores, the bushranger fleet came to the rescue. In the two and a half years it took for the bridge to be rebuilt, they carried more

than nine million passengers. And their owners saw an opportunity. Given their experience in both constructing and operating ferries, they formed International Catamarans Pty Ltd and by 1983 had conceived the wave-piercing design. This concept allows great speed, great capacity and great efficiency.

In 1988 Incat employed 31 people. By 1998 the figure was in excess of 1000, and it was turning over $120 million a year. A new shipyard joint venture was under way in China, and the world's speed record for a crossing of the Atlantic — the Blue Riband, or Hale's Trophy — was in the bag, twice. The 91-metre ferry *Catalonia*, on delivery to a customer in Spain, crossed the Atlantic at an average speed of 38.85 knots (71.95 kilometres an hour), breaking the previous record held for seven years by another Incat ship, *Hoverspeed Great Britain*. Along the way, the *Catalonia* became the first vessel to sail more than 1000 nautical miles (1852 kilometres) in a day, averaging 42.3 knots (78.3 kilometres an hour).

The *Devil Cat* can beat that. Its top speed is 80 kilometres an hour, laden with 900 people and 240 cars, or more than 90 kilometres an hour empty. In 1997/98, before its delivery to a North American customer, the Tasmanian government hired the *Devil Cat* to evaluate it for the Melbourne–Georgetown run. For four months it shuttled back and forth across Bass Strait, taking six hours for the crossing against the 12-hour overnight schedule of the regular Melbourne–Devonport car–passenger ferry, the *Abel Tasman*.

On our southbound crossing we were blessed with a perfectly flat-calm sea. The huge black ship, a jaunty Tasmanian Devil's face painted on its bow, wider than a cricket pitch, pushed along by almost 40,000 horsepower,

The Tasmanian ferry *Devil Cat* . . . stable and fast.

sliced through the sea in a dramatic illustration of its speed and stability. Inside, it was like a cavernous ballroom, with passengers having a choice of lounge or aircraft-style seats, or tables and chairs near a bar, food cafe, and poker machine or cinema sections. On our return it was much rougher, and when waves whacked against the main hull, the ship shuddered and jolted, but was barely slowed.

During both trips there was much muttering from Tasmanians that their government was being too slow and too reluctant to commission an Incat ferry for permanent use on the Bass Strait run. I have no knowledge of the economics involved, but with the evaluation trials over and the ferry withdrawn, it does seem to be a great opportunity missed — if only to showpiece an extraordinary made-in-Tasmania success story.

Tasmania, then known as Van Diemen's Land, was the second settled beachhead for the British in Australia. Ten years after the First Fleet arrived at Sydney Cove, the treacherous waters of Bass Strait had been charted, and in 1803 the flag was hoisted over a settlement of 49 marines and convicts on the Derwent River at Hobart. This was a pre-emptive move to discourage French interest in annexing land, but it was also the beginning of a convict society more harsh and repressive than New South Wales. For the next 50 years the toughest, most recalcitrant convicts were sent to Van Diemen's Land, and the worst of those were deposited in the most remote place imaginable — on Macquarie Harbour, on the island's gale-swept south-west coast. Van Diemen's Land redefined the word 'horror' for those sent there to endure it. A visit today to the Hobart museum affronts the senses: we gasped at man's inhumanity to man as we gazed on the tools of torture designed to subdue rebellious convicts. That

Strahan, on Macquarie Harbour, Tasmania . . . echoes of convict hell.

Sunset over Macquarie Harbour . . . twilight sightseeing.

Tasmania's wild western coast . . . the edge of the world.

any human would inflict these loathsome devices on any other was beyond our comprehension. There, on display among the spiked handcuffs designed to rip the flesh, heavy iron face masks and the more familiar balls and chains, were dunking boxes, where men were locked in coffin-like wooden boxes hung from a ship's yardarms and submerged in icy seas as the vessel rolled from side to side; keel-hauling contraptions designed to rip to shreds a man's back as he was pulled from one side of the ship to the other — underwater, across the barnacles; and cats-o'-nine tails, the cruel whips used to flog prisoners up to 700 times for a single punishment. Those in power said the convicts were deranged, but the same can be said of them, given the abhorrent and repulsive methods devised to subdue their prisoners.

We cruised on Macquarie Harbour, its water stained brown from tannins washed down the wild Gordon River, and passed between Sarah Island, the epicentre of convict subjugation, and a jagged rock called Grummet Island where convicts were sent into isolation for real or imagined breaches of their unconscionably strict behavioural codes. On this serene day of gentle breezes and a warm sun, we could see on Sarah Island the remnants of barracks buildings and the shape of the stone wharf, but only if we shut our eyes and dreamed a little could we hear the cries and whimperings of the poor souls consigned to this hell on earth in the 1820s.

Life was so harsh, and punishment so severe, that several convicts chose to bolt into the bush and confront the mountainous wilderness in an attempt to get to Hobart. Some succeeded, most by the expedient means of killing and eating their fellow escapees. It was hard to imagine such confronting atrocities in this calm and languid place.

Macquarie Harbour was abandoned after just ten years, but not for any altruistic reasons. It was too hard to service. It could be reached only by ship, and then with the utmost difficulty because of its slim and shallow entrance, the dreaded Hell's Gates. This narrow passage is protected from the huge waves which travel unimpeded across the Roaring Forties from Argentina by a rocky promontory tipped by Cape Sorrel. Strong winds, tides and shifting sands frequently impeded the passage of sailing ships which often had to wait for weeks before favourable conditions allowed them to thread the eye of the needle through its turbulent waters. Because of the happy convergence of gentle winds, high tides and slight seas, we were able to confidently motor through, past jagged rocks and sandy bars, to glimpse, through salt spray and summer haze, the endless beaches of the Tasmanian west coast, pummelled by towering waves, littered with wrecks, and known as the edge of the world.

In place of Macquarie Harbour, a more convenient penal settlement was established on the Tasman Peninsula, east of Hobart. Its name, too, was to become synonymous with abominable deeds: Port Arthur. Built grandly of sandstone, overlooking a calm bay and an offshore cemetery on the Isle of the Dead, it was to become in its day the harshest expression of the convict system. When transportation to Tasmania ceased in 1853,

Port Arthur was retained — as an asylum for those poor inmates it had sent mad. Today it is the major tourist attraction of Tasmania, its tales told over and over by convict-suited guides to goggle-eyed school children and adults who, like us, listen, absorb, and come away failing to comprehend how our ancestors could have done such terrible things to their own kind.

'Welcome to Port Arthur historic site,' the signs say as we swing through the gate and pay our entry fee. 'Within these majestic and beautiful grounds lies a rich and full history of Tasmania's convict past. Port Arthur staff are here to assist you with information about the history of the area . . . '

But don't mention the incident.

It's official policy: please don't ask questions about 28 April 1996, when the world's worst mass murder took place here. Thirty-five people died, but you won't find the name of the lone gunman, Martin Bryant, mentioned anywhere.

Not in the welcoming brochure. Not at the site of the cross which is a memorial for the victims. Not in the patter of the tour guides who lead their half-hourly knots of sightseers past the memorial without a glance or a word.

It's as if Port Arthur, and by association, Tasmania, is in denial. Sure, Port Arthur has a past, but it's an old, faded past of convicts, floggings, solitary confinement, bread and water, and 1000 graves on the Isle of the Dead.

The past which is Port Arthur's future as a tourist destination simultaneously showcases a prison system designed to grind down the human spirit in the name of reforming the soul, and the roots of Australia's modern history. The wounds of the more recent past are too new, too raw and too deep to be confronted.

The welcoming brochure to Port Arthur sets the policy. 'The losses were many,' it says. 'Loss of life, loss of self esteem and loss of faith in human nature. For all those recovering the aim is not that of trying to forget, but to accept what cannot be undone and strive to enjoy life once again. You can help staff and convey your respect for their grief and privacy by not asking them to provide details about the tragedy and its aftermath, including issues relating to gun law reform.'

Given that request, it's an insensitive person who mentions the unmentionable. But in talks with Tasmanians away from Port Arthur, I was told that 'loss of self esteem and loss of faith in human nature' was a coded way of describing squabbles brought on by guilt and jealousies felt by the survivors.

Some were guilty that they had survived; others compared their compensation payments with rumoured payouts to others, and were disgruntled. Some bought new cars with their payments, and were heavily criticised for being seen to be flashily profiting from tragedy. These pressures were tearing at the fabric of their small society.

But life does go on at Port Arthur, however nervously. About 250,000 people a year come here, and when we visited, the Broad Arrow Cafe, where 20 died, was a shell, with just the walls standing, their gutted windows framing the ruins of the penitentiary across the park. A temporary structure served as a cafe and as Wendy and I sat on its balcony eating a sandwich and sipping a cool drink, I counted the number of people around us. Twenty, including us. It was impossible not to

The remains of the Broad Arrow Cafe, Port Arthur, Tasmania . . . don't mention the incident.

think, what if? What if we had been here that day? What if it happened again?

But we said nothing, and turned our attention to the sanitised version of history offered by the tour guide. The hell-hole harshness of this place as a prison was somewhat glossed over in favour of its few positives: how it boasted a school for prisoners' learning; how there was a library of 12,000 books for their enlightenment; how a convict dressed himself in kangaroo skin and tried to hop past the guards to escape, only to be shot at by a guard who fancied a feed of 'roo, ho, ho, ho.

Today, the hurt, the evil, the pain, the punishment, the degradation and the induced lunacy of Port Arthur's old past is giving way to a Disneyland approach justified by the view that people want their tourism as entertainment.

Hardship, hurt, man's inhumanity to man, and death are more palatable as distant history than recent memory. Just don't mention Martin Bryant.

We swept along the east coast, past Maria Island, another convict outpost, though milder, enjoying the wild beaches and coastal towns like Bicheno which reminded us of southern English ports. Then inland, to Pyengana, known for its speciality cheeses, a nationally recognised Tasmanian niche product. But Pyengana has another claim to fame — its Pub in a Paddock, where, on the payment of 50 cents, a pig called Slops in a pen hung with signs saying 'Geez, I'm dry' and 'I'd love a beer' will skol a beer shandy for your amusement. The Pyengana pub's walls are decorated with humorous signs, many of them familiar. But one caught my eye for its defiantly Ocker male political incorrectness, and I report it here, hastening to add, utterly without endorsement!

Fifteen Reasons Why a Beer is Better than a Woman

1. *A beer doesn't get jealous when you grab another beer.*
2. *When you go to a bar, you know you can always pick up a beer.*
3. *A beer won't get upset if you come home with beer on your breath.*
4. *You don't have to wine and dine a beer.*
5. *If you pour a beer right, you'll always get good head.*
6. *Hangovers go away.*
7. *When you've finished with a beer, the bottle is still worth 5 cents.*
8. *You don't have to wash a beer before it tastes good.*
9. *A beer always goes down easily.*
10. *You can share a beer with your mates.*
11. *Beer is always wet.*
12. *You always know you're the first to pop a beer.*
13. *A frigid beer is good beer.*
14. *You can have more than one beer and not feel guilty.*
15. *You can enjoy a beer all month long.*

Tut-tutting, we carried on through twisting forest roads, the domain of hurtling timber trucks, to Scottsdale and its niche industry: opium poppies, growing by the millions, entirely legally, in neat fields of eggshell blue/green, surrounded by fences on which hang bold red signs screaming KEEP OUT. The opium farmers supply their crops by contract to the pharmaceutical industry, and the locals just shrug: this isn't the Golden Triangle of Burma; there are no warlords here; this is just another crop; just another job; just another business for us.

At Piper's Brook we paid homage to some fine cool-climate wines, and tucked some

Opium poppies near Scottsdale, Tasmania . . . a niche industry.

away in the car for long-term cellaring when we got home. They didn't survive the trip, being called on to meet more urgent needs, which I will come to later. Many Tasmanian wines are highly praised and sought after on the mainland, but little effort is made to promote them in their own backyards. At the Star Cafe in Launceston, twice named Australian Bistro of the Year, only four of the 25 wines on the cellar list were Tasmanian. 'Our customers just won't buy them,' the bar attendant explained. 'They cost us 50 per cent more than mainland wines, and people don't judge them to be 50 per cent better.' This is a paradox reflected at many levels in the niche food industry: there is a greater export demand for the clean, green Tasmanian product than a local demand. We went to the Star Cafe looking for the Tasmanian produce we had read about in brochures aboard the *Devil Cat* — and faced a choice of wood-fired pizza, Californian salad, Brunswick steak sandwich, Thai beef salad, Singapore noodles, Italian pasta and focaccia, served in a room with Spanish tiles on the floor and Italian decor. It seems to me there are opportunities being missed!

We made our way to Liffey, a quaint village at the eastern end of the imposing Great Western Tiers. There, under the towering buttress of Drys Bluff, we met Dr Bob Brown.

'My life as an environmentalist began right here,' said Bob Brown, waving at his tiny white-painted 1904 wooden home under the bluff. From its peak, world heritage conservation protection continues unbroken

Senator Bob Brown outside his home at Liffey, Tasmania . . . 'My life as an environmentalist began here.'

to South East Cape — the southernmost point of Tasmania. This, a quarter of a century after he arrived in this peaceful spot, is Bob Brown's legacy. He has no electric power at his rustic home. He had it cut off during his battles with the Hydro Electric Commission, but not to worry: the kettle boils quickly on the open wood fire in his sitting room, and he comfortably curls himself into a threadbare old armchair as we sip tea.

He's a stubborn, determined bloke. He had to be, otherwise he would have long ago crumpled before the steamroller weight of the Tasmanian Establishment, the Hydro Electric Commission, the timber industry, and every shade of political opinion other than Green. But he has stood his ground, argued his case, campaigned incessantly, gone to gaol, been elected to the state Parliament and then the

national Senate, and has, along the way, earned the respect of a nation which, sometimes begrudgingly, sees that commitment, determination and belief in the power of the individual can have its rewards. He fights on for a brave new world where children can grow up without a sense of dread; he talks of new paradigms and new ways of thinking, proposing policies which are mocked by his enemies. He stands firm, plucking from history examples of why he believes the time will come when his ideas are universally accepted. 'When the end of slavery was proposed, the idea was opposed vigorously by those who said it would wreck the economy, it would change society for the worse, it was against Biblical tenets, and the emancipists should be tarred and feathered,' he said. 'Now we take people's freedoms for granted. Revolutions in the way we think aren't new to history.'

The revolution within Bob Brown began in 1972 when he answered an advertisement for a doctor in Launceston. He knew immediately he was home in the wild beauty on his doorstep. He was invited to join a rafting trip down the Franklin River, and was hooked. 'That two weeks, with platypuses floating trip around those wonderful gorges, the waterfalls, the caves where Aboriginal people had lived 15,000 years before — the southernmost people of the last Ice Age — the ancient Huon pines and the rainforests . . . it was just magnificent,' he said. 'Then we came around a corner of the river into the Gordon, and there were jackhammers and explosions and helicopters going to and fro, and here was the first work anchoring the dam which was to flood the Franklin. So I came back and thought about it — and a little while later a group of 16 of us formed the Wilderness Society and decided to fight the dam before it was built. We had lost Lake Pedder, and we couldn't afford to fight a rearguard action. We had to get in first. Seven years later the river was saved.'

It wasn't quite as easy as Bob makes it sound. That seven years was filled with crises, challenges, political chicanery and seesawing public opinion. At first, the Wilderness Society held a 2–1 opinion poll majority in favour of saving the river, partly because Bob and some friends had bought a second-hand movie camera and made a film of a trip down the river. They bought half an hour of TV time for $800, and for the first time illustrated to people in Tasmania the value of the island's natural beauty. They also got support from celebrities like Peter Allen, Eartha Kitt and David Bellamy, and in 1975 Bob made his first run for political office.

During the campaign he acknowledged his homosexuality, a deliberate move to 'get it over with and make it history'. His opponents seized on his statement and later, in the crucial 1982 election with the Franklin River at stake, conducted a letterbox campaign in Hobart, and 'Whoosh — the opinion polls went down; I lost in the election, and so did friends all over the place. It was a disaster for us.

'Amid this anguish a very close friend took me aside and said: "Bob, we've got to stop this. We can't win. Everything is against us. You can't do this to other people." For days I had a crisis of conscience. What she said made sense. But on the other hand, I knew the Franklin gave people enormous inspiration; it was a place for relaxation and recreation, and even if we didn't save it, we had to make a stand. Where there's life, there's hope. We had to maintain our trajectory. The developmental ethos was out of hand, out of control, and wrong. We had to keep going.'

And keep going they did, in the face of threats, phone taps, rabbit guts stuffed in his letterbox, logging trucks blaring their horns as they passed his home night and day, and abuse at the graveside as he buried his mother: a cry from a passer-by as she was lowered into the grave, 'Put him in with her!'

'It was a really difficult time,' Bob said. 'My mother was a strong lady, and wise. As a kid I remember bringing home a bunch of flowers for her when we lived in the bush between Bathurst and Goulburn. I remember her saying: "Thankyou very much, I'll put them in a vase. But really, don't you think they'd be better in the bush where they could flower and make seeds for more?" I was also aware at that time that people like me — agitators — were disappearing off the streets, being tortured, and dropped from helicopters in places like Argentina, but I felt if we couldn't look future generations in the eye and say "we thought of you in everything we did," we would devalue our present, and our lives.'

Gradually, the opinion polls came back in favour of the Wilderness Society, mainly due to support from the mainland. As the society planned the 'most extraordinary civil disobedience campaign ever in this country' — a blockade of the bulldozers — a survey in Melbourne showed the anti-dam forces had 58 per cent support. About 20,000 people rallied in Melbourne, and the message was heard in Canberra. The Labor Party held its national conference and controversially approved uranium mining at Roxby Downs. The next day, in a trade-off to its left wing, angry about the uranium mine, it voted to make 'No Franklin Dam' its official policy. Seven months later Labor won office, and the High Court delivered a 4–3 judgment which confirmed the federal government's power to do so through international treaties. The rest is history.

Bob Brown's view of the future ranges from the dreamy to the jolting. He is dismissive of short-sighted local politicians who, he says, have squandered an opportunity to launch Tasmania into a new era of prosperity built on small businesses operating in dozens of speciality niches; and he argues the cause of world government. When I express surprise at this thought, he describes his vision of a global democracy with participants willing and able to make enforceable laws on the transborder issues which confront us all. This doesn't stop at familiar Green concerns like global warming, or acid rains or waste recycling; it extends to policing the global economy and regulating the flow of capital and money market

manipulation. Otherwise, he says, we will sink under the ruthless, exploitative weight of unelected multinational organisations which make their own rules to suit their own pockets. It is an interesting thought, but one at full odds with the economic rationalist philosophies which dominate world trade at the end of the 20th century. It may be a long time before Bob Brown takes his seat in a World Parliament.

Tasmania received $500 million in compensation for not building the Gordon–Franklin Dam. That money was used to build three smaller dams. 'It would have been an enormous boost to small business,' Bob said. 'The environmental tick — clean, green and clever — is hugely important; we have a reputation for the finest agricultural products in the boutique sense. We could build on that in agriculture, wine, high-quality wood-based products; benchmark products with special appeal. Up the road from here at the end of my valley, people are growing hundreds of thousands of daffodils, right up to the snow line. It's the last place in Australia where daffodils bloom, and they're selling them in the markets of Melbourne. Singapore, here we come. They're doing the same with herbs. On the side of this mountain is a native cress which grows in the rocks. It tastes a little like watercress. All you have to do is pick up some seeds, throw it into a pot, and away it goes. Somebody is going to get hold of it, grow it in a hothouse, and suddenly Tasmanian cress will be the world's new garnish. Organic products are at a premium worldwide. We — all of Australia — could be the organic basket of the world. Instead of saying it's a greenie issue, we should see it as a world market. The role of government should be to support these things: for a

Senator Bob Brown among the destruction of clear-felling . . . 'The smell is death.'

modest amount of money we can establish business incubators. If you are the only grower of cress, you might find it difficult to create a market. That needs government support.'

Bob Brown and the Greens are used to being dismissed as jam makers and basket weavers. But, he insists, Tasmanians are going through a metamorphosis by recognising that the state has unique assets. 'Tourism is the fastest growing global industry, but we get only 2 per cent of the visitors who come to Australia,' he said. 'The fastest growing end of tourism is remote eco-tourism, and we've got the best of it in our world heritage areas. But the federal government has put $100 million into woodchipping, which employs 2500 people and is still shedding jobs, while tourism employs 18,000 people. The establishment understands resource extraction and exports; they don't understand the values of standing resources, like wilderness forests, and imports — that is, bringing people here to see it. To achieve that they must promote and market the clean, green image.'

Woodchipping is a running sore on the Tasmanian landscape. We drove with Bob Brown to his favourite spot, Liffey Falls, where even the mid-summer trickle of water over the wide falls couldn't mask the sylvan beauty of the spot. He gave us a tree-by-tree description of their origins and relationship to the rainforests of Gondwanaland, in between greeting and chatting to constituents whose reactions to meeting their senator ranged from awe to gruff praise. The days of abuse may be over.

'There are still some places where I would be unwise to go,' he said. 'I'm not particularly welcome in some communities.' As we drove down a corrugated gravel road, Bob glanced several times in his rear-vision mirror. A large red Landcruiser ute with a black bull bar was close behind us. 'A problem?' I asked. 'You never know,' he said, pulling over to allow it to pass. We drove on several hundred metres and suddenly emerged into a flattened space. A tangle of tree limbs and roots covered the ripped ground; logs were piled in stacks beside the road; heavy yellow machines with long claw-like arms and bulldozer tracks parked between the stacks. This was clear-felling, where all living things had been flattened over an area of about 30 hectares. It was wanton desecration, and it stank.

This was my first encounter with woodchipping in progress. As Bob talked, in a despairing but matter-of-fact way, my brain began to hum John Williamson's lament for our forests:

What am I gunna do
What about the future
Gotta draw the line without delay
Why shouldn't I get emotional
The bush is sacred
Ancient life will fade away
Over the hill they go
Killing another mountain
Gotta fill the quota
Can't go slow
Huge machinery wiping out the scenery
One big swipe like a shearer's blow.

'It's like a cancer eating away at the rest of the natural world,' said Bob. 'This place is probably owned by someone who thinks it's OK to cut down his little patch because he

needs the money, but when you translate this into meeting the needs of six billion people, you've rapidly got nothing left at all.

'The sad thing is that it's such a waste. See that log there, which has been split by being pushed over? If that had been cut properly, it would have been a good saw log. It could have been made into something valuable. Even in China it would have ended up as spoons, or chairs or implements. Here it's going to a woodchip mill, and will very soon end up on the rubbish dumps of Japan.

Rip rip woodchip
Turn it into paper
Throw it in the bin
No news today
Nightmare dreaming
Can't you hear the screaming
Chainsaw, eyesore, more decay.

'They clear-fell because it's uneconomical to selectively cut trees. It's all or nothing. And it's so stupid. We're not getting any value from our resource. These logs are sold for $12 a tonne. When they go through the mill, they are loaded on freighters and are valued at $120 a tonne. They'll come out of a Japanese paper mill worth $1200 a tonne, and within a few months, they'll cost a lot of money to be dumped as landfill. They won't even be worth recycling as paper again, because the Japanese recycling industry is being undercut by the low price of raw materials coming out of Australian forests.'

Remember the axemen
Knew their timber
Cared about the way they brought it down
Cross cut, black butt,
Tallow wood and cedar

Build another bungalow pioneer town
I am the bush and I am koala
We are the one,
Go hand in hand
I am the bush like Banjo and Henry
It's in my blood
Gotta make a stand.

'That smell is death, and that's why there are all these blowflies around. They are attracted by the fresh flow of sap, but also by the carcasses of animals killed in this operation. When clear-felling takes place, everything goes. All the trees, all the undergrowth, and all the animals and birds that live within it. You'd be amazed at the number of species supported in forests like this used to be. But there is no way the animal life can be removed before the bulldozers move in, so it all dies. It's total annihilation; first the chainsaws, then the cable logger or snigger dragging selected logs to the trucks, then the fire-bombing with napalm-like incendiaries dropped from the air with the aim of destroying any chance of rainforest revegetation. After replanting, the zone is poisoned with 1080 to kill grazing marsupials. Gone are the animals. Gone is the arboreal habitat for owls, eagles, parrots, bats, gliders, possums and insects. It's no argument to say it will all grow back in 30 years. It takes longer than that for habitats to develop; trees must reach a maturity before limb-falling begins, creating holes for nesting birds and animals. That won't happen here. They'll probably log it again before it gets the chance.'

Rip rip woodchip
Turn it into paper
Throw it in the bin
Don't understand

Nightmare dreaming
Can't you hear the screaming
Stirs my blood
Going to make a stand.

As I took photographs and bemoaned the destruction surrounding us, Bob fidgeted. Time to get a move on. 'It wouldn't do for me to be seen here,' he said. Two days later, as we flew on a scenic flight over the South West Wilderness, I could see the extent of logging operations. Forests from Hobart to the edge of the World Heritage area at Lake Pedder resembled a chessboard with various squares flattened, others in early stages of regeneration, and others almost ripe for another harvest; pockmarks on the face of extreme beauty.

The same can be said of the road recently cut through the Tarkine Wilderness in Tasmania's north-west. Bulldozers have shoved aside the feeble topsoils supporting rare button grasses and heathlands which have evolved into unique eco-systems over millions of years, exposing a dusty white scar described by Bob Brown as the work of 'vandals breaking into the cathedral for the beleaguered human spirit'. The extraordinary thing about this road, providing a direct link between Zeehan and the hamlet of Arthur River, is that it's quite unnecessary. Both centres are already served by other roads. The sole aim of this environmental vandalism is to provide access to the Tarkine forests for woodchippers.

While this kind of official madness continues, Bob Brown's fight to preserve the natural beauty of his adopted home state will never be over.

Soon after entering the Tarkine Way we reached the Donaldson River, running fresh and clear beneath a towering rainforest. As I invited a trout to take my lure, another car turned into the parking bay.

'G'day. Where you from?'

'Launceston. And you?'

'Sydney. On the beach at Manly.'

'Manly, eh? You might know my friend, Nadia. She lived on the beach at Manly.'

And so, in the depths of the forest, on a road to nowhere, used by few people, a little mystery was solved. On our walks along the Manly foreshore we would often see a woman in grubby white leather pants, pink socks, a fur-hooded car coat, and a coloured scarf over her greying red hair. If she were not sleeping on a park bench, she would be sitting, painting her nails, and airing her worldly possessions beside her. Sometimes we saw her foraging in rubbish bins, but we never saw her with alcohol. She was our local Bag Lady, until one day, she wasn't there any more.

Our roadside acquaintance told us that Nadia was her former business partner, the wife of a wealthy businessman who lived in a salubrious two-storey house in suburban Launceston. One day she left, without a word. Two years later she returned to her home, as if nothing had happened. It's a strange world.

There were two more things I wanted to do in Tasmania: catch a trout in the mountain lakes, and visit the southernmost tip of the nation.

The trout were obliging. We set up camp at the southern end of Lake St Clair, where chubby wallabies begged for food scraps, and consulted experts on local lures. In some roadside service stations, lures are packaged according to their alleged ability to attract trout in different lakes. A Great Lake lure will be of a colour and design quite different from a Lake Pedder lure, or a Lake St Clair

Tasmanian brown trout . . . obliging.

lure, although I found it hard to credit the fish would know the difference. But in fishing, local knowledge is everything, so I took their advice and tied on a polka-dotted yellow and red number. The morning was cold and grey, with mists swirling across the water. It was touch-and-go: would we spend our day shivering and damp? But no sooner had we hit the water than the mists lifted, the clouds parted and departed, and warm sun streamed down on the mirrored waters of the lake. It was nirvana! We puttered along, sometimes casting, sometimes trolling, always enchanted by the beauty of the tall trees reflected in the water, the freshness of the air, and the splendid isolation of it all. Then whack! A brown trout snapped at my lure, and we brought it aboard, a fine specimen, thankyou very much. Then

South East Cape, Tasmania . . . next landfall, Antarctica.

Kelp clings to rocks near South East Cape . . . giant suction cups.

another; and another; and one more which spat out the hook as it came close to the boat. We kept two for dinner, and released the other. All took my yellow-and-red lure; none were attracted to Wendy's chosen lure of striped pink. But both were labelled as Lake St Clair specials. Who can explain the mysteries of fishing?

I felt satisfied by my catch. Somehow the experience balanced the barramundi caught in the rivers of the far north. In the same way, having been to the tip of Cape York, I wanted to go to the southernmost point of Australia — South East Cape.

We sauntered down the Channel Highway from Hobart, through pretty little towns like Kettering, Snug and the delightfully named Flowerpot, the mountains to our right and the D'Entrecastreaux Channel to our left. Frequently along the channel we spotted clutches of circular cages in the water; the famed Tasmanian salmon farms where millions of fine fish thrive in the cold waters destined to be smoked, steamed or grilled and served, pink, delicious and good for your heart, in homes or restaurants around the region. This new industry continues to grow apace, with Tasmanian salmon farmers finding it difficult to keep up with the demand from sashimi-loving Japan. It's another example of a Tasmanian niche industry, far more viable and acceptable than the logging further down the coast.

We picked up Sue Douglas, a friend who had quit the Sydney rat-race for a personal sea change making furniture from recycled timbers in the bucolic surrounds of Middleton. She is not alone. A combination of relatively cheap land and living, four definable seasons a year, a distinct lack of stress, intense beauty, and a growing market for cottage-industry products, has made

Tasmania increasingly popular for drop-outs from mainland cities. Sue had been in Tasmania for a couple of years, but she had never been to the South East Cape, so she willingly guided us up the Huon Valley to cross the river at Huonville, and south through Geeveston and Dover, where the pub claims to be the southernmost watering hole in the nation. Through the forests near Lune River we encountered more areas of clear-felling, and I felt saddened and angry. But in these parts it's best to keep your views to yourself. Those who make their living from the logging industry fight ferociously for their rights to continue to destroy.

Cockle Creek is as far as you can go by road. Like The Tip at the top of the country, it would require a walk to get to the bottom of the nation, but this time, instead of a kilometre or so, we were faced with a ten-kilometre trek through rocky wooded hills, across a swampy flatland and, finally, through rolling coastal rainforests. We emerged from the forests under the brow of a weathered formation called Bare Hill, where seams of black coal ribboned the surface. Below, down 79 steps, was the beach of South Cape Bay; the end of the line. From here you can see South East Cape, but cannot reach it. There are no tracks to the point where Australia abruptly plunges into the frigid sea which separates us from Antarctica. We ate a picnic lunch on the squeaking white sand, and puddled around honeycombed rocks and tidal pools filled with eight-pointed iridescent blue starfish, marvelling at giant skeins of fat kelp clinging by suction-cup to the rocks at the water's edge. We also marvelled at the walkers who approached from the western end of the beach. They had travelled down the Port Davey Track from Lake Pedder, through the Lost World Plateau, linked up with the South

Folk music festival at Cygnet, Tasmania . . . jam session.

Coast Track at Bathurst Harbour, crossed the Ironbound Range, and had two hours' walking to reach their destination at Cockle Creek after about 150 kilometres and nine days in the wilderness. You have to be keen — and fit — to do this, but in the absence of any roads it is, literally, the only way to go. Much to their credit, Tasmanian national parks authorities have invested heavily in the walking trails, building wooden walkways across sensitive areas to avoid the problems of erosion and soil compacting.

Most times, there's not much to the hamlet of Cygnet, 50 kilometres south of Hobart. Three pubs, a few shops and a community centre dotted each side of the Channel Highway, and that's about it. But we passed through on the annual Cygnet Folk Festival weekend, billed as Tasmania's folk and world music event of the year, and the joint was jumping! Over three days a dozen or so concerts were planned, featuring an Irish bazouki, tin whistles, flamenco guitars, pan pipes, Cajun fiddles and African drums. There were sessions for kids, workshops, puppets and a fancy dress dance.

We were drawn to an impromptu jam session at the centre pub. Under a stretched sail, purloined from or loaned by a local yachtie, it provided shade for an ever-widening circle of up to 20 musos jamming away their Sunday afternoon. There were guitars, accordions, banjos, violins, pipes — and plenty of Guinness. The musicians were as varied as their instruments; some young, clean-shaven and spruced up; others with hair in ponytails with roll-your-own butts

Hobart from Mount Wellington.

singeing straggly beards; some in beaten-up hats carrying badges from past festivals in out-of-the-way places; others in smart white hats or crisp caps. Their music, with a strong leaning towards Irish jigs, was wonderfully infectious. After each number one of the musicians would strum a few bars to set up a new rhythm, and the others would catch on to it, joining in with gusto, occasionally singing a few lines of chorus. I was particularly taken by a couple of local players who duelled on their banjos and fiddles like in the scene from the film *Deliverance*.

After several hours we left, toes tapping, wondering what Cygnet would be like for the other 363 days of the year.

Back on the mainland, we headed north, through the rich food bowls of the nation —

through the dairying and fruit-growing areas of northern Victoria, the plains of the Riverina, the western slopes of central New South Wales, and on to the fertile New England region. Along the way we stopped at Echuca to visit the historic wharf, a reminder that the Murray River was a vital transport link before the advent of rail; we explored the Barmah State Forest on the banks of the Murray; said 'g'day' to thousands of ostriches pecking their way over barren paddocks; and marvelled quietly at the seasonal differences between this summer drive and the last time we had been through this area. In spring the colours were green, gold and purple: green pastures, golden canola crops and the purple flush of Salvation Jane, a weed also known as Paterson's Curse. The summer had

An ancient and gnarled eucalypt beside the Murray River in the Barmah State Forest, Victoria.

transformed the landscape into a palette of beige grasslands and russet paddocks lying fallow, merging in hues of smoky blue towards the horizon.

Near Deniliquin we kept a rendezvous with Ken and Maureen Cowley at Boonoke, the famous Merino sheep-breeding stud. For more than 130 years the bloodlines of the Peppin rams were developed at Boonoke and its associated properties, their genes reaching out across the nation and underpinning both the quality of Australian wool and the popular belief that Australia rode on the sheep's back. It was another of our great myths, because although Australia did rely on farm produce as its main source of export income before the postwar manufacturing base was established, wool never amounted to more than 40 per cent of our total exports. Today it's substantially less.

To me, the son of a soldier settler wool-grower, a visit to Boonoke was an opportunity to see how the industry had progressed over four decades, and to explore the reality of modern farming: that agriculture has become agri*business*. That distinction is personified in Ken Cowley, a great Australian who has modestly never sought to elbow his way into the public consciousness as one of the nation's most influential business barons. He is a quietly-spoken, thoughtful and good-humoured man who was, for 20 years, publishing magnate Rupert Murdoch's chief executive in Australia. Today, retired from News Limited, he sits as a director of the parent News

Echuca, on the Murray River, Victoria . . . historic wharf.

Corporation, chairs Ansett International and Ansett New Zealand, is part owner of the Newslink airport shops and the R. M. Williams chain of bush outfitter stores, and is chairman of the Stockman's Hall of Fame in Longreach, Queensland. The son of a dairy farmer, he wanted to become a jackeroo, but took on a printing diploma because his father insisted he have a trade. That wasn't enough to challenge his deep spiritual feeling for the land, a hunger fed by maintaining country properties throughout his city working life.

Ken Cowley graciously defers to Murdoch when telling of News Corporation's 1978 purchase of the F. S. Falkiner properties, Boonoke, Peppinella, Wanganella, Billabong, Warriston and Barratta (added in 1986). But there is no doubt that the frustrated jackeroo was the driving force; he brought the properties to Murdoch's attention; he fanned his interest, negotiated the sale details, and has been the strategic driving force behind the businesses since. What he doesn't take credit for, though, is the fact that the properties were heavily discounted because of a prolonged drought in 1978, and two weeks after the purchase, the rains came down in buckets. That was Murdoch's luck!

It is surely an accident of history, but ironic nevertheless, that the two most famous sheep-breeding studs in the land are owned by Murdochs. F. S. Falkiner and Sons has been owned by News Corporation since 1978. In 1995, one of its strongest competitors, Collinsville stud in the mid-north of South Australia, was acquired by Paddy Handbury, Rupert Murdoch's nephew.

From the outset, Cowley insisted the Falkiner properties had to be quality businesses. 'From the day we took possession, we have concentrated on lifting the quality of the things we do,' he said. 'We have invested money and effort in genetic development of our sheep, including joining by artificial insemination, ongoing progeny testing, and benchmarking, and it wasn't by pure chance we became the first wool-growers in the world to satisfy the highest demands of the International Standards Organisation's quality assurance program. We have also made marketing and risk-management initiatives which lead the industry.'

At every stage, modern business management principles apply. The properties' executive director, Alec Morrison, recalls that Cowley's cajoling was challenging at first, but, given the tools to do the job, it was a quantum leap in farm management. Today the average value — and profit return — of every sheep is known; what nourishment they need to maximise returns; what it costs to keep them; how much wool they will produce while they graze on the flat plains; how much meat they will yield when sold; how breeding programs create finer wool quality and heavier fleece weight trendlines irrespective of seasonal variations; how fertility testing of ewes and libido testing of rams could improve lambing percentages; how managers could be given incentives and rewards for initiative and accountability; how irrigation could drought-proof the properties and create opportunities for cash crops such as rice; how forward selling of unshorn wool could minimise risk; and how the needs and demands of the stud's customers must be the company's highest priority.

In this way the clever farmers of the nation are running profitable businesses. The new

Ostrich farms provide a new income in the New South Wales Riverina district.

approaches to agribiz take advantage of new technologies — even global positioning systems fitted to headers to record the precise locations of top-yielding wheat paddocks, so that more grain can be harvested from less acreage, with consequential reductions in inputs such as fuel. As many in the bush cry out against change, and demand a return to the agrarian socialist policies of the past — support and protection, segment by segment — the smart operators are getting on with business. Today, when Australia produces four times more agricultural product than it consumes, it is said 30 per cent of farmers are producing 70 per cent of the product and 100 per cent of the profits.

'Property rationalisation is under way,' said Alec Morrison. 'There are 70,000 wool-

The palette of spring near Junee, New South Wales . . .
golden canola and pesky Salvation Jane.

growers in Australia, though perhaps only
40,000 are fair dinkum. The rest have a farm
and a lifestyle supported by off-farm incomes,
with one of the partners being a school
teacher, or whatever. Cost of production is the
major issue. You don't get maximum
efficiency until you have the equivalent of
10,000 dry sheep, which can be properly
managed by one man. But the average
Australian clip is taken from just 1000 sheep.

'A lot of farmers are looking to get out.
Their children have gone away; they don't
want the farm, and the parents are looking to
retire. All they want is enough to buy a house
in Dubbo, or Wagga or Albury, or wherever,
but this is putting downward pressure on the
value of land, which in turn is an opportunity
for those who want to get bigger.'

There are obviously big implications for
the social structure of the bush, in Alec's
assessment, but he is sanguine about it. 'That's
part of evolution. It's happening everywhere
around the world. There is a lot of fear about
the loss of community in small towns, but
when you have a look at it there's no need for
them anymore. There's no need for a pub
every dozen or so miles as there was back in
Cobb and Co.'s day, either. We have better
roads, better cars, phones, mobiles, faxes;

Boonoke, near Deniliquin, New South Wales . . .
rain is money.

increasingly we can get on the Internet with
local calls. People complain about the loss of
banking or medical services, but driving an
hour to a major centre isn't a big issue.

'The little villages have gone, the smaller
towns are going, and the bigger towns are
getting bigger. Housing is now getting very
expensive in places like Dubbo or Wagga, but
that just means the little towns get a new life
as commuter centres. Gilgandra, Narromine
and Wellington are all satellite centres to
Dubbo. These things have their own way of
sorting themselves out.'

Why do we wail so much over the decline
of country towns? Out on the Willandra
plains, the saltbush flatlands between
Hillston and Ivanhoe which the emus and
kangaroos call home, I tuned to the crackling

Fields of canola in South Australia's mid-north.

Sheep at Boonoke, near Deniliquin . . . farming is agribusiness.

voice of John Laws keeping the dream alive.

A woman called to bemoan the loss of the Australia she used to know. She appealed to Laws to 'make Australia what it was again', as if he could so by pressing one of the many buttons on his talkback radio console. 'We've had a gutful,' she cried. 'This country seems hellbent on closing down everything that's working.'

Across the Great Dividing Range at Merriwa, an 80-year-old cattle farmer was cussing the closure of the local Commonwealth Bank branch. 'This place is going to pieces,' he said.

Pessimism is a common theme in the bush. People believe Hanrahan's poetic prediction that 'we'll all be rooned'. But while some are wringing their hands in defeat, others are searching for — and finding — silver in the clouds of change enveloping Australia.

Take Canowindra, nestling in the rolling hills east of the Macquarie Ranges in central western New South Wales. It is recasting itself as a historic town and drawing tourists by the thousands. Its future is bright. Real estate prices are rising instead of falling, and the population of 1700 is growing with an influx of city slickers opting for a quieter life and cleaner air.

Australia can never again be what it was. No country Canutes can hold back the tidal waves of change. The best thing to do is adapt; to look to your strengths, find a niche, and build on it. That is what Canowindra has done through its annual hot air balloon festival, when 15,000 people descend on the town to attend a three-day event, injecting at least $1 million into the local economy.

We walked down the winding main street, its course originally defined by an old bullock trail, past the iron lace and filigree attached to wide verandas, and stopped at Finn's Old Store. Enter, and you go back in time; back to the way Australia used to be. The shelves are lined with old tins labelled Arnott's biscuits, Bushell's tea, IXL jams, Zebra stove black, Goanna oil, Moran and Cator cakes and Piccaninny floor polish. 'Imagine trying to sell that in these politically correct times,' said owner Russell Chick, a drop-out Sydney architect who moved to Canowindra almost a decade ago. Since then, he has scoured the bush sales to pick up his extraordinary collection of nostalgic wares.

'These towns have no future as service centres,' he said. 'There are dozens of places like this through the central west. They were established a day's journey by Cobb and Co. coach apart, and drew people from the surrounding district to get their supplies. But today everyone drives to Orange or Bathurst.' A heritage protection order on Canowindra's main street was bitterly opposed by some locals who launched rednecked objections to rules of preservation. They argued, 'It's my building and I'll do what I want with it' — but in the face of success in drawing tourists, their grumbles are increasingly muted.

Canowindra had two other pieces of luck going for it. It is home to the world's greatest collection of fossil fishes, 360 million years old. The locals are raising funds for a superb museum to house the extraordinary find, and paleontologists from around the globe come to visit, study and fossick.

And its position, nestled in a calm valley, makes it ideal for hot air ballooning. It has a benefactor in electronics millionaire Frank Hackett-Jones who bankrolled the annual Marti's Balloon Fiesta, named after his late mother, a local identity for many years. The festival is his gift to a community which nurtured him through his teenage years, and

Russell Chick minds his old-style shop, Finn's Old Store, in historic Canowindra, New South Wales.

Faces in the pub at Canowindra.

Balloonists prepare to fly at the annual Marti's Balloon Fiesta, Canowindra.

Sunrise at the Marti's Balloon Fiesta, Canowindra, as bizarre balloons in the shapes of a dinosaur and kookaburra prepare for take-off.

it is providing financial returns as spectacular as the 50-odd brightly coloured balloons it attracts each year.

Not all country towns have an angel like Frank Hackett-Jones sitting on their shoulders, but Canowindra has made the most of its luck. Other towns at the crossroads to an uncertain future could do well by following its example.

On to Tamworth for the annual Country Music Festival, a Mecca for fans from across the nation hellbent on aping country music fashions from across the seas. From street-corner buskers to national superstars, they strutted their stuff in a back-to-back program of song designed to wear out even the most avid fans. Families shopping in K-Mart could enjoy the Sutton Sisters doing Patsy Cline among the kitchen hardware; pubs and clubs staged morning, afternoon and night-time concerts; the big names hired the Town Hall; and everyone turned up for the climactic street parade to catch a glimpse of country music icon Slim Dusty, Ted Egan, down from The Alice, or comparative newcomers like

Balloons fly over parched paddocks near Canowindra.

Lee Kernaghan and Troy Cassar-Daley. It was a boot-scootin' week of song. But I felt I might have been in Nashville-Down-Under. Wherever we looked we were confronted with American fashions, American hats, American belt buckles, American fast food, and American songs about cowboys, not drovers, sung with fake American twangs. If there is, lurking within the Australian soul, a desire to *not* be like America, it takes a holiday during the Tamworth Music Festival. I have no argument with the notion of personal choice. To each his or her own. But each year the Tamworth organisers squander an opportunity to spotlight and showcase the best Australian country music by pandering to the belief that if it's American, it must be good.

Ireland, 1996. Four of us sightseeing around the Emerald Isle; our friends searching for their roots, posing in front of a Dublin bar bearing their family name; being entertained at lunch with United Distillers at Whiskey Corner, savouring Jameson's and Bushmills, enjoying a post-prandial singalong with a ruddy host named John Ryan. He gave us 'Danny Boy', of course, and 'Maggie', and 'I'll Take You Home Again Kathleen', and a ditty called 'Dicey O'Reilly', about a girl and the pitfalls of drink. Then he filled our eyes with tears as he mournfully sang what he called the saddest song he had ever known: Eric Bogle's lament to the futility of war: 'And the Band Played Waltzing Matilda'. We were ashamed that we could sing along with 'Danny Boy', but not with a song by an Australian which has become an internationally recognised classic.

Tamworth Music Festival… Nashville Down Under.

Eric Bogle was there, at the Longyard Hotel on Tamworth's outskirts, and I gulped with moist eyes as he sang it again. And the Bushwhackers, last seen after Opera in the Outback, belting out their brand of pure Australian anarchistic folk songs, fuelling the rugged individualism and anti-authoritarianism we like to think survives in an era of whingeing. And The Emu was there, too: John Williamson, whose 'Rip Rip Woodchip' had tunefully bounced around my head in the desecrated forests of Tasmania. At the Hog's Breath Cafe, after his sold-out performance at the Town Hall, we chatted about music, the bush, the flag and the future. And we agreed to meet again at his bush hideaway in the Gold Coast hinterland where he wrote 'Rip Rip'.

The Rainbow Country straddling the border of New South Wales and Queensland, where the Great Dividing Range nudges the sea, has long been home to a breed of uninhibited folk who have chosen to drop out of cities to commune with nature. Nimbin, in New South Wales, is the sadly tattered epicentre of this hippie haven from the seventies, a living museum of the make-love-not-war, have-another-joint, stress-free era of flared pants, beads, beards and flower-power. Originally seen by the region's long-established dairy farmers and forestry workers as a seditious threat to social order, they are now good-humouredly tolerated as harmless alternative lifestyle people whose hearts are, generally, in the right place.

John Williamson, the farmer's son from

Quambatook in Victoria's Mallee, is anything but a seventies' hippie. But in the early 1990s he bought a slice of this country just over the border in Queensland; mountain, valley, forest, creek and rainbows in the mist, because he believed it was so beautiful, and so threatened by development, that the best way to preserve it intact was to buy it and never, ever think of selling it. There was another reason: it inspires him to song.

What you see is what you get with John Williamson. He's a star, but not of the overnight kind. For more than a quarter of a century, since 'Old Man Emu' topped the charts in 1970, he's been around, singing his songs on a national stage, lending a hand to kids in crisis, koalas and the 'Buy Australian' campaign, flying his flags and making his stands for conservation and a republic. He's won umpteen Golden Guitar awards, Mo awards and an Order of Australia gong. But he's not a show pony. He's not up himself. He's a genuine good bloke; a fair dinkum Aussie. True blue.

'I didn't know I could write songs when I did "Old Man Emu",' he said. 'It never entered my mind that I could do it.' But that song hit a nerve with the Australian public in an era when gimmicky, comedy songs were popular, and it changed life's direction for John. He was, until then, a farmer. He had grown up in the sparse Mallee, a country kid who first felt the frisson of showbiz excitement attending charity concerts in Kerang, watching the last of the vaudevillians act out their era. 'I used to piss myself laughing, and I wanted to be a clown,' John said. But instead he went to boarding school in Melbourne and joined with three other school choir boys to form a group they called the John D Four — three Davids and one John. He became a prefect, and used his status

('no-one kept an eye on you if you were a prefect') to sneak out at night to haunt the jazz and folk clubs of Carlton and the city. 'It was a magic time,' he said. 'I had never heard anyone sing "Waltzing Matilda" with any gusto before, and I loved it. I didn't care about the hillbilly stuff, but I loved the Kingston Trio with their harmonies, Judy Durham was big then, and the biggest was Joan Baez singing "This Land is My Land". We moved to Moree in 1965, and I would play fullback in a local rugby team, then sing for three hours after the games in a local pub. I'd get $10 for it and spend it on wine and food. I was singing Roger Miller and Johnny Cash and a few Irish folk songs, and I'd do Rolf Harris's "Tie Me Kangaroo Down Sport". I thought it was fantastic. It got me thinking about how Australian it was, and how wonderful — the gimmick and all that — and it stuck with me. When I wrote "Old Man Emu" it was a mixture of Rolf and Roger Miller, with the jew's harp an answer to Rolf's wobbleboard. I used to sit at home at Moree and pick up 3UZ on the radio from Melbourne at nights and hear it climbing the charts, and I couldn't believe it.'

That was the beginning of the end of Farmer John. But other fates conspired. On the rich flat plains near Moree his family, including four brothers, grew wheat, sorghum and sunflowers. There were some good years, but then there were others. 'I remember one year when we lost 5000 tonnes of wheat in three days,' he said. '$1.5 million gone in three days. The frosts came and that was it. We mowed and baled it, but it rained like buggery and we got hardly anything for the bales. Farming is a way of life, but it's a tough one. It's almost a mug's game now. I probably would have gone away anyway, but "Old Man Emu" made it happen then.'

It's been a long road from Moree. Travelling, setting up in Mechanics Institute halls in one-horse towns, performing, packing up, moving on to do it all again. But on that endless road, around the nation more times than he can recall, John Williamson's soul merged with the Australian outback. 'A real Australian has the outback in their spirit,' he said. 'It's a far horizon in our psyche; a freedom we can't do without. It's so ancient, so prehistoric, it's gobsmacking. I throw myself into it. I'll stop my truck in the middle of nowhere and walk miles into a mountain range I'm driving past, feeling like I'm the only person who has ever been there. There is something special in walking up to a big boabab tree that doesn't have "I Love Jack" carved into it.

'The isolation is the best part of our country. There is always something you've never seen before, and I'm looking for that in my songwriting. I might be driving along looking at the clouds, and something goes around in my head and I'll say, "Hey, write this down: angels in the sky," and I'll use it somewhere. But mostly I write about how I feel, and I feel Australian, so I write songs about Australian people and Australian places, just like Willie Nelson writes about American places.'

If inspiration is anywhere, then the Williamsons' bush hideaway is John's favourite source of inspiration. The airy home which John and his wife Mary Kay designed themselves looks out over a precipitous rock cliff into a river valley of virgin rainforest. Mary Kay says her favourite time is when she wakes to see the valley filled with fog, the mists swirling around the trees at their bedroom window. Sitting on the balcony, listening to the whip birds, watching a curl of smoke rise from a farmhouse chimney deep below, the late afternoon light highlighting mountain bluffs across the valley; an Arthur Streeton painting, pink on distant blue. John picks up his guitar, strums and sings:

Clearing mist and morning dew
I think I'll stay in bed with you
With your warm feet touching mine
Might stay all day if the sun don't shine
I remember times like this when I'm far away
So darling give me one more kiss
One more for the road.

He wrote it where he is now sitting. He points to a partly cleared ridge below us. 'There's a beautiful rosewood there. I wrote "Rosewood Hill" after that tree. But it doesn't just depend on nature. I was watching SBS the other day, and there was this deep and meaningful European movie on. Lots of dark glances; people being pissed off with their lives of mediocrity. The girl didn't want to be like her parents, and I thought, "These silly whackers are missing out on life! They're not seeing what's worth seeing. They're stuck in their city; they've lost touch with the earth." And I wrote this song, a comment on today's society. Why are we so intense? Where's the lightness? It's my way of saying "For Christ's sake, wake up to yourselves. Look what we've got here! How could you be bored in this country?"'

Everybody's searching for a reason
Wasting time in the city
Looking for something to please them
Everybody's searching for a reason
This is not a heavy song
It's a light song
What's wrong with that?
Feeling the spirit of the earth
Spinning round round round
For God's sake seize the day

John Williamson in his rainforest 'cathedral'… 'You feel the power of the earth.'

See how the children play
How come you've got time to be
miserable
Anyway?

As the sun set across the valley, we talked about the flag and the republic. By the early 1980s John had realised his inspiration came from his Australian roots, and he began performing under the backdrop of a giant Australian flag. But it irked him to see the Union Jack in the corner — a symbol of colonialism under the southern skies — so he designed his own. It was a clutter of green and gold, the stars of the Southern Cross, and a kangaroo. Over the years there have been a number of variations, all featuring a kangaroo, and the latest merges the Southern Cross and the Aboriginal flag. 'I've copped a bit of flak for wanting a new

flag,' he said. 'They've banned me in some RSL clubs. But it's obvious it's going to happen, and I wasn't going to wait around for someone else to write a song about it, so I wrote "A Flag of Our Own". I've had people come up to me and say they fought under the present flag, and sometimes they want to punch you because they don't understand why we should change it. That's OK; it's the way they feel. But for me, the Union Jack is for England and the kangaroo is for us.

'I've been pushing the republic in concerts everywhere, but a lot of people sit on the fence. They feel some people are in it for their own agenda, and they're afraid they might open the gates to weirdos. They're not real deep thinkers, some of these people, and they say it ain't broke, so it doesn't need fixing. But to me it's all about how we feel about

John Williamson at the Best of All lookout on the New South Wales–Queensland border… 'Waking up Mt Warning.'

ourselves, and I'm amazed we didn't do it years ago. The Queen's gone.'

I asked John whether he had thought of writing an anthem for the republic. He said: 'When I wrote "True Blue", I was battling to get away from the American influence which seemed to be growing wherever you looked. So I went over the top, saying: "I'm Australian and bloody proud of it," but I've gone past that now, and I'm just writing songs as I am. I'm not pushing it anymore. I get a bit jack of everybody trying to write anthems — that's all the professional writers, the jingle writers, seem to want to do.' I said I thought that was a pity, because if anyone could capture, in words and music, the feeling of being Australian on the cusp of the 21st century, I thought he could. He didn't answer.

The next morning we were up with the sun for a walk into the heart of John's rainforest; the botanic garden of nature which attracted him to this spot in the first place, and which inspired "Rip Rip Woodchip". From the house, we could see a dark green canopy draped over the valley below. That perspective gave no indication of how steep and tough the walk would be.

As we made our way down a partly cleared and sloping ridge, greeting a pregnant roan cow contentedly chewing her cud, the singer became the botanist, naming each of the trees, explaining their origins and uses for their woods, and identifying dozens of birds by sight or call. Seriously, here was a man in love with his plot of dirt.

'That's a silky oak; there's a tamarind; they use the wood of this crow's ash here for dance floors because of its natural oils; over there is a red cedar — most of them are gone now — and a firewheel, white beech, rosewood, native hoop pines, blackbean, mountain gum, Moreton Bay figs, and that's a brushbox which is fire resistant and a favourite timber for woolshed floors.'

We spotted spangled drongo birds, kookaburras, brown pigeons, dozens of thornbills in a sandpaper fig tree, and squawking rosellas with cream coloured heads and flashing blue–grey bodies. And then the lights went out. Bashing our way through a ring of lantana, we entered the rainforest where the early morning sun could barely manage to reach the leaf-strewn forest floor. We were in a cave of tree trunks, where survival for any living thing depended utterly on its ability to command a share of the sunlight above. Huge vines, thicker than my upper thigh, hung Tarzan-like from buttressed trees feeding nutrients to the foliage clinging to branches above; elkhorns and staghorns hitched a ride on trunks and perched in branch junctions, and strangler figs criss-crossed the trunks of host trees, eventually to envelop and kill them. On the rocky forest floor, lichens and mosses covered clinking basalt, and tiny saplings stood waiting for the chance to race for the light — if a storm were to rip open the canopy in their favour.

We followed a small creek down into the valley, past a stand of bangalow palms and tree ferns, clambering gingerly over sprinkling waterfalls. When we reached the main creek, we turned upstream, disturbing a snoozing eel in a shallow rock pool, before confronting a four-metre waterfall over a solid granite ledge, where tropical rains have carved a deep hole in the sandstone at its base. 'You feel the power of the earth here,' said John. 'This is where lava flowing down this valley stopped, goodness knows how many millions of years ago. I was amazed when I found this. It's my cathedral. It's beautiful.'

It was indeed, but getting out was the next challenge. It's one thing to slip and slide *down* a steep valley; quite another to haul my bulky, out-of-form frame *up* it. But we managed, grateful for the saplings and vines to hang on to. I called it a murderous march through the jungle; he called it a quiet, pleasant stroll.

We drove around the region, stopping at lookouts and admiring the diverse beauty of the landscapes. We stood high on a ridge at the Best of All lookout on the New South Wales–Queensland border, overlooking Mt Warning, where the sun's rays first catch the Australian landmass each day. John was quiet and pensive. My bones ached.

Back at the house, he scribbled in a large notebook. 'This isn't an anthem for the republic,' he said. 'But it's something that came to me today. It's about how I feel — what did you say last night? — as an Australian about to meet the 21st century.'

I saw the sunrise on the ocean
On a day clear blue
Waking up Mt Warning
Steaming from the dew
I took a breath and thought out loud
We are lucky and we are free
I stamped my foot hard on the ground
Yes I felt Aborigine
This ancient land belongs to me
Yes I feel Aborigine
I'm Australian and proud to be
You are too if you feel like me
Oh I hurt when the south wind blows
And dries out my weathered skin
But I hold like a river gum
And fight on til it rains again
Bounding like a wallaroo
Just as far as I can reach
Across the world like a boomerang
Landing home on the beach
This ancient land belongs to me
Yes I feel Aborigine
I'm Australian and proud to be
You are too if you feel like me.

'You know,' he said. 'If we all felt the same about this place, no-one would dare to fuck it up.'

Japanese gardens, Cowra, New South Wales.

chapter twelve

Our travels came to a crunching end on a forest trail in the Barrington Tops, the woodland mountain region of the Great Dividing Range north of the Hunter Valley, in New South Wales. Most people see this place only from the air — a continuum of the precious Wollemi National Park north-west of Sydney; a place you fly over en route to Brisbane or destinations further north. It's not a place of roads, towns and people. It is deep forest of tall, straight eucalypts, thick canopies 50 metres above the ground, stinging nettles and prickly creepers, and bright verdant ferns catching shafts of light. Very few people go there. We shouldn't have been there.

I was stupid. I broke all the rules in the book. I didn't have a proper map; I had done no checking with local police or authorities about road conditions; I hadn't told anyone where we were going. I simply blundered into a situation from which we needed to be rescued.

It began as a leisurely drive back from the Tamworth Music Festival to Sydney. We came down the escarpment on Australia Day, past Burning Mountain, a smouldering coal seam which has burned for eons deep below the surface, and decided to spend the night in Scone. This is fine country; premium grazing land opened up in the late 1820s in the upper Hunter Valley. Today Scone calls itself the Home of the Thoroughbred, and a bronze statue of a mare and foal at the northern entrance to the town celebrates the famous studs nearby — Segenhoe, St Aubins, Kia Ora, and more. Even in the midsummer blaze the valleys, intersected by white railing fences, were green and lush; a crucible of fertility and wealth contained by a ragged horizon of hills capped by smoky blue eucalyptus forests. Some say this is the best land in Australia, a view no doubt shared by media billionaire Kerry Packer, whose horse stud and polo playing fields are nearby at Ellerston.

We were relaxed. This was the home run. Why push ourselves? We dropped into a pub to watch the cricket and Wendy struck a conversation with a ruddy and rotund chap named Harry, the local butcher. He talked proudly of his sausages — the best in the state, he said. 'People come all the way from Newcastle for my sausages,' he boasted, and invited her to drop into his shop tomorrow for a sample. 'Wasn't that nice?' Wendy said as we left, singing his praises as a salt-of-the-earth character.

Next morning, early, I picked up the papers from the main street newsagent. As I was getting back into the car, Harry strode towards me and thrust a plain-wrapped parcel into my hand. 'Give these to the missus,' he said. 'It's some of me sausages.' I offered to pay but he would have none of it,

so I put them in the car fridge and returned to the motel to marvel with Wendy about the warm, old-fashioned generosity of country folk like Harry.

Checking out of the motel I spotted a tourist map of the Scone shire on the reception area wall. The motel manager gave me one and I strolled back to the car, saying to Wendy: 'Look, we've got a couple of hours up our sleeves. We could take a run out here through Gundy, then on to Belltrees, where Patrick White was brought up, along this road and over this ridge, then link up with this road which will bring us back on to the main highway at Aberdeen. It's magnificent country, so let's go look.'

Wendy agreed. And so, within striking distance of home, and without a thought of special preparation, or the slightest scent of danger, we set off. We ambled through the grasslands to Gundy, and drove on to Belltrees. The historic woolshed nestled in a valley to our right as we swung into a detour to bypass an old wooden bridge which had given way under the weight of a truck. It will be replaced when the council gets around to it, no doubt with a concrete structure devoid of the charm of the old. We turned sharply right on to Stewarts Brook Road and wended our way through the valley, first on bitumen, then gravel. We slowed to pass cows and calves, chewing their cuds on the side of the road, observing us with studious disinterest. The homesteads were less grand up here; and as we went on they became more like backwoods shacks. Several times we forded the creek until the road became a track and we passed through several gates. Wendy wondered if we should be here, opening and closing gates, but I pointed to the map and said we had come this far, and it wouldn't be long before we linked up to the other road, so we might as well keep going.

A sign told us we were entering Stewarts Forest, and we admired the massive trees through which our trail wound. I could see it had carried little recent traffic, because fallen leaves lay undisturbed over the wheel tracks. It was smooth, gently rising along a ridge, with occasional water-control mounds known as 'whoaboys' cutting across the track. There had been considerable rains recently: the same rains which had kept the grazing paddocks green had left pools of water behind the whoaboys and each time we crossed one we sloshed through a muddy pool on exit. Wendy started to worry. She didn't like it when the nose of the car pointed to the sky one second, then dropped into mud the next. But, I insisted, it can only be another kilometre or two before we are over the other side.

Indeed, now we were going down. Steeply. Very steeply. On rutted tracks of mud, with sharp rocks beneath, and tree roots protruding from the sides. Through a watercourse, then another, and another, each rougher than the last. Wendy's concern was by now rising to panic as the Pajero tossed and rolled from side to side, slid down and around, crunched the bash plate under the engine and scraped over rocks, bending and twisting our running boards. I was trying to be cool about it all — it could be no more than a kilometre to go! — but I was beginning to hope the welded diff wouldn't give up the ghost at this critical stage. As we approached the fourth major creek, Wendy's panic had reached the point of hysteria. I tried to calm her, but I was unconvincing and she was definitely unconvinced! 'Darling. *Please!*' I said, sternly. 'This is hard enough without you screaming. I can't concentrate . . . '

'Stop!' she cried. 'Stop the car! I can't go through there! Let me out! I'll walk . . . I can't stay in the car! We'll tip over . . . '

I stopped. Wendy got out, shaking. We searched for her blood pressure tablets and she gulped one. She picked her way through the nettles and clinging vines beside the track as I inched the Pajero, low range, low gear, diff locked, over the boulders. They thumped on the bash plate and screeched along the driver's side running board, but we came through and Wendy, whimpering, got back in the car. She was genuinely distressed — her hands shaking, her voice trembling — but I persisted with my belief that the best way out was to go forward. The formed road could only be another kilometre or so . . .

The next crossing stopped me. I couldn't get the traction to climb a staircase of tree roots, each rising about 30 centimetres, and nor could I get a run-up to charge over the top. Stuck, I got out and piled rocks against the roots to try to claw my way over. Damn! I could hear the hiss of escaping air. I had punctured a tyre, and this was no place to repair it. Quickly, I surged at the barrier and Eureka! it worked. I bounced and skidded my way up the steep slope of rocks and roots. Suddenly there was a loud blast, a rush of air, and the awful screech of metal on rock. I'd ripped the leaking tyre to shreds, torn it off the wheel, and wrecked the rim in the process. And I was stuck on a precarious angle, facing uphill, the ruined wheel in a depression, leaving the axle no more than five centimetres above the ground. And I needed at least 20 centimetres' clearance to get the jack under the axle. This was going to be difficult.

Wendy walked forward and returned to say there was another crossing 150 metres further on, and it looked worse than any before. I didn't want to hear that, because I was jacking up the body of the car, putting rocks under it, then jacking again to try to create enough clearance under the axle. Several times, in spite of rocks chocking each of the wheels, it slid off the jack. Several times I was back to square one. I couldn't get under the car to place the jack effectively. I had to work blind, feeling my way, then scamper from my place in front of the rear wheel to crouch down behind the vehicle to see if I had effectively placed the jack. It was hot; I was sweating and my glasses were steamed and dirty. My clothes were filthy, my hands bloodied and scratched.

'Can't we call for help?' Wendy asked. 'You've got the phone. Can't you ring someone?'

'I can do it. I know how to do it. It's just that I can't do it yet.'

'Please. Use the phone. Do it for me.'

Do it for me! That's what Alfreda said when we were stuck on the beach near Robe. They are the four words which made me give in back then. 'Do it for me, dear,' she had said, and what could I say? I did it for *her*, so what if I don't do it for Wendy? She'll say I love my mother more than her. Do it for me! How can I not? But who do I ring?

I got out the satellite phone and traipsed 100 metres along the track until I found a clearing in the forest canopy through which I could get a shot at the satellite. I put the phone on a mound — and disturbed a nest of angry black and red bull ants which swarmed over the body of the phone. I snatched it off the nest, brushed them away and called for Wendy to hold the phone, its antenna carefully pointed to the north-east. She stood too close to the nest, and howled as an ant bit her on the ankle, immediately forming a large red welt. But she stood stoically as I called

the NRMA and explained our predicament. Could someone bring us a new jack? The answer was no surprise: the NRMA offers *road* service to its members, and I was not by any definition on a road. 'You're on your own, mate,' came the reply. 'We're on our own,' I told Wendy, and she silently, sullenly, tended to her ankle.

I returned to the car; to the mud, the rocks and the paraphernalia strewn about it.

I kept hearing 'You're on your own, mate' as I jacked the body of the car, propped it on rocks, then jacked it some more. I dug under the axle, chipping away and pulling stones out of the dirt. I got the jack under the axle, but still there wasn't enough clearance to get the ruined wheel off and a new one on. I dug under the tyre, scooping away the dirt with my hands which were by now bleeding and blistered. At last I was able to take off the wheel and I held my breath at the sight of the jack, precariously angled, fervently hoping it wouldn't give way as I fought to position the new wheel on the hub. Triumphantly, I spun the wheel nuts tight and repacked the car.

After this three-hour delay, we had two choices: go back, or go on. I had no wish to again face the horrors I knew lay behind us, and I still reasoned it couldn't be far before we were out of this. We went on, almost a kilometre, through two more crossings. But on the third, gunning the Pajero out of a deep mud hole, the near side front wheel bucked on a large rock and I lost control of the steering as I tried to turn hard left to avoid a tree. I clipped it. Three sounds simultaneously echoed through the bush: the crunching of metal as the bull bar and bumper bar was pushed back, the smashing of glass from my headlight, and the explosive burst of instant deflation as the edge of the bumper bar sliced through the wall of my tyre.

Stuck in the forest . . . Wendy waits for rescue.

Now we were in deep schtuck! And the sun was going down . . . In situations like this, some things are obvious. First, we weren't going anywhere tonight. Therefore, equally obviously, we had to pitch the tent and prepare for a night in an unscheduled bush camp. We had water, wine and food — including Harry's snags. Tomorrow, after a good sleep, I could winch the bull bar off the wheel and try to fit my spare tyre. But then what? Go forward or go back? Some things aren't so obvious.

If we removed from our circumstances the pretty pickle we were in, our camp was the most charming and delightful of our travels. We pitched the tent on the track — the only clear ground — a short distance in front of the car. We set up our tables, cooked Harry's delicious snags, and brought out a couple of

bottles of fine Piper's Brook shiraz purchased in Tasmania with an eye to long-term cellaring. The night closed above us, stars twinkling brightly through the gaps in the foliage; the arc of light thrown by our petrol-powered gas lamp catching the silver threads of hundreds of caterpillars lowering themselves on a single strand of silk from their leafy food supplies above. The silence was broken by occasional rustling in the trees — possums? — and the determined guttural grunts of an old man koala advertising his whereabouts to potential lovers. His 'urragh, urragh, urragh' calls were answered by higher-pitched 'chak-chak-chak' responses, tantalisingly close. We fired beams of light from our torches into the trees, but were unable to unmask the nocturnal lovers sharing our solitude. Wendy was calmer now, but unwilling to throw off our predicament in favour of enjoying this unique and unplanned camp.

By 8.30 pm, two-and-a-half hours after our crash, I had mellowed with the wine and food. 'We might,' I told Wendy, 'be able to repair the car and drive out of here. But it's a bit of a long shot. Even if I can change the tyre, do we go forward, or do we go back? And if we go back, who's to say we won't do more tyres?'

Then I said the words she was most desperate to hear: 'I think we need help.'

By pure luck, the car was parked in a spot which allowed a clear shot at the satellite, so I called the Telstra operator, got the number for the Scone police, and soon found myself talking to Senior Constable Scott Matthews. 'I'm sorry to be bothering you,' I said. 'But I've been a bloody idiot. I've broken all the rules and done everything wrong . . . I've been stupid, but the fact is I'm stuck and need help.' Scott was as soothing as an old-fashioned bedside doctor. 'Don't worry,' he said. 'Just tell me the situation, and we'll work on it from there . . . '

So I began: name, address, date of birth, car registration number, make, year, the drive from Scone, the road into the forest, the tourist map, our intended destination, and my guesstimate of where we were, and how far we had travelled. 'Are there any medical conditions?' he asked, and I replied that Wendy was on blood pressure tablets.

'How is your wife?' he asked.

'Pretty uptight. But we're all right for the night.'

'Are you sure? We can organise an evacuation pretty quickly if required.'

'Evacuation? How?'

'We can get the helicopter there within an hour or so.'

'But there's a 50-metre canopy over us.'

'Don't worry about that. Our chaps can get down through that and winch her out.'

Winch her out! My God! She's been beside herself with anxiety getting *in* here. Imagine her dangling below a chopper at midnight in the middle of this forest. She'd die with her leg in the air!

'Scott, I can assure you we're all right tonight. We're fully equipped for camping; we've got enough water for four or five days, and enough food for two or three, no problems. What we need tomorrow is a new wheel, and I'm sure we can get out OK.'

Scott accepted my assessment — for now. But he said the helicopter was still an option the next day if necessary. He told me he would get detailed maps of the area and talk to the local State Emergency Services (SES) people. We agreed we would talk again in an hour.

I told Wendy about the chopper plan. But how would they find us? How would they get through the canopy? Could she bear to be dangling on the end of a thin wire as she was pulled through the tree tops? How would they get her into the chopper? What would be worse — the winch or the horror trail?

Our next call to Scott was confidence-building. By now he had large-scale maps of the area, and again, I detailed the route we had taken as the controller of the Scone SES, Ralph Francis, listened. I gave details of my wheel size, and they told me they would set off at first light on their rescue mission. We went to bed tired, but infinitely less stressed than we had been when we arrived at this point.

We woke with the sun and the infectious laughter of kookaburras greeting the dawn. It sounded as if there were hundreds of them, cackling and chortling with the delight of a new day. Our forest was placid and beautiful, with the morning sun streaming shafts of light through the trees, catching the silk of more dangling caterpillars, and highlighting the verdant yellow–greens of the ferns beside our killer creekbed. I got out the winch and pulled the bent bumper bar off the tyre. I jacked up the wheel and loosened the nuts in readiness. I scraped together a mound of leaves to make a smoke signal for the chopper, if needed. Just before 8 am Scott rang to say he and the SES team had picked up a new wheel and were on their way. I estimated they should reach us about 11 am. Several times I thought I picked up the sound of an engine. No, just an aircraft. By 11.30 Wendy was beginning to worry.

Then I heard it. The faintest rumble of an engine. This time, it wasn't an aircraft. 'Listen,' I said. 'Here they come!' And sure enough, a couple of minutes later, an SES vehicle appeared over the hill and started down the incline towards our creek. Wendy's tears of relief streamed down her cheeks. Immediately behind, the red and blue lights of a police Nissan Patrol came into view. Ralph Francis, the SES controller, and his offsider, Bill Britt, crossed the creek, hands outstretched.

'God, I'm glad to see you,' I said. 'Embarrassed, but glad.' Scott Matthews, a young and fresh-faced burly copper from the Tamworth area — glad to be back in the country after three years on the beat at Kings Cross — followed across the creek. His demeanour was as soothing as his bedside manner the night before, and we felt safe in the hands of these three musketeers.

What do we owe these men and women who contribute so selflessly to our communities and our people? We owe them our comfort, sleeping soundly at night knowing we are safe; we owe them our speedy recovery from the natural disasters which always have and always will beset our land; and many times, we owe them our lives. We see them on the TV news, in small boats battling outback floods, rescuing people, foals or calves, and taking fodder to stranded animals; we see their sooty faces and knapsacks in the annual bushfire outbreaks, helping people, barring roads, or backburning lines of safety; and we see them at car crashes and landslides and mopping up after summer storms tear apart our notions of urban safety. They are our unsung heroes. We rarely see them at their weekly training nights, but they give up their time to learn the skills of survival and rescue so as to be constantly ready to help others. And when they're not training, most likely they're out in the community, their wives and partners helping to raise money through street stalls and raffles for the equipment they need. Sure, they receive some help from the state, but they are still massively underfunded. What do we owe them?

Scott used the satellite phone to call his HQ. 'We have located those missing persons,' he reported. Bill wandered along the track taking readings on his hand-held global positioning system. We applied the coordinates to his map and I was staggered by the result. We were miles away from where I thought we were. The information I had given the night before had missed one vital ingredient — I hadn't seen where our track divided, almost turning back on itself, about five kilometres earlier. It was like a Y-junction: if you approach it from the base of the Y, you have a choice of left or right. But if you approach from the upper right arm of the Y, the turn to take you along the upper left arm isn't so apparent. If I had taken that sharp turn back I would have linked up very quickly with Upper Rouchel Road, and all would have been well. Our

Rescued deep in the forest… Scott Matthews, Ralph Francis, Wendy and Bill Britt plan how to get out.

rescuers had followed that track, but when they didn't find us, reasoned that the only other possibility could be the lower arm of the Y — a track called Carters Brush Trail. They pressed along it, debating whether or not to go on at each of the cruddy crossings we had negotiated the day before. At one point they were going to turn back, but continued only when they recalled I had said I had driven about ten kilometres into the forest. 'We decided to search another two kilometres,' said Scott. 'About two kilometres back.' We were near Cockcrow Mountain, on a ridge above the Paterson River. It would be another 12 kilometres before we reached the end of Carters Brush Trail, so there was unanimous agreement: the only way out was to go back. But the

SES Mazda had punctured a tyre on the way in, so we had to get out with no more punctures. A zero safety net. This was going to be tricky.

Ralph led the convoy in his lightweight Mazda ute; Scott followed in the police Patrol, and Bill drove the Pajero. Twice Scott had to use his winch to help the Pajero up steep or slippery slopes. At each crossing we held our breath. Another blown tyre would complicate things. But after two careful hours, we were back on the ridge, and then on the formed roads, and then the bitumen, limping back to Scone. Ralph said he was surprised I hadn't taken more pictures. I said I was too embarrassed.

Battle-weary and bent, we bought a new tyre in Scone and made a donation to the

SES. It seemed the least we could do. Then we headed for Sydney, down the Newcastle expressway, three hours away.

Ruefully, I reflected on the lessons of our comeuppance. It wasn't that I had weighed the risks and made bad judgments. It was more to do with the fact that I simply didn't think about the risks at all. If you choose to confront the remote outback, preparation and planning are essential. But we were three hours from home, relaxed, with our minds in neutral. So we stumbled into trouble and became another statistic for the SES. There are 6700 volunteer SES workers in New South Wales alone, attending to about 18,000 incidents a year — mainly floods, storms, motor accidents, searches and rescues, and bushfires. In its 1997 annual report the SES estimates its members contributed 227,000 volunteer hours to the community. We can grizzle and grumble about perceived shortcomings in our communities, but if we bother to look at the positive side of the ledger the only logical conclusion is that the great Australian traditions of helping a mate, of looking after each other, of selfless giving in times of distress and in the wake of disaster, are alive and well. Also alive and well is this country's ability to bite you on the backside if you take it for granted. Since our occupation began a little more than two centuries ago, we have moved mountains to shape and mould it; we have sought to domesticate it and take profit from it; and we have come to see in it symbols of our freedom, through its spaces, and our good fortune, through its richness. But we have never learned to tame it.

Epilogue

With the Pajero in hospital, I flew to Canberra in early February 1998 for the Constitutional Convention. This was to be the penultimate stage in the march to an Australian republic by 1 January 2001. Would we, through the convention, make the decision to modernise our constitutional arrangements; to get our house in order, as it were, to face the 21st century? Or would we fall comfortably back into the security of a system which, though its words no longer reflect the way we are governed, has nevertheless served us sufficiently well throughout the 20th century? I felt it would be a close-run thing. Although I had been involved with the Australian Republican Movement (ARM) since its inception in July 1992, and had the benefit of endless hours of discussions with committed and enthusiastic fellow believers, briefings by eminent constitutional lawyers, extensive attitudinal research reports, public opinion polls, backyard barbecue meetings with suburban cells of supporters, debates between republicans and monarchists (including the celebrated TV stoush between radio redneck Ron Casey and singer Normie Rowe — I'm the one cowering in the foreground!), my confidence had been dented by my travels.

Throughout the past year, in cities and country towns, I had come to appreciate that the republic wasn't a top-order priority. It was not, by any stretch of the imagination, an issue burning brightly in the minds of Australians. Sure, we discussed it in the four corners of the country: around campfires with friends and strangers, in bush pubs and outback motels where we met people and chewed the fat about our travels and discoveries. But I was the one raising the subject. I never walked into a bar to eavesdrop on a group of people debating the issue. I found the levels of *support* were consistent between city and country, and the dividing line between those in favour and those against reflected what the polls had told us — that older Australians were generally against, and younger Australians generally in favour. But the level of *interest* was disappointingly low. Most people who displayed an attitude of shrugging disinterest felt there was an inevitability about the republic, and therefore there was no need to get excited about it. What will be, will be. It doesn't matter much, one way or the other. Life will go on; the sun will still come up . . .

The contrast in Canberra was electric. Gathered in the warm and gracious environs of the Old Parliament House were 152 delegates to the convention — half appointed by the government; the other half elected by the people. A century ago the Founding Fathers of Federation were all white, all male, and mostly aged; this convention's delegates were two-thirds men, one-third women; black, white and many shades in between; curmudgeonly old and inspirationally young. All had come with detailed knowledge of the issues before them; most had come with a point of view, which ranged from strong, through strident to intransigent. For the next ten days the debate and the machinations behind the scenes twisted and turned, like a wisp of smoke, and we who were living it and breathing it ran the risk of becoming oblivious of the fact that, outside the convention, life did go on and the sun did still come up.

Old Parliament House was an inspired choice as the venue for this unprecedented discussion among ourselves about our family matters. Unlike the new Parliament House higher on the hill in Canberra, this old building has a welcoming feel to it; its proportions encourage human interactivity; and its wood-panelled chambers and meeting rooms reek of history. Our history, where from 1927 until 1988 every matter of national importance had been acted out. This was a proper venue to act out the first page of history for the 21st century.

The delegates fell roughly into four camps: those opposed to change and fervently in favour of maintaining the monarchy; those who wanted an ultra-minimalist republic where nothing changed except the removal of the Queen; those who supported the ARM model of a president elected by a two-thirds majority of both houses of Parliament; and those who tenaciously fought for radical change to the American system of a republic with a directly elected president. Within each of those groups were plentiful individual variations, and as each of the delegates presented their keynote speeches, the number crunchers were wondering if the monarchists — in a minority — could split the republicans; whether minimalist republicans would side with monarchists; whether the middle-of-the-road republicans could entice enough radical republicans to their cause; and, ultimately, whether the whole convention would disintegrate into farce.

It had its moments. Very quickly, the radicals attracted public attention through the live TV coverage for their flamboyant, persistent and sometimes theatrical pursuit of fundamental democratic principles. They

threatened to be wreckers as they argued there was no point in having a president if the public couldn't be directly involved in electing that president. They played to the galleries, and to the rampant distrust of politicians throughout the land, by slandering the capacity of our elected representatives in Parliament to endorse the bipartisan appointment of a head of state; instead, favouring a process which would politicise the very office they wanted free of the taint of partisanship. As opponents of the ARM, the monarchists were courteously restrained by comparison.

As the debates wore on, there were moments of lament and times of inspiration. Neville Bonner, a 76-year-old Jagera elder from Queensland, who spent 12 years as Australia's first indigenous member of the federal Parliament, brought tears to the eyes of friend and foe alike when he spoke of his sadness at finding his world confronted with change. He received the only spontaneous standing applause of the convention as he summed up the fears and trepidation felt by many Australians of his era — regardless of race — at the prospect of the removal of another of the central pillars of their beliefs.

'You did not ask my people if you could come here,' he said, facing a depleted chamber at the weary end of the third day. 'You did not ask my people if you could occupy our land. You did not ask our people if you could stop us living our traditional lives. You did not ask my people if we would wish to live under your laws, under your government, and under your federation. [But] we have come to accept your laws. We have come to accept your Constitution. We have come to accept the present system. We believed you when you said that a democracy must have checks and balances. We believed you when you said that

Canberra... early morning balloon flights over the Constitutional Convention.

not all positions in society should be put out for election. We believed you when you said judges should be appointed, not elected. We believed you when you said that the Westminster system ensures that a government is accountable to the people. We believed you when you taught us that integral to the Westminster system is a head of state above politics . . . that Government House should be a political-free zone.

'But my heart is heavy. I worry for my children and grandchildren. I worry that what has proven to be a stable society is about to be replaced. How dare you? How dare you? You told my people that your system was best. We have come to believe you. Now you say that you were wrong, and that we were wrong to believe you. Suddenly you are saying that what brought the country together, made it independent, ensured its defence, saw it through peace and war, and saw it through depression and prosperity, must all go.

'Republicanism is a vote of no confidence in the existing system, but you forget that you have taught us to love, honour and respect that system. I ask you: what are you doing? Are you not already divided enough on other issues, real issues, real problems? From the bottom of my heart, I pray you: stop this senseless division. Let us work together on the real issues. Let us solve those problems which haunt my people — the problems of land, of health, of unemployment, of the despair and hopelessness which leads even to suicide. Let us unite this country, not divide it ever [with] that toy of those who already have too much — mere symbolism.'

Hansard recorded the next moment as: *Mr Bonner thereupon chanted his tribal sorry chant.* It was a riveting and thought-provoking moment, and it held people, inside the chamber and out, spellbound in its simplicity and purity. It was a defining moment, but it defined the past. It summed up the cry of people who feared that the rewriting of our constitutional foundations would cause all that had been built upon them to teeter and topple. But Mr Bonner's sentiments, heart-felt though they may have been, don't stand up to rational analysis. The constitutional changes proposed don't rip from the Westminster system its inherent checks and balances, or the political independence of the head of state. (In fact, it enhances that independence.) Nor will our constitutional arrangements dictate whether Australia is divided or at one on any single issue; nor whether it is at war or peace, or in depression or in prosperity. These are the outcomes of government, not constitutional, decisions. In the absence of a preamble which seeks to state who we are and what we believe in, the Constitution merely defines the processes of government.

I found inspiration in the younger delegates. They defined the future, by their presence, in their comments and, ultimately, in one young man's contribution to a final agreement. This was a debate about the future. They are our future. They were instrumental in setting this convention apart from the normal political processes: gone was the cynical rigidity of parroted party lines, and in its place a refreshing and unanimous outpouring of vigour, idealism and shared hopes for the future. Young delegates may have had different views about constitutional forms, but there was agreement about the kind of Australia they wanted: colour-blind, diverse, tolerant, compassionate, united and highly educated.

A political problem emerged from the first week's debates: the enthusiastic support for a directly elected president, pushed from the floor by the radical republicans and picked up among the TV audience across the nation. The feedback was unmistakable: by phone, fax and Internet, people were saying they didn't want to leave the choice of president in the hands of politicians. That was without doubt part of the larger disaffection with political parties and the sullen mood of the electorate, but it held the capacity to kill the entire convention process stone dead. First, the government wouldn't have a bar of it. If the convention had recommended a proposal for direct election, the government would have rejected it. Second, the political hard-heads believed it had no chance of winning in a referendum. History has shown that referendum votes, requiring a majority of the people *and* a majority of the states to succeed, don't win approval without bipartisan support. Scare campaigns on referenda questions have produced No votes on many occasions, and the concept of a radical change which would politicise the office of president, and potentially pit an elected president against an elected prime minister — each able to say at various times in the election cycles that 'my mandate is bigger (or fresher) than yours'— was a recipe for instability, and a resounding No vote. To have any chance at the referendum, the outcome had to be capable of drawing bipartisan support. But how could the two competing imperatives — giving the people a say, while establishing a non-political presidency — be achieved?

Youth delegate Jason Yat-Sen Li provided the circuit breaker. A 26-year-old University of Sydney first class honours constitutional law graduate, he was working with the United Nations War Crime Tribunal in The Hague before the convention. 'I stood for election on the platform of representing ethnic Australians and all those believing in the value of an ethnically and culturally diverse society,' he told the convention. 'My election articulates a clear message. It affirms that ethnic Australians have an undeniable interest in the future of our nation.

'I am not entirely happy with any of the three existing models for appointment and dismissal. These three models have divided the republican camp into three entrenched blocs, each pitted bitterly against the other. This is jeopardising not only the credibility of the republican initiative but also the credibility of the convention itself. As an independent delegate, unaligned to any group, I grappled last night with whether I should lend my support to any existing model, or whether I should propose a compromise of my own. I have chosen this latter course, not because I am so presumptuous to think I can solve all the problems or I can untie the Gordian knot and overnight be proclaimed the national hero for devising the ingenious Li model. I have done so because I would like to set an example that we all at this stage have to think laterally to find a compromise capable

of not only achieving consensus but also of having the greatest chance of success at a referendum.

'Compelling criticisms may be levelled against each of the existing models. However, each model has its strengths. I am concerned with preserving the strength of each model while somehow at the same time discarding its weaknesses. My proposal [is that] a two-thirds majority of Parliament elects a selection body that is gender balanced, composed of people who have the respect of the Australian people and who reflect Australians in all their diversity. That selection body receives nominations from the general public and, according to a set of transparent criteria, selects a candidate [who] must then win the support of an absolute majority of Parliament to be appointed head of state.

'This model is non-elitist [and] will produce a bipartisan, apolitical head of state. It allows for popular input without creating a massive mandate, and it removes the actual selection of the head of state from the hands of the parliamentarians, thus allaying distrust. In addition, I believe this model affords an equal opportunity to all Australians to be elected head of state.

'I was born in Australia 26 years ago. I am as Australian as anybody here. Look beyond the colour of my skin. Regardless of their origin, all Australians have a unifying commitment to Australia, to democracy and to equality. The value of ethnic diversity in Australian society is now beyond contention. The challenge, however, is for a more tolerant and inclusive democracy. Fellow Australians, I have a vision for Australia in which an ethnic Australian may be elected head of state, and it will be as absolutely normal and uncontroversial as if an

Australian of any other ethnic descent were appointed. I ask all Australians to join me in that vision.'

It took some days for Jason's proposal to come to centre stage — and then, in a modified form. But it formed the basis of the final agreement of the convention. Subject to the result of a referendum in 1999, the appointment of a president will be through a nomination procedure which, according to the convention's final communique, 'ensures that the Australian people are consulted as thoroughly as possible'. State and federal Parliaments, local government, community organisations and individual members of the public will be invited to provide nominations to a committee, balanced between parliamentary and community representatives and mindful of gender and cultural diversity. That committee will present a short-list of names to the prime minister, who will then put a single nomination, seconded by the leader of the opposition, to a joint sitting of both houses, where it will require a two-thirds majority for approval. In other words, any Australian will be able to nominate a future president, and both sides of politics must approve. In this way, only Australians of great stature and without political affiliation are

The Constitutional Convention in the Old Parliament House, Canberra... an inspired choice.

Republican delegates embrace at the end of the Constitutional Convention ... euphoric achievement.

likely to be given the task of representing us all as head of state. Jason Li's idea had evolved into an elegant solution, and the convention ended in a mood of euphoric achievement. Great strides had been taken; now there was just one more step — the 1999 referendum.

The convention also resolved that, if the referendum succeeds, a system of regular constitutional reviews should be established. This is of great significance, for it provides a way to systematically address the issues which have been gnawing at us. By calling regular conventions, where two-thirds of the delegates would be elected, we could take out of the hands of serving politicians decisions on the issues which define us. If we take the

first small step to a republic, it may embolden us to believe we can make further, more fundamental changes.

We are bound at present by the difficult processes of change. These were deliberately placed in our Constitution at Federation. The proviso that a referendum question must be approved in a majority of the states was included to guard against the more populous states imposing their will on the smaller states. That has been a major influence on the outcome of referenda: since 1901, Australians have voted on 42 proposals to change the Constitution; only eight have succeeded. This reluctance on the part of the public to fiddle with the Constitution may well have contributed to the end-of-century malaise of the political system. Many proposals sunk at various referenda would have streamlined our system of government, and may have allowed a vastly different political landscape today.

I have no doubt that if we were to start today with a blank sheet of paper and devise a system of governing Australia, we would not write the Constitution we have. We may, because of our historical links, adopt the Westminster system of parliamentary government, or we may lean to the American system of executive government. Each has its strong points; weaknesses can be argued in each. Being Australian, we would probably cobble together our own unique system which seeks to remove short-term partisan confrontation and replace it with a longer-term pursuit of national goals. If we were realistic, and alert to the way our nation operates, or could best operate in an era of globalisation, we would probably do away with the states. We would probably also reduce the number of houses of Parliament; two to a state (except Queensland) is generally regarded as excessive today. In place of the states we could have a series of regional governments, formed around natural economic zones. These could emerge from a grouping of local council areas, where common interests make far more natural divisions than the existing state borders. For instance, the fruit-growing Riverland regions of South Australia, Victoria and New South Wales could combine into a single regional government; the beef-grazing hinterlands of northern New South Wales and southern Queensland could come together; the dairying and tourism areas of the New South Wales Northern Rivers and South-east Queensland regions, or the wool-growing Western

District of Victoria and the south-east of South Australia, could speak with one voice. Other geographic and economic zones could devolve within the states: the Hunter Valley in New South Wales, Far North Queensland, the Pilbara and the Kimberley regions of Western Australia, Gippsland in Victoria, and so on. The advantage in this would be to bring government closer to, and make it more reflective of, the wishes of the people it professes to serve. There need be no more politicians: by eliminating the states in favour of smaller, regional governments, devolution would result in two tiers of government, not three: regional and federal, in place of local councils, and state and federal governments. The federal government would be responsible for all its current activities — defence, international diplomacy, taxation, a national transport system, and so on — and continue to fund regional hospitals, schools and universities. Regional governments would be responsible for policing, education policies within a national curriculum framework, and the provision of services to their towns and cities.

This is how we might have approached a system of government if we started today without any historical barriers. It is delusionary to suggest that a move to devolution could succeed, by agreement, today. Could we possibly imagine state governments voting themselves out of office? It's preposterous! But it's not impossible that, through a series of evolutionary steps, we could greatly improve our forms of government by enthusiastically embracing the constitutional review processes established at the 1998 convention. Step by step, we could redefine the way we live and govern ourselves in the 21st century. If the referendum for a republic passes, another convention will be held between 2004 and 2006, to review the operation and effectiveness of the republic, and to address any other matters relating to the system of government. A convention resolution spells out the areas for discussion: the role of three tiers of government; the rights and responsibilities of citizenship; whether the Commonwealth should have environment power; the system of governance and proportional representation; whether the mechanism for constitutional change should be altered; constitutional aspects of indigenous reconciliation; equal representation of women and men in Parliament; and ways to better involve people in the political process. In other words, all the elements of disaffection with the present system can be put on the table for discussion and resolution. That is the most empowering result from the convention. If we are bold enough, solutions to the problems which bug us rest directly in our hands.

How will we live in the 21st century? I have no crystal ball, nor any claim to prescience, but it's a fair guess to say: much as we are. We tend to think of the millennium as a major milestone, and in a sense, it is. Undoubtedly, it fuels a desire to rethink who we are, and what we are, and encourages us to make preparations for it. But it will come and go in the blink of a second, and when we emerge into the third millennium, life will be unchanged from the last moments of the second.

As the years roll by, changes will come in the same way as they have in our lifetimes. The global imperatives of consumerism will continue to lay before us new products, new gadgets and gizmos, many of which are predictable with certainty; others to emerge from technologies yet to be discovered. Marketers will tell us we must have them, and we will continue to respond by saying we want them, and want them all, and want them now! The digital rush will embrace us all, through the Internet, with television phones, and movies and other entertainment on demand. The technology is with us now; all that is to be answered is how quickly, and with what level of enthusiasm, we take it up. Facsimile technology was an invention of the 1920s, but fax machines didn't become a business or household consumer item until the 1980s. Digital communications will eliminate distance in every sense but the physical, and the pace and stresses of our lives will speed up as a result. Some of us will revolt and drop out of the cities to cope; others will embrace the chance to do more, in less time, while living longer lives. (A girl born today has a life expectancy of 100 years.) Airlines will offer sub-orbital fights across the globe — London or New York in a couple of hours — and smarter cars will take us hands-free around the suburbs or from city to city. Fashions — in dress, music and entertainment — will come and go as they always have, and parents and grandparents will tut-tut as they always have, while kids will take it all in their stride.

There is no reason to think we will be any less parochial. We will be part of a 21st century world, with divisions at every level blurring, but we will see ourselves as citizens of our towns, cities, regions or nations before we see ourselves as citizens of the globe, even if there is agreement among the nations to create a global form of authority which dictates to us all in areas involving the survival of humanity. We will still face challenges on how to best get around our cities, through the gridlocks of traffic, and how to breathe clean air and governments will no doubt put in place incentives and disincentives to try to influence our social behaviour. In the economic booms and recessions of the next century, we will still head for the beaches and the wide open spaces of this ancient land.

And we will continue to uphold the core values of humanity: that we will do all we can to provide for our families while seeking to create a better world. This instinct has driven humans for millennia, and there is no reason to suggest it will change. As the Australian brand of a global species, we will want it all. We will be diverse; we will want to be united — and we will see no incompatibility in a continued quest to be united in our diversity.

Acknowledgments

This book would not have been possible without the help of many people; some of them were long-time friends, others we met along the way. For the comfort and security afforded at all times, wherever we were, by the Telstra Mini-Sat satellite phone, special thanks to Peter Shore and Ian McMinn of Telstra. For friendship and air travel assistance, much gratitude to Ken Cowley and Gay Radd of Ansett Australia. In no particular order, thanks to Barrie Hitchon, Angelo Loukakis and Alison Urquhart of HarperCollins, Robyn Flemming, Lynette Thornstensen, Michael Ward, Ken Done, Judy Done, Debbie Then, Col Allan, Dimiti Iliuk, Tom Kantor, Peter Toyne, Lex Silvester, Alfreda Day, Jol Simpson, Geoff Hintz, William Shadforth, Bob Brown, John Williamson, Phil Matthews, Stuart Aylmer, Phil Wilkinson, Sue Douglas, Lyndey Milan, Dr John Knight and Carolyn and Stephen Beaumont who looked after our dog Claudie. And, of course, my long-suffering wife Wendy, who didn't want to go, but was pleased she did.

Using the satellite phone at the site of the 1876 Old Telegraph Station, Eucla, Western Australia.

Sydney 2000 Ansett jumbo over Sydney.